twin steer

the Bedford VAL coach and its precursors in Britain

by David Kaye and Alan Witton

a **FLEETBOOKS** publication

Cover design by Stephen Raw

ISBN   0 86047 211 6

Contents

Acknowledgements

Both the authors acknowledge with thanks help extended from numerous sources in the preparation of this book. The facts and figures could hardly have been put together without help from the publications of the PSV Circle. We would also like to single out for special thanks Messrs C Birch, R Ludgate, G R Mills, E Ogden, M Walker and G W Watts. As well as drawing on our own photographic resources wherever possible, we have been grateful for permission to reproduce photographs from the collections of Messrs D Akrigg, G Booth, P Cain, M J Fenton, T Hartley, D W K Jones, R Ludgate, G R Mills, Surfleet Transport Photographs, B A Tilley and A P Young; and also for the use of official photographs from the archives of Brown & Davies 'Trurorian Tours', London Transport Executive, Metropolitan-Cammell-Weymann Ltd, the former Northern Ireland Road Transport Board, and the former Ulster Transport Authority. Photographs by all the above are credited individually in the text.

D Kaye
A Witton
August 1983

Introduction

When they first appeared in the coach parks at various seaside resorts, or were spotted speeding along the new motorway network back in 1963, the Bedford six-wheeled VAL14 coaches caused many a hard second look by curious passers-by. For one thing, with their additional axles they seemed so near the ground. This, in itself, made them look very different from contemporary vehicles. However, whereas earlier attempts to popularise the twin-steering PSV had largely failed to win approval in the bus and coach world, this time it was not very long before the VAL became an accepted part of the British coach scene. Hundreds of operators bought them new, whilst countless others acquired them secondhand over the following two decades. Even the Soviet Union took notice of the VAL, for the USSR Trade Delegation in London bought two new ones (one of them registered JHX 4K, while the registration number of the other has not yet come to light). Other export orders went to Australia, several northern European countries, South Africa and even Fiji! British operators with household names - Wallace Arnold, Grey-Green for example - and a few municipal coaching enterprises, like Edinburgh, bought the VAL. On the other hand it also found favour with small exotically-named fleets like Claribel, Nor-West Hovercraft, and Starduster.

Although they spread all over the British Isles and to several export markets, they made their biggest impact in England where they were useful for the works outing, and the express service to the holiday camp or boarding house, which are still the order of the day. Some English firms, like Super of Upminster, bought only one batch; others, like Begg of Thornaby-on-Tees, Safeguard of Guildford and Margo of South-West London, came back for more. But by 1970 few coach firms could be considered really 'respectable' without at least one of these thirty-six footers in their depot or yard.

The modern Duple 'Dominant' or Plaxton 'Express' bodywork can effectively disguise the rest of the vehicle, so that at a distance it is hard to differentiate a Bedford from a Ford, a Leyland from a Volvo. However, one of the fascinating features of the VAL was that, by its very nature, it could be spotted (in good visibility!) a mile off.

Sadly, just as every dog has his day, so does every model in the coaching world. On this twentieth anniversary of the launch of the VAL, there are no more than a handful of these intriguing vehicles still on active PSV duties, out of over 2,000 that were built. Fortunately, however, at least half a dozen of them have already entered the ranks of preserved vehicles, and more seem likely to follow. Let us hope that we may enjoy a good representative selection of restored and preserved VALs well into the 21st century.

1 Early experiments in twin steering

The first attempt to build a public service vehicle with twin front axles, both of which were attached to the steering column, came soon after the end of the First World War. In 1922 Bradford Corporation assembled a six-wheeled double-decker trolleybus, using mainly home-made components. No. 522 (AK 9963) was 23ft 10in (7.25 metres) long, 7ft 5in (2.25 metres) wide and 14ft 7ins (4.45 metres) high. It had seats for 59 passengers and served its native city for the next five years. However, it remained a 'one-off' machine; Bradford turned to ADC and Garrett for orthodox trolleybuses thereafter.

In February 1939, Leyland unveiled their trolleybus DTD 649, an electrical version of their new 'Steer' goods chassis. DTD 649's chassis (No. 301086) had a wheelbase of just under 18ft 2ins (5.53 metres) and could take a body 30ft (9.15 metres) long. Its twin axles were situated at the extreme front of the chassis frame. Leyland also built a 70-seat rear-entrance body for it. Power was provided by a Metro-Vick 95 h.p. electric motor, driving the rear axle. After several months as a demonstration vehicle it entered the London Transport fleet in September 1939, as their No. 1671. It was classified as type X7 (the letter prefix denoted its experimental basis). It operated on route 667 (Hammersmith to Hampton Court), based at Fulwell

---

The top-heavy, tall and narrow appearance of Bradford twin-steer trolleybus 522 (AK 9963) is shown in this contemporary view (right).

The original Leyland 'Gnu' arrived with Alexander's in September 1937 as a Leyland demonstrator, but was not purchased until 1939. This view (left) shows the modern lines of P411 (WG 6608). (G BOOTH)

---

depot, until it was ousted by the new Q1 class of BUT 9641T trolleybuses in 1948. It spent its remaining days at Hanwell depot working route 607 (Shepherd's Bush to Uxbridge). In 1955 it was withdrawn from service and, unfortunately, scrapped.

Leyland Motors were also experimenting in the single-deck motorbus field at this time. At the 1937 Commercial Motor Show, Leylands proudly displayed their new 'Gnu' chassis (No. 15229), designated the TEP1. This bore a 40-seat body by Alexander, with its entrance placed some 5ft (1.53 metres) forward of its foremost axle. The wheelbase was 16ft 3ins (4.95 metres), and the overall length of the complete vehicle was 30ft (9.15 metres). At this date, of course, Ministry of Transport regulations insisted that any bus of this length must have a third axle. The normal practice was to place this third axle at the **rear** of the chassis, as in the case of the AEC 'Renown' double- and single-deckers and the Leyland 'Tiger' TS6T single-decker. The 'Gnu' was powered by a standard 8.6 litre diesel engine (114.3 mm bore x 139.7 mm stroke), which was located in a far from normal position **beside** the driver at the very front of the vehicle. Transmission was through a four-speed gearbox and a single-plate clutch, whilst the braking was by wedge-operated servo brakes. The radiator was on the **nearside**, just in front of the entrance. The chassis had an unladen weight of 4 tons 10 cwt (4576 kg). Alexander placed this coach into their own fleet as No. P411 (WG 6608).

Leyland 'Gnu' FGC 593, new to the City Coach Company, is seen here (left) in post-war years in the fleet of Thomas Wright of Southend. (SURFLEET TRANSPORT PHOTOGRAPHS)

The following year, 1938, a second 'Gnu' chassis (No. 16571) was also bodied by Alexander and became No. P436 (WG 6676). Meanwhile the City Coach Company of Brentwood, Essex, bought the third TEP1 chassis (No. 16769), which became No. G1 (FGC 593) in that fleet. This vehicle was fitted with a fully-fronted 40-seat front-entrance body by Duple. It looked vaguely like the contemporary streamlined steam locomotive, the 'Coronation Scot'. It was used on City's limited-stop route from London (Wood Green) to Southend-on-Sea.

In May 1939 Leyland constructed five of an improved 'Gnu' chassis, designated the TEC2. In many respects it was similar to the 'Steer' chassis referred to above. The radiator had been shifted to the more conventional position at the front, whilst the front axles were now situated as far forward as possible. The quintet was purchased by the City Coach Company as Nos. G2-G6 (HVW 213-217), and they were given Duple full-front 39-seat bodies, but this time with **central** entrances. Their chassis numbers were 302991-302995.

In 1940 a team of designers from Alexander's and Leyland were able to bring to fruition the 'Panda' project. The main difference between this undesignated model and the TEC2 was that the 8.6 litre engine had been repositioned **horizontally** off-centre and against the right-hand member of chassis no. 303755. A drop-frame extension had been added to the chassis, which enabled a 45-seat body with a recessed central entrance to be constructed for it. Whereas Alexander had built coach bodies for their 'Gnus', the 'Panda' received a **bus** body. As their No. P683 (WG 9519), it commenced duty in September 1941. But for the deepening wartime difficulties, the six-wheeler might have made more of a mark upon the omnibus scene in the 1940s.

Eventually P411 passed into the hands of Stanhope Motor Services in 1945. At a later date this operator modified it by removing the rearmost of its two front axles, after new Ministry of Transport regulations removed the need for a third axle for 30 ft (9.15 metre) long single-deckers. P436 was bought by Truman & Silver of Shirebrook, Derbyshire. They, too, altered their 'Gnu' by moving the radiator round to the front of the vehicle. P683 also ended up with Truman & Silver in 1946, but later passed into the hands of East Midland Motor Services, who never actually operated it as a bus.

The third TEP1 was sold by City Coaches to neighbouring Wrights of Southend in 1948. In their turn Wrights sold it to Oliver Taylor's Coaches of Caterham, Surrey. The five TEC2s were acquired by Eastern National Omnibus Co, when they bought out City Coaches in 1954. The new owners kept them for two years before selling them off again as follows:- No. 118 (HVW 213) to Symonds of South Kirkby, who passed it on to Keelings of Leeds in 1958; Nos. 119/121 (HVW 214/216) went to Heavy Motor Services of Kirkstall, Leeds; Nos. 120/122 (HVW 215/217) were acquired by the well-known dealers, AMCC Ltd of London E15.

Maybe it was the Second World War that killed immediate interest in twin-steering PSVs? Maybe it was the inveterate conservatism of the bus and coach industry? We can only surmise. All we do know for sure is that there was a gap of 21 years between the debut of the 'Panda' and that of the Bedford VAL.

However, in 1947, three rather unusual chassis were constructed by Leyland. They possessed what can only be described as 'temporary' twin-steering arrangements, pending amendments to transport legislation. The Northern Ireland Road Transport Board wanted half a dozen 30ft (9.15 metre) long 'Tigers' for the Belfast airport route. Since there were narrow lanes

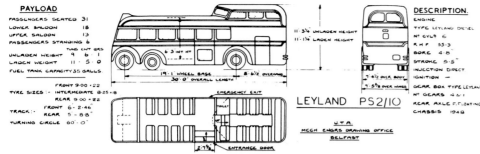

PAYLOAD

PASSENGERS SEATED	31
LOWER SALOON	18
UPPER SALOON	13
PASSENGERS STANDING	6
UNLADEN WEIGHT	9 · 6 · 1
LADEN WEIGHT	11 · 5 · 0
FUEL TANK CAPACITY	35 GALLS.

TYRE SIZES :- INTERMEDIATE 8·25 × 18
FRONT 9·00 × 22
REAR 9·00 × 22

TRACK :- FRONT 6 · 2·46″
REAR 5 · 8·8″

TURNING CIRCLE 60′· 0″

DESCRIPTION.

ENGINE
TYPE LEYLAND DIESEL
Nᵒ CYLˢ 6
R.H.P. 53·3
BORE 4·8
STROKE 5·5″
INJECTION DIRECT
IGNITION —
GEAR BOX TYPE LEYLAND
Nᵒ GEARS 4 M·I
REAR AXLE F. F. FLOATING
CHASSIS 1948

LEYLAND PS2/10

U.T.A.
MECH ENGRS DRAWING OFFICE
BELFAST

These photographs show the front nearside (in NIRTB livery) of GZ 7708, and the rear offside (in UTA livery) of GZ 7709, the two unusual 'temporary' twin-steer Leyland Tiger PS2/10s built for Northern Ireland. Note the attractive design of beading uniting the two front mudguards on GZ 7709. Above is a contemporary engineer's drawing of the plan and elevation of the design. (Official photographs of NIRTB and UTA).

---

to be negotiated 'en route', the bodies could not be more than 7ft 6ins (2.29 metres) wide. At a later date four of these chassis were cancelled from the Board's order, so that only chassis nos. 472474/472475 were actually sold to the NIRTB. These PS2/10s had a second axle in the front that would be easily removable, once the government restrictions on vehicles of that length were lifted. They were powered by normal Leyland 0600 diesel engines of 9.8 litres (122mm bore x 139.7mm stroke), and they had synchromesh gearboxes and vacuum brakes. The wheelbase had been extended from the usual 17ft 6in (5.34 metres) of the post-war 'Tiger' to 18ft 9ins (5.72 metres). The NIRTB built their own body for chassis no. 472474 in 1948 - a 27-seater central-entrance one-and-a-half-decker coach, with fleet number E8940 and registered GZ 7708. Three **years** later the other chassis was given a similar body and entered the Board's fleet as No. E8941 (GZ 7709).

The NIRTB became part of the new Ulster Transport Authority, who in 1958 removed the additional axles, replaced the bodies with their own 60-seat double-deck bodywork, and redesignated them as PD2/10s. Even the chassis numbers were altered to 473501/473500! E8941 was renumbered M659

and re-registered as WZ 659, rejoining the UTA fleet on 29 August 1958; E8940 became M660 (WZ 660), re-entering service on 1 December 1958. M659 was withdrawn by the UTA on 31 May 1971. Five years later it was purchased for preservation by Mr H Cunningham of Carrickfergus, Co Antrim. M660 soldiered on until August 1971, and by April 1973 it had become a Belfast playbus!

A solitary 8ft (2.44 metres) wide three-axle 'Tiger' (designated as PS2/11) was also constructed. Chassis No. 472473 was sold in 1949 to City Coaches, who had a rare Heaver half-cab 39-seat central-entrance bus body fitted to it. It became No. G7 (NVX 170). In 1954 it, too, became part of the Eastern National fleet, and they renumbered it as 132. Four years later, having had its additional axle removed, it was sold to Barton Transport of Chilwell, Notts. They stripped it down, redesignated it a PS2/11B (B for Barton), and had a 69-seat double-deck body built for it by Northern Counties. As their No. 794 (794 ARR), it spent much of its time on the Stamford town service, route 8. It was destined to be one of the very last double-deckers that this large independent fleet ran in service. When it was withdrawn by them in May 1975, it went to Lloyd's of Nuneaton.

The two photographs below do not look at all like the same bus; but they are! City Coach Co's 'temporary' twin-steer Leyland, G7 (NVX 170), is shown (left) in original condition before having its additional axle removed. It was later sold to Barton Transport of Chilwell with a job-lot of 'Tigers' for rebuild to double-deck form, and eventually emerged as 794 ARR with Northern Counties bodywork, seen (right) at the depot of Lloyd's of Nuneaton. (D W K JONES; A M WITTON).

2
The early VALs

These two photographs illustrate the prototype Weymann 'Topaz' body as fitted to the demonstrator that later became 472 DYK. The narrow stairwell turning to the right, characteristic of the VAL type, is clearly illustrated. (METROPOLITAN-CAMMELL-WEYMANN LTD.)

It was at the 1962 Commercial Motor Show, staged at Earl's Court, that Vauxhall Motors Ltd presented their twin-steer, six-wheeled coach to the World's transport press. The VAL was launched at the same time as its small sister the VAS, which had seats for only 29 passengers - a modern replacement for the popular OB of the 1940s and early 1950s. Three years later the range was completed by the appearance of the third model, the 45-seater VAM. Whereas the VAS and the VAM had orthodox 20in (50.8cm) wheels, the VAL had wheels of a diameter of only 16in (40.6cm). Incidentally this coincided with the successful launching of the 16in bicycle on to the home market!

In other respects the VAL was not as revolutionary as had been the 'Gnu' and the 'Panda'. It was powered by a Leyland '0400' diesel engine of 9.8 litres, developing 125 b.h.p. The engine was mounted **vertically** at the front of the chassis (hence the **V** in the designation) in the normal position, immediately behind the radiator. An American designed Clark five-speed synchromesh gearbox (with overdrive for the highest ratio) was built under licence by the Turner Manufacturing Company for the VAL14. The number '14' was the code for the type of engine fitted, as with all Bedfords at this time. The VAL's overall dimensions were 36ft (11 metres) long by 8ft 2.5ins (2.5 metres) wide. The vehicle's unladen weight varied between 6 tons 10 cwt (6610 kgs) and 7 tons 10 cwt (7627 kgs), according to the style of bodywork fitted.

At the 1962 Show there were three completed VAL14s to be seen. The first of these was 7999 MD, which had a luxurious 44-seat Plaxton 'Embassy II' body, and which had been ordered by I.T. Coach Operators. Subsequently this passed into the hands of Bloomfield's Coaches of London SE5, who upseated it to 46 passengers. Its unladen weight was only 6 tons 9 cwt 3 qr (6572 kgs). The second vehicle was at that time unregistered, but seems to have been 883 HMJ, which was tried out as a demonstrator by Edinburgh Corporation on their route 1 (Clermiston Circle) in March 1963, and by King Alfred Motor Services of Winchester in April 1963. In 1964 it was purchased by Moreton's of Nuneaton. It had a Duple 'Vega Major' coach body and had an unladen weight of 6 tons 10 cwt 1 qr (6623 kgs). There was also a Weymann-bodied chassis on the stand; it had chassis number RHD62/1 and bore the registration 472 DYK. Later the Weymann body was removed and a Plaxton one substituted. By 1966 it had become a racing car transporter for Jack Brabham - probably the first such conversion of a VAL. A fourth early chassis (No. LHD62/3) was given a 49-seat Plaxton body, the one later transferred onto RHD62/1.

A bus version of the VAL appeared during 1963 in the form of 525 LMJ, a demonstrator with a 53-seat Willowbrook body. At this point it is important to emphasise that Willowbrook and Duple (Midland) bodies were identical, and were both built at the same works at Loughborough. Whether a vehicle bore a Willowbrook plate or a Duple (Midland) one seems to have been according to the personal preference of each operator! In December 1963 525 LMJ went up to Scotland for trials. On the 2nd and 3rd of the month it was used by McGill's on their Paisley (St James's Street) to Fairway Avenue route. From the 17th until Christmas Eve it was operated on Edinburgh Corporation's route 1. For the remainder of December it was on loan to Scottish Omnibuses Ltd for their Edinburgh - North Berwick run. After its stint as a demonstrator it was sold to Moreton's of Nuneaton, joining 883 HMJ as we have noted above. Later it passed into the hands of West Coast Motor Service at Campbeltown, Argyllshire.

The impending success of the VAL14 was demonstrated at the 9th British Coach Rally, held at Brighton in April 1963. Eleven VALs were entered, but 883 HMJ and Jeffways & Pilot's 52-seater Duple 'Vega Major' bodied 7771 BH failed to turn up. However, the Show prototype 7999 MD was present, as was another Duple-bodied VAL14, 246 JTM, belonging to Taylor's Reliance Coaches of Shefford, Bedfordshire. There were no less than six Plaxton-bodied examples, of which five had

Two relatively unusual types of bodywork for the VAL are illustrated on this page. The Yeates 'Fiesta' body as supplied to Whippet of Hilton on 390 GEW (top right) shows the flamboyant style associated with the Loughborough manufacturer. On the other hand, the two Harrington 'Legionnaires' (below) are angular in concept though no less attractive than the generous curving lines usually expected from Harrington's. Barton's 994 (994 VRR) (below left) was one of eight of the type delivered to the Nottingham company. Yelloway had four, of which CDK 409C is shown in later life (below right) in typical seaside boarding-house country while owned by Baker's of Weston-super-Mare. (G R MILLS; P CAIN; P CAIN.)

'Panorama' bodywork (AML 148A, 6 JNM, 293 LG, 776 LG and 3711 RU); one (AME 719A) had the special 'Val' bodywork. Apart from the two with LG registrations, with seating for 49, the rest had seats for 52 which was to become the

normal layout for the VAL14.

A third coachbuilder represented among the VALs at that event was Yeates of Loughborough. They had adapted the 'Fiesta' body design for 390 GEW of Whippet Coaches, Hilton, Huntingdonshire. In all only ten other VALs were to receive bodies from that particular works, and of these only three (plus the original Whippet) were in the form of coaches; they went to Gibson of Barlestone, Leicestershire (179 CNR and 407 EAY) and Rickards of London W2 (No. 1, AYV 92B). The latter was one of the very last to receive a Yeates body before the firm discontinued its body-building activities to concentrate on dealing in buses and coaches.

The long-established firm of Harrington's of Hove designed the 'Legionnaire' body for the VAL, bearing all the distinctive hallmarks of that bodybuilder. Taylor's Reliance Coaches' 72 MMJ and Gill of Sheffield's 166 JWA carried this body. In all Harrington's built 42 'Legionnaires' before they sadly faded from the scene, and these were shared by no less than 21 different operators. The largest helping by far went to Barton Transport of Chilwell, who bought eight (Nos. 989-996, 989-996 VRR). Richmond of Epsom bought five (531-533/535/536 LOR); Yelloway of Rochdale four (CDK 409-412C, the last two being for their subsidiary, Cream's); and several firms purchased two apiece, viz: Abbott, Blackpool (AFR 17B/27B), Ewer Group, London N16 (ALR 451B for Grey-Green and ALR 453B for Batten), Heaps Tours of Leeds (CNW 154C/155C), Interline of London WC2 (LMG 951C/952C) and Leigh of Bolton (AWH 371B and DBN 642C). Instances of a single purchase of a 'Legionnaire' are:- Aston, Marton

Two views of the Weymann 'Topaz II' body are shown (right). The top view shows a 'Topaz II' under construction at the Addlestone factory, bearing a mysterious 'registration' which **might** have been a works reference. Below is seen FWW 809C in service with Billie's of Mexborough. (METROPOLITAN-CAMMELL-WEYMANN LTD; D AKRIGG).

(AWD 217B), Jackson, Chorley (CTJ 706B), Lacey, London E6 (YHM 606), Lloyd, Nuneaton (FAC 101C), Morris, Bearwood (8750 HA), Shadwell, Warrington (BED 366C), Shamrock and Rambler, Bournemouth (100 BRU) and Summerbee, Southampton (CCR 963C). For a manufacturer so popular in the London area and along the South Coast, it is ironical that only ten 'Legionnaire' bodies, less than a quarter of the total built, were bought by operators in Harrington's normal clientele area. Again, it seems strange that only Harris and Leigh placed repeat orders with Harrington.

By 1965 two other coachbuilders were providing bodies suitable for the VAL chassis. Weymann, having tried out their 'Topaz' body, with its overhanging hoodlike roof fore and aft, produced the 'Topaz II'. The original 'Topaz', of which only one seems to have been built, was originally fitted to the VAL demonstrator, 472 DYK; after it was replaced by a Plaxton body on that chassis, it was transferred to BMK 345A for Rowson's of Hayes. The 'Topaz II' found very little custom; Wallace Arnold was the only large operator to show sufficient interest to take delivery of a 'Topaz' (CUM 494C). The others went to smaller fry - Billie's Coaches of Mexborough (FWW 809C), Clarke of London SE20 (KRO 545C), R I Davies of Tredegar (No. 50, FAX 6C), Fox of Hayes (JNK 686C) and Jones of Aberbeeg (No. 122, FAX 314C).

The other newcomer in 1965 was Marshall of Cambridge, but their bodies were for bus use and come under the province of our next chapter.

3
The VAL as a bus

Although the vast majority of VALs sold not only had coach bodywork, but spent most of their days on coaching duties, there was a sizeable minority of these six-wheelers that were either specifically designed for bus work, or else were used by their owners on stage carriage work for much of the time. In the latter category, for example, came a batch of 52-seat Harrington 'Legionnaires' that appeared in the Barton fleet (Nos. 989-996, 989-996 VRR), alongside a quartet of 52-seat Plaxton bodied VALs bought earlier (Nos. 970, 414 SRR; 971, 971 SRR; 972, 650 SVO; and 973, 433 TAL). Likewise No. 1000 (ANN 700B), which had appeared in the demonstration park at the 1964 Commercial Motor Show at Earls Court, also sported a coach body – this time by Duple. On the other hand, Barton's initial intake of VALs was made up of dual-doorway bus-bodied examples by Yeates (Nos. 963-969, 963-969 RVO) of which the first four had only 50 seats, compared with 56 seats in the last three. Later Barton bought out Hall Brothers of South Shields, and as a result took a further nine VALs into their fleet. The oldest (renumbered 1120, JFT 259) had a 52-seat Plaxton body, whilst the remainder (Nos. 1121-1128, BCU 281C/282C, CCU 276/277/768/769D, DCU 584/585D) had 52-seat Duple 'Vega Major' bodies. Another secondhand acquisition by the Chilwell-based firm was 1060 (ARY 693B), a 52-seat Plaxton 'Panorama', which had originally been No. B8 in the fleet of Provincial of Leicester. This made their total stock of VALs up to 30.

A & C Wigmore of Dinnington, now in South Yorkshire, also built up a fair-sized fleet of VALs; at various times they owned 16 of them, all with bus bodies, as follows:- 27 GWX, DWW 838B, HWU 402/403C, NWR 788D, OWW 686/787E, SWU 654F, VWW 982F, WWU 787G, YWY 949G, BWU 314H, FYG 663J, GWX 159J and HWU 519J. Of these, the ones up to and

Barton's first batch of VALs were these unusual dual-door models with Yeates Europa bodywork. The 'IN' and 'OUT' labels (the latter obscured by the sliding door) on 969 (969 RVO) leave no room for doubt! (P CAIN)

Above are shown two Barton coaches with apparently similar Duple 'Vega Major' bodies but very different life histories. 1000 (ANN 700B) (left) was the celebrated 1964 Commercial Motor Show model, and was photographed in the demonstration park outside Earl's Court; note the unusual provision of fixed windows instead of sliding ventilators. On the other hand, 1121 (BCU 281C) was one of the fleet of VALs acquired by Barton when they took over Hall Brothers and Taylor Brothers in South Shields and North Shields respectively. It was photographed, however, in classic 'Barton country' at Peterborough. (D KAYE; D AKRIGG).

---

including OWW 687E had Duple (Midland) plates, whilst the remainder bore the Willowbrook name. In addition Wigmore purchased AJS 110B from Mitchell of Stornoway; this, too, had a Duple (Midland) plate. The last-mentioned vehicle had 53 seats, 27 GWX had 54 seats, but all the rest provided seating for 56.

The North Western Road Car Co Ltd needed some specially designed buses to squeeze under the 8ft 9ins (2.67 metres) low bridge under the Bridgewater Canal at Dunham Woodhouses, on their route 98 into Warrington. It was decided that the answer lay in a combination of a VAL14 chassis and Strachan body. Ten of these buses were constructed, with 52-seat bodies, and were numbered 130-139 (AJA 130-139B) in the North Western fleet. They remained in service until 30th June 1971, when they were ousted by equally special Bristol RELL6Ls with ECW 49-seat bodies (Nos. 373-381, SJA 373-381J). The Bedfords and Bristols shared a most distinctive domed roof profile to fit the contour of the bridge. After withdrawal in 1971, some of the replaced Bedfords were shipped across to Ireland. AJA 131B had a spell with J E Coaches of Brackley

Wigmore's of Dinnington had – and still have – a rapid turnover of rolling-stock; it has proved easier to photograph their buses with subsequent owners than with Wigmore themselves! The first of the long line of Wigmore VALs was 27 GWX, (top left) which was run to earth at the Troon depot of Dodd's Coaches, a member of the AA Motor Services co-operative. A later model (top right) was VWW 982F, seen with Gem of Colsterworth carrying a school party at Three-kingham, Lincolnshire. In total contrast are the domed-roof VALs bought by the North Western Road Car Co to solve their low bridge problems. 135 (AJA 135B) is seen (bottom left) entering Altrincham bus station to the accompaniment of a cheerful smile from the 'clippie'! (D AKRIGG; D KAYE; A M WITTON).

before being sold to the GAA Club of Hilltown, Co Dublin. AJA 135B passed through the hands of R Ward of Kirkby on its way to the 6th Newtownards Sea Scouts in Co Down,

16

Northern Ireland; they in their turn resold it to the Ulster Defence Association.

Other rare bus bodies came from the works of Marshall's of Cambridge. Burton Cars of Brixham, Devon, had one such VAL14 – COD 925C – which later saw service with Tally Ho! Coaches of Kingsbridge; unfortunately this unique vehicle, the only VAL bearing a normal Marshall body other than those intended for airport work, was scrapped during 1982.

Two BEA airport buses – and the fate of a third – can be seen in these three views. 6561 (OYF 262F) is seen in BEA red and white livery at Heathrow Airport Central (top right), while ex-Shearings Group coach 6559 (GMB 111C) is photographed at the same place (bottom left) similarly bedecked. On the other hand, Marshall 'airside' bus LMG 155C later passed to the British Airports Authority at Stansted (bottom right). (A M WITTON (2), G R MILLS).

17

The last of the three VALs delivered to the ill-fated fleet of Tailby & George (Blue Bus Service) of Willington was Willowbrook-bodied BRB 674G, seen (top left) at Burton bus station. It was fitted with semi-coach seats. One of the most photographed VALs - at one of the most commonly-chosen locations! - was Seaview Services ADL 321B, (bottom left), representing the independent stage operator among a mass of Tilling green Bristols in Ryde, Isle of Wight. (D AKRIGG; D KAYE)

In the latter category of airport buses, British European Airways purchased three small batches of Marshall-bodied buses for carrying airline passengers within airport precincts, mainly at Heathrow. They were LMG 155-164C, OGO 337/340E, and OYF 262-269F. Actually the two 'E' registered buses were really part of the last-named batch, but arrived in time to receive the earlier year suffix. They all had 40-seat bodies with access from either side. Similar vehicles RAR 267-270D, delivered to Interline of London WC2 for airport work, eventually ended up with Whyte's Airport Services in 1975.

Blue Bus Services of Willington, Derbyshire, was a well-known North Midlands independent firm during the heyday of the VAL. Their trio used on stage carriage routes consisted of KRB 426D, a 52-seat Duple coach, and YRB 203G and BRB 674G, both 56-seat dual-purpose Willowbrooks. They were allocated 'book' fleet numbers BD6/8/9 respectively, although by the time they arrived the practice of showing fleet numbers on Blue Bus vehicles had ceased. All three passed to Derby Corporation, when they purchased Tailby & George's Blue Bus Services business in 1973. They were numbered 35/36/38 respectively in the municipal fleet. Sadly the oldest VAL and the only coach-bodied one, KRB 426D, was destroyed in the disastrous fire at the Willington garage premises on 5th January 1976. The two Willowbrook-bodied ones had already been sold out of service by Derby Borough Transport by January 1976, and so escaped incineration.

The relatively flat Fenland country and parts of adjoining counties have formed a happy hunting ground for the VAL. Leon of Finningley, near Doncaster, have owned a sizeable number including bus-bodied 65 (ARR 720B) (top left), numbered like all Leon vehicles in a single chronological series. In more rural parts, coaches often tend to masquerade as buses, as with Fowler's of Holbeach Drove whose OWT 297K (top right) was seen at the firm's depot. (G R MILLS; D AKRIGG).

Seaview Services on the Isle of Wight purchased a 54-seat Duple (Midland) bodied VAL for their sole stage carriage route, between their depot and Ryde. ADL 321B was still on active service on this popular summertime route fifteen years later. All this operator's other VALs were coaches, viz: BDL 214B, FDL 585D, HDL 454E, NDL 313G, PDL 823H and SDL 838J. In addition they acquired one VAL secondhand – 44 EMO from Eagle Line of Swindon. Since at peak holiday times two vehicles were needed to operate the stage service timetable, and sometimes reliefs or duplicates may have been required, most of these VALs must have served as buses at some stage of their careers.

Leon Motors of Finningley near Doncaster, on the South Yorkshire/Nottinghamshire borders, bought one new 53-seat Duple (Midland) bodied bus, which became No. 65 (ARR 720B) in their fleet. It was later joined by OWW 686E and SWU 654F from Wigmore's of Dinnington, which became Leon's Nos. 77/80 respectively. In addition Leon's operated several VAL coaches. Nos. 64 (448 VAL) and 70 (LAL 547E) were bought new, and to this pair was added a couple purchased from the Ewer Group's Grey-Green fleet – SYX 576/577F. It is worth noting that 448 VAL has a plausible claim to be the longest-serving VAL with its original operator; it was delivered in February 1964, and was not withdrawn until July 1981, nearly seventeen and a half years later! It would be quite difficult to beat this record, as the model has only been available for twenty years.

In Lincolnshire, where many rural routes run only to market towns on market days, and then carry pretty full loadings, the VAL came as a great boon. Appleby of Conisholme on the Lindsey Marshes bought two new (DBE 921C and PFU 163G), as well as buying PSC 230G from Lothian Transport. Although they were coaches, these vehicles were used on stage services into such towns as Caistor, Grimsby and Louth. Their neighbours, Grayscroft of Mablethorpe, have used a succession of coach-bodied VALs over the last two decades; the last of these, GVO 266D, was only withdrawn from their daily Mable-thorpe - Louth service in 1982. Daisy Bus Company of Broughton run routes into nearby Brigg and Scunthorpe and have used a number of VALs over the years, including 22 EFW, ABE 300B, GBE 300D, JBE 522E and MFU 196F (all new), together with secondhand KTC 550F, VAA 107H and PVE 592J. In what used to be the Parts of Kesteven, Wing of Sleaford have operated both new (ETL 899D and OCT 990H) and secondhand (91 MMJ, CCT 732C and SJJ 589F) VALs on their network of routes into Billingborough, Boston and Bourne. Even in 1983, Fowler of Holbeach Drove, right in the southern Fenland tip of the county, is using a secondhand six-wheeler (OWT 297K) on their main Spalding to Wisbech route.

Yeoman's of Canon Pyon, Herefordshire, had one Willowbrook-bodied VAL bus (No. 9, CVJ 800C), as well as several VAL coaches (700 CVJ, CVJ 500C, MCJ 800F). Irvine of Salsburgh, now in Strathclyde, had two VAL buses (BVD 828/829C), whilst operators with a single example included Ford of Fairburn, West Yorkshire (351 GYG), Jolly of South Hylton, Co Durham (BUP 148B), Martlew of Donnington Wood, Shropshire (3170 NT), Richmond of Epsom, Surrey (4230 PE) and Whittle of Highley, Shropshire (the re-registered JNT 252E).

VALs made ideal high-capacity transport for workers, which is probably why Maltby Mines Transport purchased a pair (4940 ET and DET 909D). As well as the British European Airways buses referred to above, BEA stationed a mixed bag of VALs at Abbotsinch, consisting of AXD 526/527B, DME 976A, GMB 111/112C, HMA 588C and HTU 881-884C, for service at Glasgow Airport. Some of these saw service at Heathrow as well. Silver Fox of Edinburgh used DLG 652F on their route to Glasgow Airport. Another firm associated with the airport business was Rickards of Brentford, whose ten VALs (Yeates-bodied AYV 92B and Duple-bodied LBY 169-177D) were regular visitors to Heathrow Airport on the firms various contract services for passengers and airline staff.

The VAL as a country bus, with the unusual refinement of a no-ticket farebox, is represented by CVJ 800C in Yeoman's attractive dark green livery in Hereford bus station. (A M WITTON).

4
The VAL as a coach workhorse

It was primarily for the long-distance coach operator and the tours firm that the Bedford VAL was designed. Its small wheels, and the fact that there were four of them at the front of the vehicle, was reckoned to ensure safety at high speeds on the new motorway network that was beginning to be built in Britain in the mid-1960s. After all, it had been on 2nd November 1959 that the then Minister of Transport, the colourful Ernest Marples, had declared open the first 45-mile

Two views of the Wallace Arnold Group's large VAL fleet are shown below. 229 HUM (left), one of the early ones, is seen in Wellington Street Coach Station in its home town of Leeds – interestingly carrying both 'Val' and 'Panorama' bodywork badges! EUG 914D (right) of the subsidiary Kitchins Tours fleet, is seen arriving at Torquay. (P CAIN; D AKRIGG).

We have referred in another chapter to the question of names on Bedford VAL coaches; but Heaps Tours of Leeds 104 (CNW 155C), with a Harrington Legionnaire body, must have been the only VAL to run with the name 'Leopard' - Leyland Motors would not have been amused! The coach was photographed at Torquay. (D AKRIGG).

---

stretch of the M1; until the advent of Barbara Castle at the Ministry, the motorways were to have no upper speed limit. Coaches regularly achieved speeds of well over 80 m.p.h. on this new 'race track'.

Wallace Arnold of Leeds is one of Britain's largest operators of extended tours, and they seem to have been well pleased with the VAL. Starting off in 1963 with a batch of three, 132-134 FUA, they continued to put batches in service at the beginning of each new season for some years, viz. 222-237 HUM (1964), BNW 615-623/636-641/643C and the Weymann-bodied CUM 494C (1965), EUG 904-916/919/921/926/927D and EUM 401D (1966), JUA 318-322E (1967), MNW 700-703F (1968) and RUA 713G along with SUB 666-668G (1969). The split between the VAL14 and the later VAL70 version came after MNW 700F. Some of these VALs were originally in the fleets of Wallace Arnold's various subsidiaries; Feather's ran 226 HUM, BNW 615-617C, EUG 904/916D; Kitchin operated 227/228 HUM, BNW 641C, EUG 908-911/914/915D; Wardways took in BNW 619C and EUG 919D; and all the final 1969 batch went to Woburn Garages (Evan Evan Tours) of London, which had become a Wallace Arnold subsidiary only in February of that year. In addition five VALs reached Wallace Arnold from the fleets of undertakings taken over. OTS 603 was acquired from the fleet of Dickson of Dundee in 1963, and was retained by Wallace Arnold until 1968; EJY 328D, JDR 285/418F and NJY 992J came from Embankment of Plymouth in 1974, but all except the last-mentioned had been withdrawn by the new owners within a few months.

Another, but smaller, Leeds operator, Heaps Tours, also took some of these coaches into stock, consisting of 73 FUM, 770 JUA, CNW 154/155C, EUM 242D and HUB 542/543E.

Across the Pennines, in Cheshire there were several groups of firms who were very interested in the VAL. The Godfrey Abbott Group, based in Sale, bought nine. Into their own fleet they injected 1347 LG, AMB 888B, and HMA 597/598C, whilst for their subsidiary Pride of Sale Motor Tours they purchased 129 TU, CMA 298B, UMA 615E, DLG 652F and JMB 399G. On 21st March 1967 Abbott took over Altrincham Coachways, previously a subsidiary of the North Western Road Car Co Ltd, who had taken delivery of a pair of VALs the previous year (Nos. 990/991, FJA 990/991D).

In Altrincham itself the Jackson/Pleasureways/Ribblesdale/Shearing Group was the complicated-sounding name of the domin-

In the early years of its production, the VAL was an inveterate rallygoer, and literally hundreds of them must have been shown off at one time or another to admiring coachmen at Blackpool or Brighton. Bostock's 14 (OTU 602D) is seen brand-new at the Blackpool Coach Rally in 1966 (left). (T HARTLEY)

---

enthusiastic users of the VAL coach in the business, and altogether they took delivery of forty VALs new (plus the odd one or two secondhand purchases) between 1963 and 1969. Indeed, 800 YTU, which arrived in April 1963, was one of the very first production models to be sold. There followed AMB 666B and CTU 888B of 1964 (the former passed by a devious route to Grenville's of Camborne, with whom it is still in daily use in 1983); GMB 111/112C, HMA 577/588C, HTU 881-884C and KMB 900C of 1965; NMB 301/302/304/305D and OMA 501-505D of 1966; ULG 21-23/27/30/31/33-35/38/39E (1967); ATU 50-58F (1968); and HTU 88-92/96-99G (1969).

At Congleton another fan of the six-wheeler was E J Bostock & Sons, who had one of the longest associations with the VAL of any operator. Starting off with 776 LG (1963), they progressed through BMB 680B (1964), JLG 326C (1965), OTU 602D, PMA 246D, RMA 326D (1966), VLG 76E (1967), BMB 560/561F (1968), HTU 762-765G (1969), PLG 762-764H (1970), WTU 690J (1971) and finally DMB 860/861K, FLG 360K (1972).

In contrast to this long run by Bostock, the well-known

Even nowadays, coaches seldom stay long in the Whittle's of Highley fleet; in the VAL era it was a case of one year maximum. JNT 252E, bought secondhand in April 1967, lasted a mere nine months with Whittle's, for whom it was the last full-sized bus bodied vehicle they ever owned. So we have to illustrate it here (left) in use later by the well-known Somerset independent stage carriage operator, Wake's of Sparkford. (P CAIN).

firm of Smith of Wigan, including their subsidiaries such as Blundell, Happiway-Spencers, and Webster Brothers, had only a mild flirtation with the VAL. The group bought XWM 75 in 1963 (apparently for Blundell, hence the Southport registration), followed by BEK 98C, BEK 316C and CFY 956/957C in 1965 and CEK 53-57D in 1966. They also purchased 222 CYG secondhand.

Whittle's of Highley in Shropshire seems to have been a more interested customer, taking in the VAL model in most years up to and including 1972. Their purchases were 4023 AW (1963), AAW 320B (1964), CUJ 309/313C (1965), FAW 100/118D (1966), HUJ 506-508/515E (1967), LAW 105-107/120F (1968), NUX 105-107/120G (1969) and XAW 505/506/514/550K (1972). Of these, FAW 100D and XAW 550K were in the livery of their associated company, Corvedale of Ludlow. They also bought JNT 252E secondhand from Phillipson of Shiptonthorpe, Yorkshire, who had registered this bus-bodied vehicle LWY 820D but had never used it under that number. During the 'VAL years', it was Whittle's practice to replace their entire fleet of 30-odd vehicles every year; so the above schedule of 26 VALs were never there at one time and seldom accounted for more than a small proportion of the fleet strength, which was mainly made up of smaller Bedford models like the SB and VAM.

Moving down to the East Midlands, the only operator (apart from Barton, dealt with in the previous chapter) to use the VAL at all extensively was Skills of Nottingham. They borrowed an early production coach (307 NOF), which led them to order ten of their own - Nos. 41-48 (41-48 SAU) and 49/50 (ATV 49/50B). These did not stay very long with the fleet, but this was no reflection on their value, as Skills have quite a rapid turnover of stock.

In the West Midlands, Don Everall of Wolverhampton supported the six-wheeler, but from 1966 until after its takeover by the NBC it deserted Bedford for Ford. In the first year of VAL production Everall's took delivery of 9800-9805 UK, followed by 140-144/153 EJW in 1964, and CUK 501-506/526C in 1965. Extra VALs came secondhand; 1211 DH from Central Coachways of Walsall in 1966, ANK 399B from Harpenden Motors in 1968, and ULG 34E from Pleasureways of Altrincham in 1970. For a short while Don Everall's 153 EJW had been with Central Coachways, where it joined 1211 DH (with which it was re-acquired by Everall in 1966), along with 1212 DH and BDH 510/511C. In Birmingham itself the VAL found favour principally with Allenways, Smith, and Stockland. Allenways had 648 JOC, EVP 369/370D, and

Apart from 'Leopard', another 'copyrighted' name carried by a VAL was Mulley's of Ixworth 101 (FCF 602D) 'Rover Roadliner', at the time when the Daimler Roadliner chassis was beginning its brief vogue! Bury St Edmunds coach park is the venue. (A M WITTON)

HOV 224E. Smith's Imperial Coaches bought theirs in two periods with a three-year gap between them, viz. COP 500/600C, GOA 100D, followed by UOL 400H and DOE 111K. Stockland bought 22-24 JOC, COH 25/26C, FOC 1-4D and JOK 10E.

In East Anglia, support for the VAL came mainly from medium-sized independents such as Kenzie of Shepreth, Cambridge-shire (CVE 666C, GCE 999E, JJE 55F and LVE 617G); Mulley of Ixworth, Suffolk (VGV 88, XGV 222, FCF 602D and LCF 999F); and Young of Rampton, Cambridgeshire (JER 584F, NER 823H and PVE 592J, plus secondhand CCU 769D, GBK 995E, PUE 952F and DWT 890H). Whippet of Hilton, Huntingdonshire (now in Cambridgeshire) was an early buyer of the VAL, as we have already noted in chapter 2. They followed up 390 GEW with FFL 86D; they then bought no less than ten of the VAL70 model, UFL 498H, VEG 244H, VFL 584H, AEG 371/564/565J, AFL 384-386J, and finally PEW 946K. Between 1966 and 1969 Whippet also took in four second-hand VALs, namely OMA 505D (ex-Jackson, see above), JVR 250F (ex-Mayfair, Wythenshawe) and SWP 734/735F (ex-Regent, Redditch).

Along the South Coast, Shamrock & Rambler of Bournemouth purchased the coach, 100 BRU, which they entered for the 1963 British Coach Rally at Brighton. In 1966 they added FRU 420D. After their takeover by the Tilling Association Ltd, on behalf of the then Transport Holding Company, in 1967, Shamrock & Rambler received JEL 850E, followed by MEL 987-989F; the last two of that trio actually became Nos. 88/89 in the fleet of Charlie's Cars of Westbourne, who had also been taken over by the Tilling Association in 1967. Subsequent deliveries were PEL 994-997G, SRU 252/253H and VLJ 231-233J. VHT 911H was acquired secondhand from National Travel (South West) Ltd (see below). The newly-formed National Bus Company gave control of Shamrock & Rambler to Hants & Dorset, who themselves took delivery of a pair of VALs, WEL 804/805J, in 1971 for the Bournemouth coach fleet. In 1964 Wilts & Dorset had been placed under the same management as Hants & Dorset, and were completely absorbed into the latter company in 1972. Wilts & Dorset bought a baker's dozen of the six-wheelers, namely 920-923 (LMR 731-734F), 924-927 (PEL 903-906G), 928-930 (SLJ 756-758H) and 62/63 (WEL 802/803J). All but the first four were registered in Bournemouth not Salisbury, reflecting the Hants & Dorset company's control.

It was across the Solent, in the Isle of Wight, that the VAL really reigned supreme. For two decades thousands of holidaymakers and day-trippers have enjoyed a ride in a VAL for the traditional 'Round the Island' tours, calling

The independent King's Cross coach station, London, has migrated to several sites in recent years. Whippet's secondhand VAL, JVR 250F, bought from Mayfair of Wythenshawe, is at the York Way site on the firm's Huntingdonshire express route in 1969. (A M WITTON).

at such places as the dinosaur-infested Blackgang Chine, the picturesque thatched village of Godshill, and Alum Bay with its multi-coloured sandy cliffs. The representative of the NBC on the Island is the Southern Vectis Omnibus Company, and they went for this type of coach in quite a big way. Commencing with Nos. 401/402 (ADL 109/110B) in 1964, they added Nos. 403-405 (EDL 992-994D), 406-409 (HDL 228-231E), 410 (PDL 351H) and 411/412 (SDL 743/744J). The two last-named vehicles can claim several distinctions; they were the last VALs delivered new to the Isle of Wight, and the only Plaxton-bodied examples ever bought new by an NBC subsidiary.

In 1967, Shamrock & Rambler took over three Isle of Wight-based coach operators - E H Crinage & Sons Ltd of Ventnor, Fountain Coaches of Cowes, and H Randall & Sons of Ventnor. The coach fleet thus built up, still trading under the names of the three acquired undertakings, was transferred to Southern Vectis control in 1969. Two ex-Shamrock & Rambler VALs, the original 100 BRU and PEL 994G, thus became Southern Vectis coaches nos. 114/118. They had been transferred to Fountain Coaches while the firm was under Shamrock & Rambler control.

The Hants & Dorset, Wilts & Dorset and Shamrock & Rambler companies had a substantial stock of VALs until fairly recently. Shown here are (bottom left) Shamrock & Rambler 525 (JEL 850E), bearing the name 'Chichester', at the garage at Holdenhurst Road near Bournemouth railway station; and (bottom right), Wilts & Dorset 920 (LMR 731F), the first VAL delivered to the Salisbury-based fleet. It was seen parked in Chepstow Street, Manchester, at the northern terminus of one of the numerous Forces leave services on which Wilts & Dorset VALs were regular performers. (A M WITTON (2)).

On the Isle of Wight the biggest, though far from the only, VAL fleet was that of the resident NBC company, Southern Vectis. Their 409 (HDL 231E) was photographed on Ryde sea front with the town's famous pier (which still carries BR trains and used to have petrol-driven trams as well!) in the background (top right). The adjacent fleet number was a somewhat different vehicle – 410 (SDL 743J), a VAL70 with one of the only Plaxton bodies delivered new on VALs to the NBC, seen in Shanklin bus station (bottom right). (D KAYE; A M WITTON).

We have dealt with Seaview Services, of Seaview near Ryde, fully in chapter 3. Shotters of Brighstone bought new 228 BDL, HDL 793/794E and NDL 556/557G, along with secondhand 878 KOU and URO 925E. Some of these Shotters later sold to their neighbours, Moss Motor Tours of Sandown, who also had their own new VALs (52 BDL, ADL 252B, EDL 783D, NDL 360/361G and PDL 816H). As well as the influx of secondhand vehicles from Shotters, Moss also bought 140 EJW from Don Everall and HBW 120D from Plants Coaches of Rishton, Lancashire. West Wight Motor Bus Company of Totland Bay ran three secondhand six-wheelers (5188 RU, OOR 320G and ROT 353G) while nearby Coaches (IOW) of Thorness Bay used their new pair, NDL 699/700G.

Down in the West Country, Western Roadways of Patchway, Bristol, bought nine VALs in all – 223 THU, EDD 883C, GDG 467D, NDF 630F, OAD 173F and Caetano-bodied RDF 878-881G. Also based in Bristol, Wessex Coaches had only four VALs – JAE 927/928D, MHU 926F and VHT 911H. Further west, in Devon, Embankment Tours of Plymouth, as well as operating the quartet mentioned above as being sold to Wallace Arnold, had earlier run YCO 313/314 and BDR 256B. Burton Cars of Brixham had a trio. In addition to the Marshall-bodied VAL (see chapter 3), they also used JOD 529E and AXF 379F. It is worth noting that Tally Ho! Coaches of Kingsbridge, nowadays one of the largest coach operators in those parts with a fleet of some 50 vehicles including double-deckers, never bought any VALs new but did acquire

A contrast in radiator styling and general design is provided by these two VALs running for Isle of Wight independents. Moss Motor Tours 140 EJW (above left), a one-time member of the Everall of Wolverhampton fleet, is seen at Whippingham Church on the traditional 'Round the Island' tour, in 1978 – appearing in excellent shape for a 15-year-old coach! A later VAL70, OOR 320G (above right), belonging to the West Wight Bus Company of Totland Bay, shows a recognisable family resemblance to the earlier coach, being built just before the revolutionary changes in Plaxton's body designs; it was seen at Ryde. Finally, VHT 911H was one of a few independently-owned VALs that passed as such to the National Bus Company; it is seen, (below right), wearing the characteristic Wessex livery, at the NBC coach park at Battersea Wharf, London, in 1973, just before the business was transferred to Wessex National Ltd. (G R MILLS; D KAYE; A M WITTON).

London's VALs naturally spent much of their time shuttling between the capital and the various resorts of the south and east coasts. Banfield's 'Empire's Best' subsidiary basically operated a London - Clacton route, but their Duple-bodied VAL CMD 206A - a precursor of the A-prefix registrations that will be around by the time you read this! - was seen (left) in Coulsdon, Surrey, heading down the A23 London - Brighton road in 1969. It was in the middle of the London - Brighton HCVC rally of that year, but was presumably not an entrant! (A M WITTON)

a large number secondhand. Their stock of used six-wheelers peaked at nine a couple of years ago, including COD 925C, the ex-Burton Marshall-bodied bus, which unfortunately went for scrap in the summer of 1982. In spring 1983 they still ran six, which were regularly used on local school contracts.

In the London metropolitan area the principal support came from the George Ewer Group, but even here the VAL never represented more than a small proportion of the 150 or so vehicles in the Group's fleets. Of the George Ewer constituent companies, Grey-Green took in 448 GYR, ALR 451B, CLK 700B and SYX 576/577F; Orange Luxury Coaches had 450 HLW and ALR 452B; Batten took ALR 453B; and Fallowfield & Britten used AYL 463 /464B. Later the Ewer Group acquired secondhand LLY 60D, ATU 55F, BAR 828F, HTU 741F and JUR 582G from Universal Cream Coaches Ltd, of Edmonton. Charles Banfield of Peckham bought several VALs in the initial stages of the model's production run - 75-77 (CMD 204-206A), 78 (EMH 811B), 79-82 (EMP 798-800/808B) and 89-92 (LGT 801-804D). Nos. 76, 77 and 79 were actually for the long-established subsidiary company, Empire's Best Coaches.

Richmond of Epsom, trading as Epsom Coaches, had a series with different body makers, viz. 4230 PE (Duple Midland), 531-533/535/536 LOR (Harrington), BOT 544C (Duple), NOR 635F (Plaxton) and VYT 493-495G (Duple Northern). Premier-Albanian of Watford invested in a total of ten VALs - 592/593 PUR, GAR 401-403C, CRO 161/162F, and OAR 67-69H. Charles Rickards Tours, with their extensive network of tours around Central London and also their important activity carrying airport passengers, bought ten VALs (Yeates-bodied No. 1, AYV 92B, and Duple-bodied Nos. 11-19, LBY 169-177D). Frames Tours, with whom Rickards were later amalgamated and finally lost their identity altogether on 1st January 1983, tried only four - Nos. 141/142 (MRO 144/145D) and 150/151 (TRO 706/707E). Timpson's, the BET subsidiary based in Catford, had the demonstrator 883 HMJ on trial for a few weeks in 1963, before ordering four VALs at a much later date - SJJ 587-590F. Also in South-East London, the Royal Arsenal Co-operative Society bought another four, Nos. 118/119, MMC 308/309C, and 120/121 (NYE 717/718E), as well as purchasing a pair for their subsidiary, Duval's (Nos. 69/70, RLD 96/97E). Some new firms began life with the Bedford VAL70, as in the cases of Pagan of Sutton (JUR 581-584G, RAR 675/676H and SKG

709H), Guards of London (TAR 183-189J) and Limebourne (NUR 471-474H). Although there were no large-scale VAL operators in the capital and its environs, yet, when they are all added up, London's VALs came to well over 400, being at least 20% of all UK sales! Of course, these 400 coaches were never all in service at any one time.

In Scotland, pride of place must be given to the civic fathers of Edinburgh, who found a good use for the VAL on city tours for all those who flocked to the 'Athens of the North' for either the 1970 Commonwealth Games or else the annual Edinburgh Festival. The coaches came in four consignments, viz. 213-218 (213-218 SC), 223-225 (MSF 223 -225F), 228-230 (PSC 228-230G) and 235-237 (SSF 235-237H). All but the first six ended up with the new Lothian Regional Transport undertaking after local government was reorganised in Scotland in 1976. They were frequently to be seen, with their smaller cousins in the same fleet, on the transport department's tour coach stance on Waverley Bridge, by the railway station.

Apart from the bus version (already dealt with in the previous chapter), at least thirty-three other VALs are known to

---

It wasn't just London among Britain's capital cities that used the VAL. Edinburgh Corporation's handsome black-and-white liveried coach fleet included no less than fifteen of them, together with other Bedford and Ford models. 217 (217 SC) was photographed in the Central Bus Garage (left), whilst later model 228 (PSC 228G) is set off by the handsome archi-tecture of the city's 'New Town' in St Andrew's Square. (D AKRIGG; A M WITTON).

A number of VALs came to fiery ends, as a result of accidents, depot fires or occasionally simple arson. One which was burnt out was NWN 786F of Morris of Swansea. It had just under a year of life remaining to it when photographed on a sunny day in Llanelli, in August 1976. (A M WITTON).

have been bought new by Scottish operators, three-quarters of them going to firms in the Southern Division of the Scottish Traffic Area. Few firms bought more than one VAL new, and only Park of Hamilton (371 FVA, NVD 648F, SVD 20/21G, AVA 238J) and Galloway of Harthill (GVA 91D, LGE 427E, NVA 561F and VVA 259H) bought more than a couple. Interestingly, although some of the earliest six-wheelers went new to operators North of the Border, only a handful of the VAL70 version were sold in Scotland.

The smaller and less populated Principality of Wales welcomed over 30 VALs as new. R I Davies of Tredegar bought seven of them, 16 JWO, EAX 888C, FAX 8C, FAX 697C, JAX 444D, JAX 634D and JAX 932D. Jones of Aberbeeg's share was four new ones plus a pair secondhand:- Nos. 122 (FAX 314C), 10 (JAX 384D), 11 (JAX 898D), 115 (JWO 794D); the secondhand ones were 104 (FWB 778C) ex-Littlewood of Sheffield, and 91 (FWH 354D) ex-Leigh of Bolton. Of the 'area agreement' companies in Wales, Rhondda Transport alone purchased any VALs - a mere three, 395-397 (395-397 WTG). Unlike the Scottish firms, some Welsh operators came back for second, third or more helpings. For example, Jenkins of Skewen (between Neath and Swansea) entered the VAL market late, well into the VAL70 era, buying VNY 987G, VTX 195G, YTG 528H, DTX 504J and DTX 942J. On the other hand, Eynon of Trimsaran (near Llanelli) was one of the pioneers, purchasing 695 ETH, BTH 987C, ETH 260D and FTH 989E. Similarly Demery of Morriston (on the outskirts of Swansea) took in 290 HWN, FCY 815D, GWN 8D, and finally NWN 786F. The last operator in this group is Morlais of Merthyr Tydfil with AHB 892B, CHB 213D, CHB 959E and DHB 863F. The holiday resorts on the North and West Coasts of Wales saw a few new VALs:- the users included Creams of Llandudno (BCC 1/6C, ECC 770E), Davies (Voel) of Dyserth (ODM 100E), Hollis of Shotton (NDM 1E), Lloyd's of Bagillt (KDM 792D), the Penmaenmawr Motor Co (MJC 172 and the oddly-registered URO 926F), and Royal Red of Llandudno (800 ACA, BCC 795C, DJC 886E). These eleven vehicles, however, although they were later joined by some secondhand purchases, seemed an inadequate share of VAL production for such a vast area containing several populous holiday resorts.

We have already discussed VAL purchases by the Tilling (later NBC) companies in Hampshire, Wiltshire and the Isle of Wight, and the handful purchased by BET subsidiaries such as Rhondda and Timpson's. Apart from these, only two companies taken into the NBC had any new VALs in their fleets. Cumberland Motor Services purchased four, viz. Nos. 1300 (FRM 618C), 1301 (GAO 38D), and 1302/1303 (LAO 580/581E). The West Riding Automobile Company, which was independent of the

Cumberland Motor Services' small fleet of four VALs carried two distinct styles of Duple bodywork, and the opportunity was taken to paint them in different styles to suit the body designs. The first, 1300 (FRM 618C) was photographed (left) in the open yard attached to Whitehaven garage, whilst 1303 (LAO 581E) of the second batch, is seen (right) in Dumfries. (P CAIN; G R MILLS).

---

big groupings until 1967, bought nine VALs during its independent era:- 992-994 (YHL 992-994) in 1963, 997-999 (2997/2998/2980 HL) in 1964, and finally 1-3 (EHL 470-472D) in 1966. The first two batches were retained for only a two-year life with West Riding, after which they were sold for further service with smaller fleets. 1-3 were kept until 1971, so joined the small group of VALs in NBC ownership. Midland Red acquired a couple of secondhand VALs in 1973 during their takeovers of several smaller firms within their operating area. DAW 825/826C, formerly of Cooper's of Oakengates (now part of Telford New Town) were numbered 2137/2138 in the Midland Red fleet.

Yelloway Motor Services of Rochdale was one of the few operators who, in the end, used the VAL for long distance express coach routes. Their stock was 6691-6694 DK, CDK 408-412C, EDK 389-393D, HDK 44-46E and KDK 547/548F. Of these, 6691/6692 DK, CDK 411/412C, EDK 392/393D, and KDK 548F were in the livery of their associated company, Creams. They were frequently to be seen working Yelloway's routes from the North-West to Clacton (joint with Premier Travel), Cheltenham and, until a service exchange with National Travel in 1976, London.

The photographs on this page demonstrate the wide variety of duties performed by the 14 VALs delivered to Manchester City Transport. 203 (GNB 517D) is seen (above left) in the forecourt of Ringway Airport on the City Centre – Airport express service which was the VALs' first duty. 210 (JND 210F) was photographed, amid typical North-West industrial scenery, at the Stockport (Mersey Square) terminus of the marathon Trans-Lancs Express route – the name shown on slipboards below the windscreen (above right). Finally, 213 (MND 213G) was seen (below right) in the suburban surroundings of Halebarns, with the inn sign of the 'Bull's Head' in the foreground, on the occasion of the launching of the luxury 'Executive Express' service in 1970. (A M WITTON; D AKRIGG; A P YOUNG).

Some of the best known independents tried out only one or two VALs. Lloyd's of Nuneaton, for example, had FAC 101C and HNX 187D; Harper Brothers of Heath Hayes bought Nos. 75/76 (KRF 875/876B); Bere Regis & District of Dorchester bought two secondhand, 7 JNM and CDK 412C; York Brothers of Northampton took delivery of a pair, Nos. 90 (90 DBD) and 91 (ABD 91B); King Alfred Motor Services of Winchester took in CCG 704C and EOU 703D, both of which were taken into Hants & Dorset stock when that NBC company took over King Alfred in 1973.

Few municipalities were interested in this type of vehicle. If they had steep hills, then the VAL was not one of the most efficient mechanical mountain goats in the world. Neither had many local authorities contemplated going into the excursion and private hire business with coaches, twenty years ago. So we have to look for special needs when it comes to examining the reasons why Manchester, alone among the English municipalities, decided to buy six-wheelers. The initial answer lies at Ringway Airport. There were ageing Leylands working the service between the city and the airport, and the VAL14 seemed to be an ideal replacement. The first two batches had rather eccentric fleet numbering, viz. Nos. 201/203/205 (GNB 516-518D) and 202/204/206 (GND 111-113E), presumably caused by their being delivered in penny numbers over the change-over period for year suffixes! Only two or three were needed at any given time for the Ringway route, leaving the remainder for private hire duties. The latter seem to have flourished sufficiently for a fresh order to be placed for another six which arrived as Nos. 207-212 (JND 207-212F). They were followed by Nos. 213/214 (MND 213/214G).

No sooner had the last two VALs arrived than Manchester City Transport was absorbed into the new SELNEC Passenger Transport Executive. SELNEC found work for 207-212 on a new 32-mile express route linking the 'outer ring' of towns in Greater Manchester, from Bolton via Bury, Rochdale, Oldham and Ashton to Stockport, extended at certain times to Ringway Airport. This 'Trans-Lancs Express' kept four VALs busy at all times to provide an hourly headway, until they were replaced in 1970 by new Seddon 'Pennine' coaches, which later still gave way to double-deckers for the sake of increasing capacity. The newest two VALs became regular performers on the 'Executive Express' service, also pioneered by SELNEC for commuters to Manchester city centre from the stockbroker suburb of Halebarns. The fleet of 14 VAL coaches continued to act as the nucleus of a private-hire fleet, which developed into the present Central Coaching Unit operating under the well-known Charterplan, Warburton's and Godfrey Abbott names. 213/214 survived long enough to be transferred in 1974 to the new Greater Manchester Passenger Transport Executive as nos. 13/14.

The other English municipality to take any VALs into stock was Barrow-in-Furness Corporation. In 1972 they acquired the coaching business of Hadwin's of nearby Ulverston. At the time of the takeover Hadwin's entire fleet was made up of six-wheelers, viz. ETF 330B, ETJ 778B, LTJ 306C, VTB 568D, ATF 740E, DTD 154E, KTC 361/362F, PTC 597/598G, VTJ 611/612H and DTJ 632/633J - a grand total of fourteen vehicles. Barrow Corporation retained Hadwin's distinctive red and cream livery, and used the VALs extensively for private hire and excursion duties. Finally, although the older ones had by then been replaced by more orthodox coaches, Barrow sold six of the newer VALs, together with the goodwill of the Hadwin's business, to Shaw's of Silverdale in 1977.

Although 49, 52 or 53 were the usual seating capacities of VAL coaches, some operators modified them to carry less for various reasons. For example, some of the earlier Manchester ones sat only 47 passengers, in order that small tables might be added for the convenience of travellers. As we saw in chapter 2, one of the early demonstrators, 7999 MD, sat only 44 passengers; nor was this unique, for so did Plaxton-bodied JTB 400F belonging to Mills & Seddon of Radcliffe,

A rather un-municipal looking vehicle was PTC 597G, of the Hadwin's fleet run by Barrow Corporation for several years. Although Barrow gave them 'book' fleet numbers and housed them alongside the buses in Hindpool Road garage, the Hadwin's coaches kept their red livery and separate identity. This one was photographed (left) next door to a blue and cream liveried bus whose side destination blind must be every southerner's prejudiced impression of Barrow-in-Furness! (A M WITTON)

Lancashire, and MEB 150G of International Progressive of Cambridge. Hill of West Bromwich was down to 43 for their Duple-bodied FEA 440D. However, even that low figure was four more than the 39 seats fitted to both HEB 333 of A J Cater of Wisbech, Cambridgeshire, and 226 PMJ of Cook of Biggleswade. They hold the joint record for the least number of seats fitted to any new VAL according to our researches. However it is worth noting that seats on most modern coaches are designed to be easily moved, and many of the vehicles we have listed must have run with fewer seats at some time in their lives. Apart from the ones that were rebuilt for non-passenger-carrying duties such as horseboxes, mobile showrooms and the like, the least seating capacity of any VAL during its life seems to have been that of ROT 356G, which passed to Hinckley Venture Scouts in 1980. They rebuilt it as a 29-seater and fitted it with a toilet - a most unusual refinement for a VAL!

5
Later developments

As 1967 drew to a close, a second version of the VAL appeared on a stand at the SMT Show in the Kelvin Hall, Glasgow. This was the VAL70, powered by a new Bedford 466 diesel engine with a capacity of 7.634 litres. To mark its debut, Duple had brought out a body to replace their 'Vega Major', called the 'Viceroy 36'. The new body still sat 52 passengers in its standard form, but in 1969 a modified 'Viceroy 37', an extra foot longer, increased the seating capacity marginally to 53. However, this slightly longer body allowed a little more leg room.

Plaxton modernised their coachwork too, replacing the 'Panorama' with the 'Panorama Elite'. The later VAL70s (normally the ones bearing 'J' and 'K' suffix registrations) had yet another variation of this popular bodywork – the 'Panorama Elite II'. As with the Duple ones, both marks of 'Panorama Elite' had 53 seats in their 37ft (11.29 metre) bodies.

VAL14s were still being bodied as late as New Year 1968, but by then several VAL70s were already in service. As far we have discovered, the first two of this new breed were delivered to Ashmore of Smethwick (LHA 588F) and Seamarks of Westoning, Bedfordshire (NXD 660F) in August 1967. Other early VAL70s were LCG 101F of Coliseum, Southampton, in September; HTH 279F (Jones, Login, at the foot of the Prescelly Mountains in South Wales) in November, and DHB 863F (Morlais of Merthyr Tydfil) in January 1968.

By the late 1960s the time seemed to be ripe for the entry of continental manufacturers into the British market, just as they had done forty years earlier. One such foreign competitor was Caetano of Portugal, working through their UK agency, Moseley Continental of Loughborough. The 53-seat 'Estoril' (named after a holiday area near Lisbon) looked quite different from anything being produced on the home market at that time. Maybe it was this fact that attracted certain operators to include one in their fleet?

The first of the score of 'Estorils' that have been traced went to Gath of Dewsbury (FHD 856G) and R & S of London W8 (UYC 799G) in March 1969, followed by Bold of Melling with RTC 409G, and Grayline of Bicester with TBW 718G, in the following month. The early summer of 1969 saw seven more entering service with English fleets as wide apart as Eddie Brown of Helperby in North Yorkshire (PPY 551G) and Western Roadways of Bristol (RDF 878–881G – the only order for more than one body!); Nor-West Hovercraft of Fleetwood bought STB 450G, whilst Bryan of Didcot, Berkshire purchased TJB 78G. The only other Caetano-bodied VAL70 to be sold that year was VHU 666H, which went to G P Smith of Bristol in the November. A further half dozen were delivered between March and August 1970, viz. LXC 583H (Ardenvale of Knowle, Warwickshire); OKX 234H (Bletchley Self Drive, Bletchley, Buckinghamshire); OVU 858H (Stubbs of Manchester); VAA 107H

The rather flashy lines of the Caetano body for the VAL are shown in this view of WAF 734J of Brown and Davies ('Trurorian') of Truro, one of the later ones to be built. The irregularly-shaped first nearside window is a particular recognition point when trying to identify Caetano bodies. Only 20 VALs were bodied by Caetano, although the firm's products were far from uncommon on other types of chassis. (BROWN & DAVIES - TRURORIAN TOURS).

(Cowdrey of Gosport, Hants); WAF 734J (Brown & Davies trading as 'Trurorian' of Truro); and YYB 239H (Clevedon Motorways of Somerset). By the time that 1971 dawned the days of the six-wheeler were already numbered, and only two Caetano-bodied VAL70s entered service that year:- BBW 939J with Hambridge of Kidlington, Oxford, and CFD 300J with Mills of Gornal Wood, a suburb of Dudley.

The Dutch company Van Hool (whose agency for the British Isles was in Dublin) had even less success than Caetano, selling a solitary example. This went to All Seasons of London W2; RAR 690J was used on tours under the name 'Swinging London'. It later passed to Boulton's of Cardington, near Church Stretton in Shropshire.

After 1967, Duple transferred their production of bodies for the VAL70 from Hendon to the former Burlingham coachworks at Blackpool, where they were turned out under the Duple (Northern) nameplate. Here a 3-digit prefix code for body numbers (e.g. 229/35) was employed, rather than the 4-digit code (e.g. 1158/1) used at Hendon. So it was to the Lancashire coast that the chassis of Southern Vectis's Nos. 406-409 and Edinburgh Corporation's Nos. 228-230 went for their bodies to be built.

One of the few unique VALs was RAR 690J, the only British VAL coach bodied by Van Hool. It is seen at the premises of Home James of Liverpool in June 1973 during a brief sojourn with that operator. (M J FENTON)

The advent of the non-driving Mrs Barbara Castle at the Ministry of Transport had resulted in a 70 m.p.h. speed limit being enforced on all motorways. Blow-outs at high speed on these highways had been comparatively few. So two of the main selling points of the VAL had vanished. The Ford R226 (metricated to the R1114), the Bristol RE, and the various versions of the Leyland 'Leopard', had resulted in many former VAL enthusiasts turning to other manufacturers to meet their needs. After an initial boost of over 450 sales in 1963/1964, the VAL14 had settled down to a steady production rate of 200-300 vehicles per annum for home consumption until 1968. The rate began to slump with the 'G' registrations (down to 202), fell again the next year (131), and then proceeded to plummet, with only 111 bearing a 'J' suffix, 65 a 'K' and 22 an 'L'. Ousted by the orthodox two-axle YRT, a stable-mate for the 45-seater YRQ which had replaced the VAM, VAL70 production ceased after a run of some 2,000 vehicles for the home market and about 50 for export. The last two delivered in the UK seem to have been ANO 395L and MRO 200L, both with Plaxton bodies, entering service for McIntyre of Roydon near Harlow in July 1973. At least one export VAL entered service with a New South Wales operator as late as 1974; the delay was probably due to the time taken to ship out this chassis to receive its Australian-built body.

Plaxton introduced its new-style bodies, with fixed panoramic windows and rounded lines, about 1968, but the Duple output remained similar to earlier products, displaying a much squarer look; the Duple 'Dominant' range of bodies did not appear until after the VAL era had ended. Both styles had their admirers among operators; some continued to buy both side by side. Typical late-model VAL70s shown below are (left) Plaxton-bodied DUR 980K of Ben Stanley of Hersham, seen running out through its home village on contract duties; and (right) Duple-bodied FAR 739L, with the Glenway fleet, in a snow-covered winter scene at the Ripponden depot. (A M WITTON; D AKRIGG).

6
Special treatment

One way in which some operators gave special treatment to their VALs was to make their external appearance more attractive or flamboyant. A good instance of this happening was in the case of Delaine Coaches of Bourne, Lincolnshire. They had their fleetnames made out of polished chrome; these were affixed to the sides of Nos. 61 (ETL 726D), 62 (GTL 825E) and 70 (UTL 283K), as with all their vehicles. When the vehicles are sold to other operators, the chrome fleetname plates are removed and re-used on the replacement vehicles.

A second method is to give the coaches their own individual names. Thus Shamrock & Rambler of Bournemouth called their 1967 batch after towns of Roman origin, viz. JEL 850E 'Chichester', MEL 987F 'Chester', MEL 988F 'Ilchester', MEL 989F 'Dorchester'. Subsequent VALs were named after a mixture of hawks, summer migrants and crows! Thus PEL 994G was 'Kestrel' (until it went to the Isle of Wight as noted in Chapter 4), PEL 995G was 'Merlin', PEL 996G 'Swallow', PEL 997G 'Swift', SRU 252H took PEL 994G's name of 'Kestrel', SRU 253H was 'Falcon', VLJ 231J 'Gannet', VLJ 232J 'Skua' and VLJ 233J 'Raven'.

Heaps Tours of Leeds chose three diverse Christian names for some of their VALS, viz. 770 JUA 'Magdalen', EUM 242D 'Michael', HUB 542E 'Sally'. Southern of Barrhead, Strathclyde bought GSN 710E secondhand, after it had been repossessed from its previous owner (Cunningham of Drymen Station on Loch Lomond) by an HP company, and Southern gave it the title 'Southern Princess'. Meanwhile, down in

One of the best-loved independent fleets in the Fenlands is Delaine Coaches of Bourne, with their screw-on metal fleetname plates proclaiming 'The Delaine' in manuscript style. Delaine 61 (ETL 726D) is seen in Bourne on the joint Bourne – Spalding run shared with Lincolnshire Road Car Co (the latter's service 34). (D KAYE)

Moss Motor Tours EDL 783D, 'The New Yorker', which was exhibited at the New York World's Fair as an unregistered Vauxhall demonstrator, is seen on more prosaic duties at Ryde Esplanade, the Isle of Wight's major picking-up point for tours. Its 'Boston' destination is being shown off, presumably as a proud memento of its transatlantic trip! (D KAYE).

the Isle of Wight, Moss of Sandown ran EDL 783D in a distinguished livery of gold and beige, bearing the title 'New Yorker'. This name derived from the fact that it was exhibited on the Vauxhall stand at the 1966 New York World's Fair. Later 878 KOU was painted in a similar fashion and given the name 'New Yorker II', although it never crossed the Atlantic. Fowler's of Holbeach Drove, Lincolnshire, gave HEB 333 the apt name of 'Fenland Queen'.

The registration of the last-mentioned vehicle had been transferred by its previous owner, A J Cater of Wisbech, Cambridgeshire, from a Bedford SB3. To some superstitious persons the treble three is an omen of good luck, whilst to others, triple seven also augurs well for the future. Other operators going for these 'lucky' numbers included N & S of Leicester (333 DAY), Derwent of Swalwell, near Gateshead (CPT 333B), Baxter of Moggerhanger, near Biggleswade, Bedfordshire (AMJ 333C), Thomas of North Muskham, near Newark, Notts (GNN 333D), Beach of Staines (TPK 333F), Rowson of Hayes, also in Middlesex (YLT 333H), Topping of Liverpool (777 JKA), Jeffways & Pilot of High Wycombe, Buckinghamshire (DPP 777B and BKX 777F) and Head of Lutton, near Peterborough (SNV 777G). Then there are those who, doubtless, as children tried to write the last entry in a friend's autograph book, and have always hankered after triple nine ever since! Maybe for them the VAL was not only the last word but also the last number as well? So we find one of the very first VAL14s registered DME 999A, followed by Shirley of Meriden, Warwickshire with their NUR 999D, Kenzie of Shepreth, Cambridgeshire with GCE 999E, Mulley of Ixworth, Suffolk with LCF 999F, Price of Wrockwardine Wood near Telford New Town with LUX 999F, and Jeffs of Helmdon, Northants, with NNV 999F.

Other operators just loved triples for the sake of their uniformity, and perhaps for giving them a sense of 'one-upmanship'? The principal exponent of this cult was Tours (Isle of Man) Ltd. Based on Corkill's of Douglas and taking in many other coach operators, from 1966 Tours (IOM) re-registered nearly all acquired vehicles with a '111' mark; there were several cases where two vehicles successively carried the same registration, in accordance with the policy of re-issuing registration marks where necessary in the Isle of Man. (See Appendix 2 for a full list of VALs re-registered in the Isle of Man).

Triple number registration plates were standardised by a wide variety of different kinds of coach operators – from Tours (Isle of Man) Ltd, nearly all of whose re-registered ex-mainland VALs turned up with '111' marks, to the Shearing/Jackson/Pleasureways group of Altrincham, who favoured 'triples' in the early days of their VAL purchasings. Two Tours coaches, PMN 111 and JMN 111, are shown (above right); the former is also mentioned in this chapter as having previously been Yeoman's of Canon Pyon MCJ 800F. A former Shearings VAL, AMB 666B, is depicted (below right) in its present home town of Camborne, Cornwall; Grenville Motors of that town acquired it from the Penryn & Falmouth Motor Co as long ago as 1973. (G R MILLS; A M WITTON).

In the search to obtain triples every time, so much depended upon having a co-operative local vehicle licensing officer! This was very necessary, too, for other firms who preferred to see complete hundreds on the registration plates of their coaches. In an earlier chapter we came across Yeomans of Canon Pyon doing this, but there were others in that league. The most prolific of these was Tatlock of Whitefield, on the edge of Manchester, with eight VALs with 'hundreds' plates, viz:- LTJ 900C, MTF 900C, UTF 100D, UTJ 100D, CTB 400E, JTB 400F, JTJ 400F and KTB 100F. Those with three such vehicles included Hanworth-Acorn of Hounslow, Middlesex with OHM 300E, OHM 400E and LYE 800D, along with Creamline of Bordon/Liss & District down in Hampshire with 100 HOR, 300 HOR and FHO 900D.

Obviously there must have been considerable satisfaction for those operators in the Nottinghamshire area who managed to 'bag' a reversed VAL registration in 1963. In November that year Wilfreda Luxury Coaches of Ranskill near Bawtry were able to get into poll position with 1 VAL, followed by Brumpton of Dunham-on-Trent with 100 VAL, Sherwood of Worksop with 440 VAL, and Leon of Finningley, situated just over the border in the then West Riding of

Two 'made to order' registrations are illustrated above. Leon Motors of Finningley was one of the four lucky operators in Nottinghamshire and neighbouring areas who registered a VAL coach with a VAL number! Their 64 (448 VAL) went on to become one of the longest-lived of the type with nearly seventeen and a half years' service with the one operator (left). On the other hand, Abbott's of Blackpool merely insisted on all their numbers ending in '7', a policy which is continued (when they can get away with it!) to the present day. Harrington Legionnaire bodied VAL AFR 27B was seen in the depressing-looking East Street coach station in Manchester, now long defunct. (D AKRIGG; A M WITTON).

Yorkshire, with 448 VAL.

Another interesting example of a case where the index **letters** of a registration were significant was an amusing second-hand purchase. LAW 897F, which had been new to Jones of Market Drayton in Shropshire, was sold in 1972 and entered the fleet of **Law** of Hoddesdon, Hertfordshire! Perhaps it was just a happy accident; but perhaps the sight of his name already written on a coach in the dealer's yard drew the proprietor's attention and confirmed the sale?

Telephone numbers also feature sometimes in registrations; this appears to have been the case with Brunt's Coaches of Potter's Bar, Herts, who booked a '510' registration for virtually all their new vehicles for at least twenty years. The VALs affected were HRO 510C, LHX 510C, WJH 510E, JUR 510G and LUR 510L. Note that the LHX one was registered in the neighbouring county of Middlesex in order to obtain the coveted '510' mark! Another operator who insisted on a particular number in all registrations was Niddrie of Middlewich, Cheshire, who registered new vehicles with the number '461', including Bedford VALs 461 YMA, AMB 461B and BMB 461F. Abbott's of Blackpool have the 'trademark' of registering all new vehicles with a number ending in '7', so AFR 17B and AFR 27B, their two Harrington-bodied VALs, were so treated. However, the longest series of VALs registered with a single serial number that we have been able to discover was the procession of seven '310s' delivered to the related Orsborn and Coales fleets of Wollaston, Northamptonshire. Their run consisted of ABD 310B (Orsborn) of 1964, ENV 310C (Orsborn) of 1965, KRP 310E (Coales) of 1967, SNV 310G, SRP 310G and TBD 310G (Coales) of 1969, and finally VBD 310H (Coales) of 1970. During the same period all other new purchases for the group fleets were registered '310' as well.

7
Put out to grass?

By 1983 some VALs have been scrapped; others lay idle in depots up and down the land; but for some there has been a new lease of life in an altered form. This particular model is long and low, and as such makes an ideal ambulance. That is what happened, for example, to VBD 301H, which became the property of the Leicester & District Multiple Sclerosis Society. They were able to use it to take members on trips to the seaside, for instance. Other similar conversions affected EMH 811B, which became a mobile first-aid unit for the St John's Ambulance Brigade in Weybridge, Surrey, in 1976; GPC 340C which spent a couple of years (1978-1980) with the Hillingdon Association of Voluntary Social Service in north-west London; FOG 32D which, like the first-named vehicle, was used by the Multiple Sclerosis Association in Atherstone; SNN 219F similarly employed in Loughborough; and, to extend the concept of 'welfare' to dumb animals, there is LUP 478D which has become possibly the country's only mobile veterinary surgery, based at Rothbury, Northumberland.

Another role found for a few VALs has been the carrying of mobile exhibitions. ABD 310B was rebuilt to carry a model railway layout (the Coacharama Model Railway Exhibition), whilst 213 SC was sent by its owners, Edinburgh Corporation, to Florence in 1966 to drum up tourist interest in their region of Scotland. VALs have been used as mobile showrooms by various commercial firms, including BNW 620C with Mountain Management of London W1; LMG 159C (one of the ex-British Airways Marshall-bodied airside buses) with Island Records of London W6; and OWJ 501E with Barnard's of Melton Mowbray, Leicestershire. BNW 620C and LMG 159C

One of several uses which have been dreamt up for pensioned-off Bedford VALs has been that of the mobile first-aid unit. EMH 811B, suitably modified and decorated for its new role, is seen at Wembley Stadium in 1978. (G R MILLS).

In a chapter dealing with an odd selection of VALs, one of the oddest looking is MNG 645V of Robert Brownlie Ltd, Kings Lynn. The angular bodywork style houses a mobile exhibition unit which is available for hire. It was seen in its home town. (G R MILLS)

were withdrawn from use as showrooms in 1979/1980 respectively. If you need to hire a mobile showroom based on a Bedford VAL, you could do worse than approach Robert Brownlie Ltd of King's Lynn, Norfolk, who own MNG 645V. It was once 4940 ET, originally a Willowbrook-bodied bus with Maltby Miners' Transport in South Yorkshire. They would have a hard time recognising it now, as apart from the changed registration it has a modernistic new body with which to fulfil its new role.

Many VALs have been used by Juvenile Jazz Bands. This title is somewhat of a misnomer, as these groups have relatively little connection with Duke Ellington and the like! They are marching bands in which uniformed children and young people play drums and wind instruments under the leadership of adults. They are particularly commonly found in the traditional mining areas of County Durham and Tyneside, South Wales and the East Midlands. They take part in regional and national championships for which transport is essential, and no less than 55 Bedford VALs have finished their days running for a Jazz Band – indeed many are still in use for this purpose. Another 16 VALs are or have been in use for dance and Morris groups, marching bands and similar organisations in various parts of the country; to complete the musical score, 12 VALs are used by a variety of other musical groups including (at

The Cardiff East Moors Bluebirds Jazz Band travelled to their engagements in ex-Edinburgh VAL 216 SC until it was sold for scrap recently. It is seen here (bottom left) at the Annual Jazz Bands Competition at Caister-on-Sea, Norfolk, in 1980. (G R MILLS)

Of the battalions of Bedford VAL caravans, only one is known to carry a Mercedes radiator badge! Ex-Barton 996 VRR is seen at Siddal near Halifax. (D AKRIGG)

---

least) one full brass band.

The 6th Newtownards Scouts in County Down had AJA 135B for a time. Other Scout groups that have owned VALs to carry them around include the 14th Aylesbury (YHL 993), the Gloucester Guides and Scouts Band (350 JEA - possibly this should have been included in the previous paragraph!), the 42nd Leicester (BRX 539B), the Stifford Sea Scouts of Grays, Essex (MFU 196F) and the Hinckley Venture Scouts' ROT 356G, referred to in a previous chapter.

At least 12 schools have operated VALs, and so have six churches or church groups. In the latter category, ARO 238F of the Spring Terrace Tabernacle in Swansea is unusual as it has been cut down to a low-loading lorry! The Assemblies of God in Dundonald, Belfast, have used JWX 235D. Skill's 47 SAU was bought by Revd David Hathaway, who runs Crusader Coaches. This particular coach became front-page news when this minister was arrested by the Czech Government for trying to use the coach to smuggle Bibles and other religious literature into Eastern Europe.

Over 70 VALs have been converted to caravans, or have been purchased in order for such conversion to be undertaken. The spacious interior dimensions of the VAL make it suitable for living accommodation for a medium-sized family, or perhaps even a youth group or other party on holiday. Some VAL caravans are mobile, for use perhaps as holiday homes or as transport for circus people and the like; others are used as stationary accommodation. One or two have been converted to site huts for the use of contractors' employees. At least three caravans have acquired names - ACG 77C is 'The Family', while 1542 DH is titled 'The Flying Barn', and ex-Southern Vectis EDL 993D carries the name 'Ivy-Lee'.

One of the most interesting life-histories of any VAL which ended as a caravan is that of RUW 990E. New to Homerton Coaches of London E9, this coach passed in 1975 to no less a body than the London Transport Executive, and was set upon by the boffins of Chiswick Works in a attempt to design a radically different type of London bus. If this had material-ised as a twin-steer model, this book might have had a very different ending! However, the design project came to an end, and so far as is known RUW 990E seldom if ever stirred outside the confines of Chis-wick Works during its six years with LT. In 1981 it was sold to a private owner in Northamptonshire, converted to a caravan and re-registered KBD 453Y!

Probably one of the least-photographed of all VALs, at least for several years, was RUW 990E. Outwardly appearing like a normal passenger-carrying coach (top left), it was actually the only VAL (and only the second twin-steer vehicle of any kind!) to serve with London Transport, as an experimental vehicle at Chiswick Works. It is seen here, without a vestige of any sign of LT ownership, surrounded by the workshops where London's buses are designed. (LONDON TRANSPORT)

However, humans are not the only live things to be transported. The Pathfinders Alsatian Display Team of Northampton transport their canine friends in a specially modified coach, JXE 307D, which has more recently been supplemented by SRP 310G. Six former passenger-carrying VALs have been converted by their present owners to carry horses - 931 XBF, ACG 992C, CDC 495C, DBN 642C, RDJ 828F and WUR 870J have been so treated. The last-mentioned vehicle is owned by the Kirkhill Lodge Hotel of Dyce, Aberdeenshire, who have converted it to a combined horsebox and executive suite! Presumably the horse is comfortably looked after in the former, while the jockey, trainer and owner celebrate their win in appropriate style in the latter!

As racing car transporters, with double rear doors, VALs proved to be ideal. Indeed KTF 863F was constructed new for this purpose (see next chapter for details). Probably the first VAL to become a racing car transporter was the very first to be built, demonstrator 472 DYK, whose strange history is also recounted in the next chapter. Its conversion to a transporter started a veritable stampede

Compared with the coach in the previous illustration, JXE 307D (bottom left) gets out quite a lot - with a payload of Alsatian dogs forming the 'business end' of the Pathfinders display team of Northampton. It was photographed at the 1982 Traction Engine Rally at Carrington Park. (D KAYE)

of conversions of pensioned-off PSV VALs, and at least 111 of them are known to have been rebuilt to carry vehicles of one kind and another. Most carried racing vehicles - racing cars, stock cars, 'hot-rods' and racing motorcycles - but some were used by garages and other organisations in the car trade. Several received new custom-built registrations to suit their role and (perhaps) conceal their age! These included KEK 674 which became 1 AGU with Mannion of Wallington; 9 BRV which was re-registered BWH 586A for Blanshard of Barrow; and KWF 4E which became WER 99 as a stock-car transporter based in Cambridge. Others received year-suffix registrations current at the time they were converted; they included ULG 22E, WJH 510E and RDF 881G which became respectively BUK 899T, EOL 83V and HAB 154X with Dave Fuell of Redditch, a major car transporter owner; EOL 83V later passed to Quaife of Tonbridge, Kent. Although the X-suffix registered VAL seemed impressive when it appeared, it has now been upstaged by the Y-suffix caravan referred to earlier.

In a similar vein, at least three VALs have been converted as recovery vehicles for use by garages. They are FML 127B with the Halfway Service Station, Congresbury near Bristol, ABD 310B (the one previously mentioned as a model railway exhibition vehicle) which has been converted to a third use as a recovery vehicle with Pilning Garage, also in the Bristol area (see the photograph on this page) and HAY 400D with the Bridge House Garage, Barlborough, Yorkshire. The last two vehicles mentioned have been rebuilt by having their bodywork cut away aft of the first window bay. BMW 398C has been converted to play a unique role (so far) as a transporter of water skis!

If you are travelling by road and feel like a drink or a snack, why not obtain it from one of the Bedford VAL mobile cafes? Although we cannot vouch for the present location or even existence of these vehicles, recent reports show that 7104 UP is to be found on the A64 Leeds - Scarborough road near Tadcaster, Yorkshire; 593 PUR is a tea bar on the A505 at Royston in Hertfordshire; or if you travel up the A64 and miss 7104 UP at Tadcaster, you might go through to Scarborough in the hopes of finding 994 VRR in that area. Other possibilities are EMP 799B on the A500 road, exact location unknown; EKL 732C at Stockley, Kent; RMA 326D alias the 'Mobile Chef' snack bar on the A30 near South Zeal, Dorset; DJM 450E is not far away on the same road at Nyland, Dorset; while CWU 391H's present location

Only a few VALs have had two different non-passenger carrying roles since their service as coaches came to an end. One such is ABD 310B, whose first conversion produced the 'Coacharama' mobile model railway exhibition based in Bath. Only a short distance away geographically, but a million miles apart in concept, it has now lost most of its original bodywork and is a recovery vehicle for the Pilning Garage, near Bristol (right). (G R MILLS)

48

is unknown, a challenge for intrepid cafe-hunters! The latest recruit to the 'cafe society' is ENE 454D, which appeared only in June 1983 as a mobile cafe on the A43 at Silverstone. You probably won't be allowed to patronise ONR 350F, JUR 588G or NED 537G, which are owned by contractors responsible for providing food for film location crews and the like. If you do get inside any of these vehicles you can probably expect a full meal, not just a snack!

A remarkable member of the battalion of car transporters is ALR 453B, which attained fame as a 'film star' after being converted to carry BMC Minis with a rear ramp that could be raised or lowered. Readers may recall the exciting scene in the film 'The Italian Job', in which the three escaping cars were picked up in this way by this coach, at speed along an 'autostrada'. This vehicle has since become a more ordinary vehicle transporter, owned by the Crow's Nest Hotel of Anstruther in Scotland.

Allied to the filming role is that of television. CED 764C starred in the Silver Jubilee edition of 'The Countryman', televised on 22 January 1978, carrying many of the residents of Ashton-under-Hill, deep in 'Fred Archer' country near Worcester. The three VALs which were built new as television outside broadcast units - GNF 951E, HXJ 846F and OOW 999G - are fully described in the next chapter.

One ex-Wallace Arnold VAL coach, EUG 905D, became an extra-large mobile home at the Fenland airfield of Holbeach St John, Lincolnshire, in 1977. Two years later, the Circus Hoffman was employing ex-Don Everall CUK 502C as living quarters during their touring season. 7771 BH was converted as a showman's vehicle for 'Davey's Circus Spectacular' during 1978.

The vehicles described in this chapter necessarily only 'scratch the surface' of the subject. There are probably many non-passenger carrying VALs, both custom-built and rebuilt from PSVs, that we have not been able to find out about. It should not be too difficult to recognise the distinctive three-axle VAL chassis, however exotic (or everyday) may be the style of bodywork that is mounted on it. The authors would be only too happy to hear from any reader who can positively identify any VAL, especially of the custom-built variety, that is not mentioned in this chapter or in chapter 9. Who knows, you may be able to add a whole new volume to our knowledge of this interesting and adaptable vehicle!

8
Across the Irish Sea

These views show the utilitarian and workmanlike exterior (left) and interior (right) of Ulster Transport Authority 118 (2318 GZ), the only VAL to be delivered new to a Northern Ireland operator. The body was constructed by UTA in their own workshops but is described by some sources as a 'UTA/MCW' body; it would be interesting to know in what way MCW helped in the construction of what would have been the only bus body for a VAL to bear their name. (ULSTER TRANSPORT AUTHORITY).

Very few new VALs were purchased by Irish operators. The first to cross the Irish Sea, as an unbodied chassis, was chassis no. 1054 for the Ulster Transport Authority. They fitted it with a 56-seat bus type body of their own manufacture, and it entered service in 1964 as no. 118 (2318 GZ). Although the UTA and Ulsterbus, and for that matter CIE south of the Border, have since bought large fleets of Bedfords for school bus and similar duties, 2318 GZ was and remained the only VAL to be supplied new to an Irish public-sector bus company.

Robinson's Coastal Bus Service of Portrush, Co. Antrim, purchased six VALs secondhand from English operators. 22/23 JOC arrived from Stockland's of Birmingham in 1968; SRN 920, AWT 351B, BWE 755B and CTD 324B came in 1969. All six passed to Ulsterbus as nos. 1271-1276 when they took over the Coastal business in April 1974. At least three were passed on for further service by Ulsterbus:- 1271 (CTD 324B) went to the 6th Newtownards Scouts and later became a car transporter for John Rea of Temple Patrick in 1978. After an Ulsterbus fleet renumbering had removed the initial digits of their fleet numbers, 273 (AWT 351B) went to Keenan of Bellurgan Point, and 274 (SRN 920) went to Lavery, Dublin, both in the Republic. It is worth noting that AWT 351B, which had been delivered new to Store's of Stainforth near Doncaster, had arrived at Store's with the registration 144 GWX which was changed prior to entry into service. Subsequently it spent its life with Store's in England, Coastal and Ulsterbus in Northern Ireland, and Keenan's in Eire – four different owners in three different vehicle registration territories – but it apparently kept AWT 351B throughout!

Returning to the subject of new VALs delivered to Irish operators, three VAL coaches were sold new to operators in Eire. In 1967 Kelly of Inchicore bought XZJ 8, a VAL14 with a Plaxton body. In 1969 a Plaxton-bodied VAL70 was delivered to Flynn of Waterford (CWI 418), whilst a similar chassis with Duple Northern bodywork, FZU 875, went in the same year to Shannon-Greyhound of Dublin. The only other VALs which seem to have crossed the Irish Sea in unused condition were five chassis ordered by Aer Lingus and delivered in 1971. They were bodied as 'airside' buses for use at Dublin Airport, with bodywork built by Duffy of Dundalk who have also bodied many of CIE's vast fleet of Bedford SB5 school buses. Since the Aer Lingus VALs were not used on public roads they remained unregistered, but they were given the fleet numbers 300-304. Their bodies had seats for about 40 passengers, with room for a similar number standing, and they ousted an assorted fleet of Leyland 'Tiger' PS and OPS models which had been used at the airport until 1971. It is not known whether these five interesting vehicles are still in use.

One of the largest collections of secondhand six-wheelers could be found at Urlingford, Co. Kilkenny, among the various Kavanagh operators. At various times the Urlingford operators have had at least 12 VALs in stock, most of which are probably still there; others have been passed on to smaller operators over the years. P Kavanagh's intake included AGV 235B in 1979, FML 126B in 1972, HTU 92G and NDL 699G in 1978 and LUR 600L in 1979. B Kavanagh's share was ATV 49B (re-registered 3124 IP) in June 1970, EUG 915D (3276 IP), GND 111E (3277 IP) from the Manchester City Transport 'airport coach' fleet, HUJ 506E in about 1974, and PTG 658F (3123 IP). Other members of the clan bought one each; M Kavanagh bought another Manchester airport coach, GNB 516D, in 1974, while J J Kavanagh received JVR 250F in 1978.

Apart from Ulsterbus and Coastal, only four other VALs seem to have entered PSV service in Ulster. Three of them went to the coastal area of County Antrim, viz. FBM 706E (GIA 9946) with Mulholland of Carrickfergus, LVX 320C (KIA 1777) with Mahood of Glengormley, and 792 XYB with Boyd of Eden. The fourth Northern Ireland VAL entered the fleet of Kerr of Dungannon as recently as November 1980 – FDL 585D (FJI 1262).

In June 1978 KIA 1777 (the Irish version of 'lucky' numbers?) was sold to an operator in the Republic, Crosson Transport

Standing in the fast lane of a motorway to take bus photographs is seldom recommended! However, it was perfectly
safe near Manchester at Whit weekend, 1982, when the Pope
visited Heaton Park. Two motorways were closed off and
reserved as coach parks. One of the most interesting of
the many vehicles seen there was 134 TZO (right) of
Lavery's of Dublin, a late-model Plaxton-bodied VAL previously registered TAR 185J and new to Guards of London
WC1. It joins a large number of VALs from a wide variety
of sources in what has probably now become the most
numerous VAL fleet in the British Isles. (A M WITTON).

of Drogheda, Co. Louth, where it was cannibalised. Another
cross-Border sale also went to Crosson, being BPL 920B,
which arrived with them via Hanna of Belfast. Five others
which came direct from the British mainland to this firm
were BVD 829C, EGD 160C, GMB 749C, OWW 687E and FCF 602D.
BVD 829C has since been passed on to Keenan, Bellurgan
Point, with the registration YIY 684.

Lavery of Dublin has specialised in acquiring VALs from the Isle of Man. Since May 1976 this large fleet has taken in
MAN 618, MAN 615, BMN 111, JMN 111, MMN 111, NMN 111, OMN 111 and PMN 111, 111 HMN and 111 KMN. Several of these,
already re-registered once in the Isle of Man, are known to have received third registrations in Eire; the table
(Appendix 2) will make this clear. One of them (MMN 111, formerly FWH 354D with Jones of Aberbeeg) has been re-
registered 284 HZC and passed on to Barron of Dublin. In addition Lavery bought one VAL from Ulsterbus (SRN 920), and at
least four direct from England; 407 EAY in 1977, CAL 227C (re-registered 1129 ZB) in 1981, LRP 1E in 1982, and TAR 185J
(re-registered 134 TZO) circa 1982; the last-named vehicle was the only representative of Irish coaches at the visit of
His Holiness Pope John Paul II to Heaton Park, Manchester, in May 1982.

PAB Tours of Dublin purchased three secondhand VALs in April 1968, re-registering them:- 1462 TF (VZL 179), CTD 576B
(VZL 191) and 132 FUA, the very first VAL to have entered the Wallace Arnold fleet (VZL 192). All three were passed on
to coach operators in various parts of the Republic after PAB had finished with them.

On the non-PSV front, AJA 131B was found useful for a time by the GAA Club of Hilltown, Co. Down, whilst AJA 135B and
BPL 920B both served for a spell with the Ulster Defence Association. One of the few VALs to fall victim to terrorists
was, unfortunately, the unique UTA No. 118 (2318 GZ), which was destroyed by an IRA bomb on 27th November 1973.

This chapter would not be complete without reference to another island 'across the Irish Sea', though not so far across
- the Isle of Man. At the start of the VAL era the Manx coaching industry was served by a multiplicity of firms, mainly

A couple of the unusual Strachan-bodied VALs of the North Western Road Car Co saw non-PSV service in Northern Ireland. AJA 135B (top left) ran for a time with the 6th Newtownards Sea Scouts - who put it in very 'shipshape' order. It is seen attracting admiring - or perhaps just curious - glances from three young passers-by. (R LUDGATE)

---

small, most of which used secondhand ex-UK coaches of various types. No VAL was ever delivered new to a Manx operator, but with the wide and well laid-out roads in the Island, several Manx coach firms found a use for second-hand VALs over the years. The first arrived in 1969, being KCU 701 which was re-registered MAN 615 with Shimmin of Douglas. Sixteen more were sent to the Island in the next ten years, ten of them to the conglomerate company, Tours (Isle of Man) Ltd, which had taken over nearly all the Douglas-based coach operators in the late 1960s and early 1970s. Tours inherited from Corkill's, previously the largest coach company and the nucleus of Tours, two VALs and the tradition of registering all their coaches with '111' registration numbers. By 1982 the Tours empire had crumbled, but already by that date the VAL had become extinct in the Tours fleet. One independent operator, Roberts' 'Amy Tours' of Bucks Road, Douglas, never joined the Tours company and still runs a small coach fleet today. They bought three second-hand VALs (ULG 23E which became MN 8964, GNP 140C which became MAN 72D, and XPK 77G which became MAN 958F) in 1974/1975. ULG 23E (MN 8964) was

---

The first VAL on the Isle of Man was ex-Hall Brothers KCU 701, which was re-registered MAN 615 with Shimmin of Douglas, and later passed on takeover to the Tours (Isle of Man) fleet (bottom left). The 3ft gauge tram track in the foreground identifies the location as Douglas sea front. Note also that all Tours vehicles carried, in addition to the Tours name on the rear locker door, the name of Corkill's, the major constituent and motivating force behind the Tours amalgamation. (G R MILLS).

sold for scrap by Roberts in July 1981, but one or both of the others may still be operating for Amy Tours today. If so, they are the last VALs in PSV service on the Island.

A full list of re-registrations in the Republic, Northern Ireland, and the Isle of Man, is given in Appendix 2. Compulsory re-registration of ex-UK vehicles was introduced by the Government of Eire during 1976; many vehicles ran in the Republic using their UK registrations until then. Irish registrations have not yet been reported for all ex-UK VALs believed to be still operating in the Irish Republic. In all, 86 VALs have been reported as sold to operators in the Irish Republic from various parts of the United Kingdom, as well as the eight (three coaches and five airside buses) delivered new. In some cases the Irish owners are not known, and some of the vehicles may never have entered PSV or indeed non-PSV service in Eire. Northern Ireland's score is more modest – 11 second-hand vehicles have gone there, plus 2318 GZ, the solitary new one.

9
The ones that never were

The Bedford VAL was originally conceived as a passenger-carrying vehicle, and the vast majority of the 2,000-odd that were built carried passengers for at least most of their lives. However, at least 35 VAL chassis were originally fitted with non-passenger-carrying bodywork, mainly by specialist concerns. They included outside broadcast units for television companies; pantechnicons for furniture manufacturers and the like; mobile exhibition units; horseboxes; and no less than six pigeon transporters for pigeon racing clubs and individuals concerned in the sport. Despite our best endeavours we have been unable to find a photograph to illustrate these 'odd men out'; but we felt that a separate chapter was necessary to describe them in some detail. They were, of course, additional to the many VALs that were rebuilt for non-passenger-carrying work (principally as car or motorcycle transporters) after finishing their first career carrying passengers; they are described in Chapter 7.

The first 'special' VAL we shall describe is special in more ways than one. Unlike the others in this chapter, it was originally built as a passenger-carrying coach; like the others, it was never licensed as a PSV or used as such. It was none other than the original prototype, exhibited at the 1962 Commercial Motor Show with Weymann body no. M504. Bedford gave it a prototype chassis number, RHD62/1, and it was registered 472 DYK. Later the Weymann body was removed, apparently to be fitted to production VAL chassis 1183 which entered service with Rowson's of Hayes in 1963, with the registration BMK 345A. The resultant bare chassis RHD62/1 received the Plaxton body, suitably modified, from left-hand-drive VAL prototype LHD62/3 (this was Plaxton body no. 2225 of 1962).

472 DYK was not destined to spend much of its life as an ordinary coach, and as far as we know it never became a licensed PSV. In July 1966 it was sold to the Jack Brabham racing organisation as a racing-car transporter, the first of many VALs rebuilt for this purpose. By 1976 it had been sold to F Hall of Stanford-le-Hope and then, towards the end of 1979, it passed to a Mr Bescoby of Droylsden near Manchester, still as a racing-car transporter.

One VAL was constructed new as a racing-car transporter. This was KTF 863F, which was based on a left-hand-drive chassis. Its body had a front end constructed by Willowbrook; the registration suggests that it was probably new in 1967/1968 to a Lancashire purchaser, although neither of these details are known for certain. It passed to Ran Racing by September 1976, and to David Price Racing by February 1978.

The earliest VAL chassis to be bodied from new for a non-passenger job was FFM 105C of 1965, based on VAL14 chassis no. 1860. It was used as a caravan transporter, but no other details about it have come to light so far.

1966 saw the first of three VAL horseboxes to enter service. GOU 764D was based on VAL14 chassis no. 6872684 and was delivered new to J Rolls of Appleshaw. Its bodywork was built by Lambourn, a name perhaps unfamiliar to most PSV enthusiasts but famous within their own field of horsebox manufacturing. The other two horseboxes were both based on late-model VAL70 chassis. DDP 828K bore a Vincent body on chassis no. 2T475511. GNR 844L had a G C Smith body (no. 34617.73) on VAL70 chassis no. 2T473224; both were new in or about 1973. Ownership details are not known for either of these; any bus enthusiasts who habitually visit racecourses should perhaps look out for them!

The six pigeon transporters were ushered in by CTE 688E, new in 1967 to Chris Catterall of Hambleton, Lancashire. It later passed to the Welsh North Road Federation; by 1974 it had been sold to the West Wales Pigeon Association of Tumble, Dyfed, who in turn passed it by 1978 to Mr J O Davis of Neath. It is thought to have had bodywork by Cocker with a front built by Plaxton, and its chassis number was VAL14 7832388. Chris Catterall next bought KTE 328F which arrived in 1968, a similar machine to its predecessor but this time based on a VAL70 chassis, no. 7T453964. The next was OED 881G which, despite its Warrington registration provided by the body builders, arrived with the Welsh North Road Federation in April 1969, being VAL70 chassis no. 9T456643 (some sources quote 9T465643) with Marsden bodywork.

PTA 263G is somewhat of a mystery vehicle, but it is known to have had a VAL70 chassis and is thought to have been new to the West of England Pigeon Association in 1969. The last two of this group were late-model VAL70s. VED 948J, another Marsden product with Warrington registration plates, went to the Coalville & District Pigeon Racing Association based at Hugglescote, Leicestershire, in 1971. The last one was LPL 456K, fitted with a Duple cab and, presumably, front end; it went to the Thames Valley Federation of Racing Pigeon Societies, with whom it was in service by 1977; it is not known for certain whether it was delivered new to this group. Chassis numbers for these last two were ?T484622 (VED 948J) and ?T473066 (LPL 456K).

Two mobile outside broadcast television units were delivered in 1967, and a third joined them later. The two original ones, GNF 951E and HXJ 846F, were both based on VAL14 chassis and were fitted with bodywork by Road Transport Services (Hackney) Ltd (body nos. 4030/4031 respectively). RTS were, of course, the company that gained fame by 'vintagising' several double-deck buses to the order of the Guards/Vintage Bus companies in London. The two TV units were probably new to Granada Television in Manchester, as suggested by the Manchester registrations; by 1972 GNF 951E had passed to Thames Television in London, and HXJ 846F was sold at about the same time to Race Course Technical Services Ltd – where it was quite probably involved in recording 'photo finishes' for racehorses carried in some of the VAL horseboxes listed above! A later report quotes 'JOW 951E' as a mobile TV unit with the National Coal Board in Nottingham; it seems possible that this could have been GNF 951E under another guise, but this is not certain. The third and apparently the last VAL to be fitted out as an outside broadcast unit was OOW 999G, which became Outside Broadcast Unit 2 of Southern Television, based in Southampton. It differed from its predecessors in having bodywork by Dell Coachbuilders Ltd on a VAL70 chassis (no. 7853351).

KJU 797E was the first of a number of VALs built as pantechnicons. It was VAL14 chassis no. 6860116, and carried a Crawford, Price & Johnson body. It was new in March 1967 to Clarkes Boxes Ltd of Mountsorrel, Leicestershire. 1970 saw two more pantechnicons, with Marsden bodywork this time, delivered to Sharnaware (Manufacturing) Ltd of Droylsden near Manchester. As we have learnt to expect, they were registered in Warrington by the bodybuilder. TED 125H (chassis

0T478771) arrived in June 1970, and UED 108J (chassis 0T478790) followed in September. YED 661K on chassis 2T472255 was the last VAL pantechnicon to arrive at Sharnaware. A fourth Marsden pantechnicon somehow managed to avoid registration in Warrington, and was delivered to Ace Associated Woodwork of London SE15 as KMP 111K; it was based on VAL70 chassis no. 1T491053. A pair of pantechnicons with Abrams bodies, VXJ 397/398L, were delivered to Duncan Tucker Ltd (Solent Furniture Systems) of Bridport in 1972, based on VAL70 chassis nos. 2T474241/2T473527. Two other L-registered pantechnicons were UWR 144L (2T473249) with Marsden bodywork, new in December 1972 and later passing to Lawrence & Hall of Harrogate; and HNR 455L, which is believed to have had a G C Smith body and passed successively to Palatine Delivery (by 1975) and ACE Industries (by 1978).

Several of these 'odd men out' were built to carry passengers, though not in the ordinary way. CGU 78H was fitted out by Sparshatt (body no. 810/0869) as a mobile classroom for the Road Transport Industry Training Board (MOTEC) at High Ercall, Shropshire. It entered an assorted fleet of vehicles of all kinds kept at High Ercall to teach drivers and other transport operatives their skills, and acquired MOTEC fleet no. 301. It arrived in 1970; its chassis number was 9T462311. In the same sort of category were mobile exhibition or display units like PSG 858H (VAL70 with unknown chassis number) with a Duple body for British Gas, Edinburgh, delivered in 1970; and MXE 667K, the only British VAL apart from the PSV RAR 690J to carry Van Hool coachwork. Its Van Hool body was finished and modified by Coventry Steel Caravans; its original owner was the Kent Group who registered it KNT 1, in October 1970 (was this the first-ever 'cherished' registration mark to be applied to a VAL?), and it was later sold to GKN Rolled and Bright Steel of Cardiff, bearing the K-suffix registration quoted above. It was VAL70 chassis no. 0T477416, and Van Hool allocated it their body number 4869.

VMO 770H is a VAL70 about which very little is known. It was sold to Gordon Spice of Staines in September 1971 (who may not have been the original owner). By 1977 it was working for Catric Components Ltd of Caerphilly, Glamorgan. Its main claim to fame is that when with Catric it became the only VAL ever to be fitted with a fourth axle, manufactured by York Trailers!

GLF 352J was registered in London as a mobile film location unit. It spent most of its life with Filmstrasse AG, 76 Lavaterstrasse, Zurich, Switzerland, and was therefore almost certainly the only VAL to be owned by a Swiss company. It was delivered to them around 1972.

There was a small group of true passenger-carrying vehicles conceived as glorified 'ambulances'. They were designed to carry disabled passengers (precursors of today's 'Mobility Buses'), and therefore had much reduced seating, and chair-lifts were fitted. The earliest one of this type that we have discovered was RJE 414J, built on chassis 0T478741 with a Smith-Appleyard body seating 38 passengers. It was delivered in June 1971 to the Ida Darwin Hospital at Fulbourn, Cambridgeshire, and passed in May 1979 to the Vale Hospital, Swainsthorpe. YSN 10K was new in 1972 to the Broomfield & Lanfine Hospital of Kirkintilloch Scotland, with a DP16C body built by S.M.T.; CWG 753L followed it in 1973 for the Central Regional Council. A second English hospital bus was LBD 529L with the Northamptonshire Health Authority, who received it in 1973. The last-named vehicle had seats for only 20 passengers; it seems likely that the others were similar in design, but no information has yet come to light on the bodybuilder or the seating capacity of CWG 753L.

Finally, the Royal Navy operated two mass radiography units for the staff at H.M. Dockyard, Portsmouth. The first arrived in 1966 with Services registration 18 RN 22 and VAL14 chassis no. 6831783. The second came in 1971, possibly as a replacement for the first, and was registered 13 RN 11 with chassis no. 1T485306. There are rumours that the Royal Ordnance Factory at Euxton, Lancashire, ran a fleet of five or six VAL buses for staff transport, but no further details have come to light; the Portsmouth Dockyard X-ray buses are the only Government-owned VALs (in a vast fleet run by the Services and various Government departments, which includes most other Bedford PSV models) that we have been able to trace for certain.

10
The ones that got away

At least 42 Bedford VAL chassis were exported new as passenger-carrying vehicles outside the British Isles. In addition several VALs which were new to British operators went abroad later, and at least one of these subsequently returned to Britain. A few VALs were used by British-based operators of international services, to the Middle East and Pakistan; it is not known for certain whether any of these vehicles went abroad regularly, or if they were merely used to ferry passengers from British pick-up points to the Channel ports.

The biggest single importer of new VALs was Australia; we have discovered 16 VALs which went there, all to New South Wales operators. Bedfords were prominent in many Australian fleets for many years, although recently General Motors decided to close down Bedford's sales organisation in Australia. Australian Bedfords were an odd lot to British eyes; many incorporated unusual combinations of chassis and engine; several Australian VALs and VAMs were rebuilt locally by setting back the engine behind the front axle and fitting an 'observation coach' type of body, as popularised by the Greyhound company in America. This had a flight of steps leading to a high-floored section set well above the driver. This peculiarity applied to six of the 16 VALs that we have traced to Australia.

Other countries that bought VALs new, with the number exported shown in brackets, were as follows:- Belgium (4), Denmark (2), Fiji (3), Luxembourg (2), Netherlands (3), New Zealand (2), Pakistan (2), South Africa (8). A left-hand drive version of the VAL14/VAL70 chassis was offered by Bedfords from 1963 until about 1970, when it was discontinued. It is understood that less than 24 left-hand drive VALs were built. One of them was one of the original demonstrators, while another was KTF 863F which was bodied as a racing-car transporter for use in Britain. Of the others, we have traced 11 in the list above, namely those that went to Belgium, Denmark, Luxembourg and the Netherlands; possibly also Fiji's three were left-hand drive models. There were almost certainly others sent out, possibly as non-passenger-carrying vehicles or to countries where they have not yet been identified. VALs exported to English-speaking countries like Australia, New Zealand and South Africa were of course right-hand drive models as offered in the British Isles.

Information on some of these VALs is sketchy; we have felt it best to set it out in order of the countries involved.

<u>Australia</u> – The 16 Australian VALs went to nine different operators. Before continuing, it would be best to explain that New South Wales buses are registered with the prefix mo. (Sydney metropolitan area) or MO. (rural areas of the State); the mo. prefix actually appears on the licence plates with the m above the o, thus m , but we have used the form mo. for ease of typography.   o

Touring coaches have registrations prefixed TV.; this applied to Pykes' Motor Tours TV.619/620 and to Kogarah Bus Service's TV.501. Kogarah was actually the first Australian operator to receive a VAL, mo.4820, which was delivered in 1964 with a Coachmaster 50-seat bus body with dual doorways. They followed up with TV.501 in 1966, also bodied by Coachmaster but this time with a 44-seat luxury coach body. The next VAL in our list arrived in 1969 for Katen & Heath, the first of a fleet of five, all fitted with CCMC bodywork. mo.5393 arrived in July 1969 with a 48-seat coach body, followed by mo.5653 in May 1970 with a 50-seat dual-doorway bus body. The 1971 arrival was mo.5703 which once again was a 48-seat coach, while 1972 saw the arrival of mo.5821 which was another 50-seater two-door vehicle but this time with dual-purpose bodywork. Finally in 1974 came mo.5973, a 48-seat coach of 'observation' layout, which was almost certainly the last VAL coach to enter service new anywhere in the world.

Offner's Bus Service of Wellington, NSW, had one VAL70 - MO.5129 with a B49F body by Coachmaster, delivered in 1968. 1971 saw the arrival of a pair of VAL70 touring coaches with Pykes Motor Tours of Sydney, with Van Hool C49F bodies - the only Australian VALs fitted with a European make of body as far as is known. As mentioned above, they were registered TV.619/620 and carried Van Hool body numbers 4833/4832 respectively. On 1st July 1975 Pykes Tours was merged with two other operators to form Australian Accommodation & Tours, and the two VALs were transferred to the new operator. 1971 also saw the arrival of the first of a pair of VAL70 buses - both with CCMC 51-seat bodies, twin doorways and raised rear sections - for Gosper of Windsor, NSW. mo.064 came in December 1971, and its sister mo.581 arrived in September 1972.

July 1972 saw the arrival of two 'one-off' VALs for New South Wales operators. The Chester Hill - Bankstown company got mo.5827, with a CCMC 50-seat bus body with dual doorways, while Evans of Nimmatabel received MO.219, bodied by PMC as a bus with 53 seats, front entrance and raised rear section. Two more 'one-offs' arrived in 1973 - Duffy's Bus Lines received MO.3434 with CCMC 'observation' coach bodywork for 49 passengers in March, and Hubbard's of Milton took delivery of mo.5849, with a similar body but with 48 seats only, in August.

One of the earliest Australian VALs, Kogarah's TV.501, enjoyed a curious after-life after withdrawal by Kogarah in 1973. Its body was placed on a second-hand ex-British Leyland 'Leopard' chassis, previously that of bus no. 470 of Ribble Motor Services. The resultant hybrid retained the Bedford badges and the (empty) engine cover which had been fitted to the Coachmaster body when originally fixed to the VAL chassis. As a 'new' vehicle it was re-registered mo.5156 and entered service with Oatley Bus Service in 1973.

Chassis and body numbers for most of these Australian VALs are known and, to avoid needlessly cluttering up the text, these details are tabulated in Appendix 3.

Belgium - The first Belgian VAL was delivered with a 46-seat coach body by A Verleure and received the registration 079.P.9, but it is not known who ran it. Also somewhat of a mystery is the 1967 Brussels Motor Show vehicle, which was exhibited without a registration and carrying a Van Hool C53F body (no. 4201). It would be interesting to know whether this vehicle ever worked for an operator in the Low Countries or anywhere else. There is less mystery about the next two, 327.P.7 and DUG.172, both of which were delivered to L Gevers van Hove (fleetname 'de Blauwvoet') of Balen, Belgium. 327.P.7 was based on VAL14 chassis 1506 and was delivered in 1964; it is understood that at some time in its

The handful of VALs delivered to Continental coach firms had a variety of bodywork makes, most of them looking strange to British eyes. 327.P.7 (top right) of Gevers van de Hove ('de Blauwvoet'), Balen, Belgium, received a Stoelen body and was photographed at the operator's premises as recently as 1981. (M J FENTON)

---

life it was fitted with a DAF engine, which was probably unique! DUG.172 had chassis no. 141243 (indicating that it had been constructed on the Dunstable production line normally reserved for smaller vehicles). Both had coachwork by Stoelen, 327.P.7 having seats for 50 passengers.

Denmark - Two VAL14s are understood to have been delivered to Danish operators, one each to Vikingbus and Selandia. The Vikingbus one carried a C48F body by Soro and was registered AS 99.252. We have been unable to turn up any information about the Selandia one.

Fiji - This interesting outpost of VAL operation in the South Seas had three examples, all apparently delivered in 1971. Island Buses of Suva, Fiji's principal bus operator, had W 707 and X 33, based on VAL70 chassis nos. 9T463336 and 9T463170. Both were bodied locally as buses by Lal, with 64 and 56 seats respectively. Like most Fijian service buses, they had unglazed window panels to spare passengers from the stifling summer heat. A visitor to Fiji in 1975 reported that both vehicles were derelict, so they do not seem to have had a long life. The third Fijian VAL was based on chassis no. ?T463051, but other details, including the operator's name, have not come to light.

'Wonderful, wonderful Copenhagen' is the setting for this Soro-bodied VAL14 of Vikingbus (bottom right). The body design seems to be ideal for enabling tourists to gaze up at tall buildings; the Bedford badge and twin-steer layout are about the only features that would attract a British enthusiast's attention. (B A TILLEY)

Illustrated on this page are three of the nine VALs which were delivered new to operators in the Benelux countries. Perhaps the most interesting is LO486 of Rapid Canach, Luxembourg, which inherited the Jonckheere body from its predecessor of the same fleet, 77001 – an unusual example of a Continental VAL with service bus bodywork (top left). Below are shown two of the three Dutch VALs described in detail on the following page. Verharen of Rijen's pair included AB-10-29 (bottom left) with a van Rooijen body, while Gebo of Nijverdal had BA-61-72 (bottom right) with Van Hool bodywork. Both were photographed at their respective operators' depots. (M J FENTON (3)).

Luxembourg – The Grand Duchy's two examples of the VAL had an interesting link with each other – both of them successively carried the same body! VAL14 chassis 1224 was delivered to E Weber's 'Rapid Canach' fleet of Canach, Luxembourg, with a Jonckheere dual-purpose 51-seat body

with two doorways (body no. 9772). It was registered 77001. In 1972 a VAL70 arrived, on chassis no. 1T494593, with the same Jonckheere body, refitted with service bus seats but still carrying what appears to have been the chassis number of the original vehicle! This second bus bore the registration L0486.

Netherlands - The Verharen fleet of Rijen took delivery of two VAL14s. The first was registered AB-10-29 and was based on VAL14 chassis no. 1866, delivered in 1966. The second had the registration AB-99-34, chassis no. 6831218, and arrived in 1968. Both had 49-seat coach bodies by van Rooijen. A third vehicle, BA-61-72, this time a VAL70, was delivered to the Gebo company of Nijverdal in 1970; its chassis number was ?T480819 and it had a Van Hool C50F body.

New Zealand - Two VALs have been traced to New Zealand, both with South Island operators. Jenkins Motors of Gore had CW.2206, with VAL14 chassis no. 1303 and a McWhinnie 40-seat coach body, which was delivered in 1964. Less details are known about the other one, which bore a 36-seat coach body by Midland and was placed in service by Turnbull's Southern Coachlines of Dunedin, but it is not known when.

Pakistan - Two VAL70s were delivered to an unknown operator in Pakistan around 1971. No other details are available.

South Africa - Six of South Africa's quota of eight VALs were bodied by Duple, the only instance we have come across so far of Duple-bodied VALs being exported new. Three of these were delivered to United Transport in Durban, while the other three went to Greyhound Bus Lines. Quibel's of Capetown had CA.18017, a VAL14 with coach bodywork by Blankenberg. Little has been reported about the eighth vehicle except that it is understood to have gone to a Capetown operator.

So much for VALs exported new. At least nine VALs were exported outside the British Isles second-hand, bringing the type to three countries which had never bought them new. The first example is somewhat of a 'yo-yo', as after being exported privately to West Berlin it returned to Britain for further non-PSV service. It was RWA 188E, which went to West Berlin at about the middle of 1978. It returned to Britain in May 1980 and became the property of the Wythenshawe Community Trust in south Manchester, passing later to the Barrow-in-Furness Community Trust in Cumbria.

Three VALs were sent secondhand to Sri Lanka, which has long been a home for secondhand British buses and coaches. 4220 TE and KTC 128C were both exported in February 1981 to Karunaratne of Sri Lanka, receiving the Sri Lankan registrations 29-Sri-5726 and 29-Sri-5727 respectively. The third vehicle went to Ebert Silva of Colombo, Sri Lanka, in January 1981, and was registered 29-Sri-5555. It has not been possible to establish the identity of this coach beyond all doubt, but it is strongly suspected that it was ECK 946E, sold by Smith of Swanley, Kent, in June 1979 for export to Sri Lanka.

Other 'one-off' secondhand exports were Harrington-bodied 535 LOR to Reneeus of Den Haag, Netherlands, in May 1975; GAR 401C which went to Dacca, Bangladesh, in March 1977; LMG 162C (one of the British Airways 'airside' buses) which went to Oda, Ghana, in January 1980; HMJ 469F, exported to an unknown destination in 1980; SJJ 590F, which had been damaged by fire with Timpson's of Catford in 1970, and whose chassis was exported to Australia in February 1977 for spares; and YWJ 665G which went to Pakistan in September 1979. The most recent report of an exported VAL concerns ex-Wallace Arnold EUG 912D, which was bought by Costain's, the contractors, who sent it out to Saudi Arabia.

Of course, many British-based VALs went abroad at some time or another. At least three were owned in Britain by operators of international services. FEA 430D and HDK 44E were acquired by Moreton's of Birmingham in October 1975 and December 1976 respectively, for the operation of a Birmingham - Istanbul service. British law does not require a vehicle to be licensed as a PSV if no journey is wholly inside the United Kingdom, so these two coaches, which presumably worked through to Istanbul regularly, were run by Moreton's as non-PSVs - a sort of Bedford answer to the 'Orient Express'! The third vehicle in this category was 536 LOR, a sister to 535 LOR which went to Den Haag. 536 LOR seemed to have duties taking it still further afield, as it was owned from December 1974 by Bradford - Lahore Transport of Bradford, West Yorkshire. However, as it appears to have been licensed as a PSV, it is possible that it was used either wholly or partly for journeys within the United Kingdom.

Appendix 1 — VAL14 and VAL70 passenger vehicles in the British Isles

This Appendix lists the full details, including registrations, chassis and body numbers, body makes and types, first owners, and dates of entry into service, of all the VAL14 and VAL70 PSVs known to have been produced for operators in the British Isles (including the Irish Republic). Details of VALs known to have been sold new to operators outside the British Isles will be found in Chapter 10 and in Appendix 3 (Australian vehicles). Those built new as non-passenger carrying vehicles are detailed in Chapter 9.

Because of the sheer volume of information presented and the work which has been involved in processing it, we would be foolish to promise total accuracy! However, we have done our best with the sources available, which occasionally give conflicting information. We have not used or requested access to the official records of Vauxhall Motors Ltd, any of the bodybuilders or any of the operators. We have quite extensively used the records and publications of the PSV Circle, in which all of these vehicles have appeared at one time or another. We are most grateful for the help given by the Circle's editors, librarians and others in helping us to prepare this tabulation.

The following information is shown in the order stated (left to right):-

The **page heading** shows whether vehicles on the page are VAL14s or VAL70s, or both. (If both, vehicles of one of the two types are distinguished by an asterisk).

Column 1 shows the original registration number, whether British or Irish. Re-registrations of vehicles going to the Isle of Man, Northern Ireland, or the Irish Republic, are shown in Appendix 2. A few vehicles were re-registered while remaining in mainland Britain; details of these are shown in footnotes referred to by marks against the vehicles concerned.

Column 2 shows the chassis number. The original series of chassis numbers for VALs ran upwards from 1001 and reached 1913. These numbers were reserved for VALs only, other parallel series being used for VAS and VAM types built during the same years. In late 1965 a new series was started, and all Bedford large passenger chassis were numbered in the same series. Numbers were in the series 68xxxxx for vehicles built in the 1965/1966 season, and 78xxxxx for vehicles built in the 1966/1967 season. Thereafter all large Bedfords were given 6-figure chassis numbers, starting with the figure 4, and prefixed by 7T, 8T, 9T, 0T, 1T or 2T to indicate the year of manufacture as some of the 6-figure numbers were used more than once. This system continued until the end of VAL production in 1973.

Column 3 shows the body manufacturer and vehicle type and seating capacity. Body manufacturer codes are those used by the PSV Circle and are as follows:- Co Caetano, DM Duple Midland, DN Duple Northern, Du Duple (Hendon), Hn Harrington, Ml Marshall, Sn Strachan, UTA Ulster Transport Authority, VH Van Hool, Wk Willowbrook, Wn Weymann, Ys Yeates. These are followed by a code indicating the type and layout of bodywork, around the **original** seating capacity as delivered (as far as we have been able to ascertain it). The seating capacity is prefixed by B for a bus, C for a coach or DP for a dual-purpose vehicle. The suffix shows the position of the entrance(s); almost all VALs were built with front entrances (F), but the Yeates-bodied VALs for Barton had dual-doorway layout (D) and a few vehicles built for 'airside' passenger carrying at Heathrow and other airports had central doorways on both sides (C). Thus the typical standard VAL coach would be coded C52F (coach, 52-seat, front-entrance); a typical service bus might be B56F (bus, 56-seat, front-entrance) and so on.

Column 4 shows the manufacturer's body number, except in a few cases where we have not been able to ascertain this information. Duple and Duple Northern bodies were numbered from 1 in batches indicating the body design and date of manufacture; thus the first batch of Duple (Hendon) bodies for VALs were numbered 1158/1 upwards and thereafter all Hendon-built bodies had four-digit prefixes. Duple (Northern) bodies for VALs were numbered upwards from 179/1, 182/1, 200/1, 213/1, 229/1, and 241/1, always using three-digit prefixes. Plaxton body numbers were prefixed with a 2-digit code indicating the year of manufacture, but this was a season (from autumn to summer), not a calendar year. For most of the years during which Plaxton built bodies for VALs, each type of coach represented in their output was allocated a block of numbers to itself. In some years VALs 'overflowed' their number allocation and had to be numbered in blocks originally reserved for another type (such as the VAM). Other body builders generally numbered their bodies in a single series in order of output, irrespective of type. Caetano did not at first use body numbers at all, but later started a 'year prefix' system. Most manufacturers fitted a body number plate somewhere on the vehicle (on Plaxtons for example this was usually on the entrance step risers), enabling enthusiasts to record these and note changes of bodywork. So far as is known only one British VAL received a brand-new second body after accident damage to the first one.

Column 5 shows the date of entry into service with the original owner, with month and year if known. In a few cases, notably those VALs delivered to Wallace Arnold and Yelloway, we have not been able to ascertain the exact month.

Column 6 shows the name of the original owner, together with a code showing the Traffic Area (in mainland Britain) or other territory in which the owner's place of business was situated. The codes for Traffic Areas are the official ones, thus (A) Northern T.A., (B) Yorkshire T.A., (C) North-Western T.A., (D) West Midland T.A., (E) East Midland T.A., (F) Eastern T.A., (G) South Wales T.A., (H) Western T.A., (K) South-Eastern T.A., (L) Scottish T.A. Northern Division, (M) Scottish T.A. Southern Division, (N) Metropolitan T.A. In addition we have used the following unofficial codes for other territories:- (I) Republic of Ireland, (IOM) Isle of Man (second-hand vehicles only in the case of VALs), (NI) Northern Ireland. Addresses in the London postal districts are followed by the district number. Where the original owner is known to have given the vehicle a fleet number, this is shown after the owner's name and location and before the Traffic Area code. However, many of the smaller undertakings changed these fleet numbers at fairly frequent intervals. The Traffic Area letter is prefixed X, thus (XB), (XN) etc, if it is known that the vehicle was not licensed as a PSV when delivered to that owner. This includes the 'airside' buses referred to above, staff buses used by employers to transport staff free of charge, and of course various non-passenger carrying subsequent uses such as car transporters, breakdown tenders etc. The letter (X) on its own or accompanied by a question mark (X?) means that the owner was known to be a non-PSV operator but his Traffic Area is not known. Similarly the prefix Z indicates that the owner did not use the vehicle at all during the time it was in his possession; the prefix P indicates that the vehicle was purchased with a view to preservation.

Column 7 gives similar details for the most recent ownership which we have traced for each vehicle. Information shown is the present or most recent owner's name, place of business and Traffic Area, followed by one or more dates. The first date shown is that on which the vehicle entered service when it arrived most recently with the last recorded owner. (Some VALs have passed through the hands of one owner on two separate occasions, for example when coaches have been transferred between subsidiaries of the same group). If the vehicle is known no longer to be with that owner, prefixed by 'sold', 'scr' (scrapped or scrap), 'burnt out' etc to indicate the circumstances. If the vehicle is known no longer to be in use with that owner, the date (or approximate date) when it was last used is shown, prefixed with the abbreviation 'wdn' (withdrawn). Where the vehicle was known to be still in use with the owner at a certain date but we have not been able to ascertain its movements since then, the last date for which we have firm information is shown in brackets at the end of the entry. Thus 'Guscott, Halwill (H) 2/81 (3/83)' means that the vehicle entered service with Guscott's in February 1981, and was known to be still running for them in March 1983. The second date does not indicate that the vehicle has been withdrawn unless the code 'wdn', 'sold', 'scr' etc. is shown.

Finally - if you have read this far! - a few vehicles have special stories which can only be described in footnotes. The footnote references are on the right of the page, and the footnotes themselves appear at the very end of the table.

We hope this table is found to be as accurate as possible, but a few mistakes are almost inevitable. If you can prove that we have made a mistake, please let us know - especially if you have recorded the correct information! We cannot promise to reply to all such letters, but we would like to eliminate any 'howlers' as time goes on. Thank you - and happy hunting!

VAL14 (* - VAL70)

CWI 418*	9T466832	Pn C48F	(692460)	/69	Flynn, Waterford (I)	
FZU 875*		DN C52F		6/69	Shannon-Greyhound, Dublin (I)	PMPA Coachtours, Dublin (I) -/74
HCU 955	1008	Du C52F	(1158/9)	4/63	Hall, South Shields (A)	Locker, Marton (B) 12/74, wdn 2/76
HCU 956	1131	"	(1158/60)	"	"	Griffin, Lydbrook (H) 5/76, wdn 12/77
HEB 333	1174	Du C39F	(1172/1)	1/64	Cater, Wisbech (F)	Shephardson, Barton-on-Humber (E) 5/75, wdn 2/76
JEX 3	1083	Du C52F	(1158/34)	5/63	Seagull, Great Yarmouth (F)	Mascot-Seagull, Great Yarmouth (F) burnt out and scr 9/75
JEX 5	1098	"	(1158/52)	6/63	"	Truman, Drayton (XF) 9/77
JFT 259	1161	Pn C52F	(632682)	2/64	Taylor, South Shields (A)	Gateshead Juvenile Jazz Band (XA) by 7/77
KCU 701	1263	"	(632874)	"	Hall, South Shields (A)	Shimmin, Douglas (IOM) MAN 615, 5/69; to Lavery, Dublin (I) 8/77
KCU 702	1264	"	(632873)	"	"	Robin Hood, Ilford (N) 5/77, wdn 6/77
KCU 703	1265	"	(632875)	"	"	Mobile caravan, Birmingham (XD) 11/75
KCU 704	1266	Du C52F	(632864)	"	"	Transporter ?/??, dumped beside Newry Ulsterbus depot 5/82
KEK 674	1078	Du C52F	(1158/76)	6/63	Unsworth, Wigan (C)	Mannion (racing car transporter), Wallington (XK) as 1 AGU by 7/78
LSY 477	1142	"	(1158/69)	"	Hunter, Loanhead (M)	Irvine, Law (M) 1/73 stolen and burnt out c2/74

Reg	No	Body	(Chassis)	Date	Operator	Disposal
MJC 172	1050	Du C52F	(1158/32)	6/63	Penmaenmawr Mtr Co, Penmaenmawr (C)	Adkins, Upper Beddington (E) 9/73
OHG 988	1184	Pn C52F	(632628)	5/63	Sandown, Padiham (C)	St Gregory's School, Cheltenham (XH) 9/73, sold c11/79
OHG 989	1095	Du C52F	(1158/68)	7/63	"	Stevens, Rainham (N) 3/73, wdn 5/76
OTS 603	1116	Pn C49F	(632544)	5/63	Dickson, Dundee (L)	Nutley, Parkwell (ZG) sold -/79
OYJ 550	1109	Du C52F	(1158/50)	"	Watson, Dundee (L)	Moffat, Cardenden (L) 6/74
PEF 370	1469	Pn C49F	(642281)	4/64	Beeline, West Hartlepool (A)	Sturt, Lincoln (XE) 11/74
PEF 371	1468	"	(642282)	"	"	Guest, Runcorn (C) 12/74
RTS 463	1413	Pn C52F	(642244)	"	Watson, Dundee (L)	Watson, Dundee (L) wdn by 2/81
SRN 919	1032	Du C49F	(1158/14)	3/63	Overland, Preston (C)	Merseyside Coachways, Liverpool (C) 2/76 wdn 8/78
SRN 920	1048	"	(1158/15)	"	Majestic, Preston (C)	Lavery, Dublin (I) by 3/76
TSN 710	1250	Du C52F	(1172/8)	4/64	Cunningham, Drymen Station (M)	B Whorton (stock car transporter), Lichfield (XD) by 12/78
UCK 875	1432	Pn C49F	(642170)	"	Premier, Preston (C)	Kelly (?Reilly?), Borris (I) 4/77
UTK 301	1140	Du C52F	(1158/91)	8/63	Rendell, Parkstone (K)	Smurthwaite, Copthorne (N) 6/78, wdn 6/79
VGV 88	1067	"	(1158/45)	5/63	Mulley, Ixworth 86 (F)	Semmence, Wymondham (F) 8/73 wdn 7/78
VJT 907	1229	Pn C52F	(632855)	1/64	Bluebird, Weymouth (H)	Hudson, Rowlands Castle (K) 7/73 wdn 11/79
VPR 77	1267	Du C52F	(1172/27)	"	Sheasby, Corfe Castle (H)	Seldon (transporter) (X?) by 5/79
VPR 78	1328	"	(1172/39)	"	"	Caravan by 4/81
VSD 488	1029	Du C52F	(1158/4)	4/63	A1 (Docherty), Ardrossan (M)	Clarke, Ardrossan (M) by 7/78 wdn by 12/81
WCT 590	1065	Pn C52F	(632552)	"	Blankley, Colsterworth (E)	Ford, Gunnislake (H) 3/72, wdn 6/77
WGR 676	1384	"	(642041)	3/64	Carney, Sunderland (A)	Revill, Langtoft (B) wdn 6/79
WGR 677	1378	"	(642042)	"	"	Fairburn Racing Team (transporter), Louth (XE) 7/81
XBA 938	1202	"	(622409)	4/63	Fieldsend, Salford (C)	Field, Maidstone (K) wdn 2/74
XGV 222	1365	Du C52F	(1172/57)	5/64	Mulley, Ixworth 95 (F)	Stone, Edenbridge (N) 9/77, sold 1/79
XRJ 193	1042	Pn C52F	(632554)	4/63	Wheatley, Patricroft (C)	Unknown owner (transporter) (X?) by 7/79
XRJ 417	1039	"	(632555)	5/63	Fieldsend, Salford (C)	Hardie, Chester le Street (A) 9/71 wdn 5/73
XUD 969	1119	Du C52F	(1158/85)	7/63	Gray, Bicester (E)	Williams, Talywain (G) 6/75, sold by -/76
XWM 75	1130	Pn C49F	(632626)	5/63	Blundell, Southport (C)	Fletcher, Skelmersdale (C) 9/71, wdn 5/75
XZJ 8	7835429	Pn C52F	(672570)	7/67	Kelly, Inchicore (I)	Chassis only ex Silverdale, Dublin (I) to Kirkby (dealers) 9/74
YCO 313	1038	Du C52F	(1158/19)	5/63	Embankment, Plymouth (H)	Caravan, Stretford (XC) by -/80, sold for scr 5/82
YCO 314	1049	"	(1158/28)	"	"	Sabelis, Bugbrooke (E) 1/73
YHL 992	1135	Pn C52F	(632613)	6/63	West Riding 992 (B)	Winlon, London W12 (N) 9/69 written off after accident 10/72
YHL 993	1182	"	(632614)	"	" 993 (B)	14th Aylesbury Scouts (XE) 3/75
YHL 994	1178	"	(632615)	"	" 994 (B)	R Craig (racing car transporter), Chesterfield (XB) 5/77
YHM 606	1374	Hn C52F	(2930)	4/64	Lacey, London E6 (N)	Riverside, Liverpool (C) 9/74, wdn 5/75
1943 AP	1121	Du C52F	(1158/54)	/63	Rutherford, London E11 (N)	Burnt out with Jenkins 8/71
1944 AP	1082	"	(1158/57)	/63	Bradley, London E17 (N)	Tally Ho!, Kingsbridge (H) 10/71 (12/82)
1945 AP	1118	"	(1158/56)	6/63	Victor, London N15 (N)	Sayer, Ipswich (F) 11/71, wdn 7/77
2870 AP	1166	"	(1158/83)	"	Leighton, Barking (N)	Pentland, Loanhead (M) 3/68 wdn -/71
4023 AW	1005	Du C49F	(1158/10)	5/63	Whittle, Highley (D)	Bowater, Shirebrook (E) 1/74, wdn 4/76
6145 AW	1056	Du C52F	(1158/31)	6/63	Cooper, Oakengates (D)	Gilbert, Hanley (D) 10/72, wdn 7/78
6146 AW	1062	"	(1158/35)	5/63	"	Cloud Engineering (transporter), Brentford (XN) by 5/78
7771 BH	1012	"	(1158/12)	"	Jeffways & Pilot, High Wycombe (N)	Daveys Circus Spectacular (showman's vehicle) by 3/78
7873 DF	1024	"	(1158/65)	6/63	Perrett, Shipton Oliffe (H)	Mike Taylor Racing, Gloucester (XH) by 8/78
1211 DH	1063	"	(1158/48)	"	Central, Walsall (D)	Bassett, Holsworthy (H) 11/77, wdn 8/78
1212 DH	1084	"	(1158/49)	"	"	Thomas, Chorlton (C) 3/66 wdn 5/71
1542 DH	1197	Pn C52F	(632680)	"	Dawson, Walsall (D)	'The Flying Barn' (caravan), Alderley Edge (XC) by 3/76
1543 DH	1196	"	(632664)	7/63	"	Thomas, Cardiff (G) 9/72 sold 4/73
4070 DH	1492	"	(642284)	4/64	Pearson, Walsall (D)	Dane-Line, Petersfield (K) 8/77, broken up 9/78
6691 DK	1312	"	(642045)	/64	Creams, Rochdale (C)	Morgan, Monmouth (G) -/71, sold to breaker -/76
6692 DK	1315	"	(642044)	3/64	"	Unknown owner (transporter) 3/79, broken up 4/80
6693 DK	1375	"	(642061)	/64	Yelloway, Rochdale (C)	Transporter (X?) 3/79
6694 DK	1380	"	(642062)	/64	"	Cheek, Wealdstone (ZN) 1/78, sold c6/79
9797 DP	1369	Du C52F	(1172/56)	3/64	Smith, Reading (K)	Carter, Foulden (F) 9/72 wdn 3/79

Reg	No.	Body	Chassis	Date	Operator	History
3217 EH	1449	Pn C52F	(642279)	5/64	Copeland and Bowers, Hanley (D)	Downs, Newcastle under Lyme (D) 5/70 (12/78)
4940 ET	1199	Wk B54F	(CF688)	10/63	Maltby Miners, Maltby (B)	Brownlie, Kings Lynn (XF) as mobile showroom regd MNG 645V by 9/80
7322 FD	1092	Pn C52F	(632542)	5/63	Kendrick, Dudley (D)	Mobile caravan, Cannock (XD) by 11/75
7323 FD	1137	"	(632543)	"	"	Being converted to caravan in Preston area (XC) by 10/79
2318 GZ	1054	UTA B56F		/64	Ulster Transport Authority 118 (NI)	Ulsterbus 118 (NI) destroyed in terrorist attack 11/73
8750 HA	1361	Hn C52F	(2927)	3/64	Morris, Bearwood (D)	Caravan (XE) c9/82
8982 HA	1258	Du C52F	(1172/6)	4/64	Mann, Smethwick (D)	Goodenough, Scawsby (B) 7/76
2980 HL	1419	Pn C52F	(642277)	5/64	West Riding 999 (B)	D J Clarke, Elmswell (F) 4/74 (4/80)
2997 HL	1393	"	(642275)	"	" 997 (B)	Grouptravs, Luton (N) 11/77, wdn 12/77
2998 HL	1403	"	(642276)	"	" 998 (B)	Racing car transporter, noted Ipswich (XF) by 7/81
2222 KF	1124	"	(632420)	4/63	Sunniways, Liverpool (C)	P S J Autos, Tipton (XD) by 7/77
3883 KF	1064	Du C52F	(1158/42)	5/63	Topping, Liverpool (C)	Topping, Liverpool (C) wdn 7/71
4699 KF	1089	Du C41F	(1158/59)	7/63	James, Liverpool (C)	Bellaires Jazz Band, West Bromwich (XD) by 8/81
4799 KP	1433	Pn C52F	(642278)	5/64	Margo, Bexleyheath (N)	Foster, Glastonbury (H) 9/68 wdn 3/79
7 KX	1077	"	(632546)	4/63	Todd, Whitchurch (E) (Note 1)	Re-registered 814 XAF 5/76 (q.v.)
293 LG	1051	"	(632425)	"	Lofthouse, Mickle Trafford (C)	Landliner, Birkenhead (C) 2/71 sold by 7/73
776 LG	1076	Pn C49F	(632545)	"	Bostock, Congleton 2 (C)	Alpine, Woking (N) 6/71 sold 10/73
1347 LG	1103	Pn C52F	(632610)	"	Abbott, Timperley (C)	Caravan, Wakefield (XB) by 7/80
2522 LG	1043	"	(632426)	5/63	Bullock, Cheadle (C)	Gould, Pilton (H) 8/69 sold for scr by 7/80; engine to YYB 239H
2523 LG	1170	Du C52F	(1158/79)	"	"	Henderson, Carstairs (M) 7/69, wdn by 11/78
7654 LV	1385	"	(1172/55)	/64	James, Liverpool (C)	Burntwood Sailing Club, Burntwood (XD) by 10/81
7999 MD	1009	Pn C44F	(622224)	/63	Bloomfield, London SE5 (N)	Salmons, Corringham (N) 3/74 wdn 12/80, preserved by them by 12/81
3170 NT	1247	Wk B54F	(CF674)	1/64	Martlew, Donnington Wood (D)	Smith, Wilmcote (D) 9/78 wdn 11/80, to shed at garage 6/81
8488 NU	1362	Pn C52F	(642063)	4/64	Branson, Chesterfield (B)	Fowler, Holbeach (F) 3/74, preserved by Fowler (PF) since 9/80
4230 PE	1134	DM B54F	(CF627)	11/63	Richmond, Epsom (N)	Beverley Eagles Jazz Band (XB) 2/80
1539 PG	1171	Pn C52F	(632660)	8/63	White, Camberley 8 (K)	Underground, London SW16 (XN) 4/74, wdn 1/75, scr or exported
4208 PH	1169	"	(632422)	5/63	" (K)	White, Camberley (K) sold 4/76
3711 RU	1021	"	(632540)	4/63	Excelsior, Bournemouth (K)	Byley Garage, Byley (C) 10/67 wdn 9/80
5188 RU	1096	"	(632541)	5/63	"	West Wight, Totland Bay (K) 5/66 wdn by 12/81
213 SC	1333	Du C52F	(1172/67)	1/64	Edinburgh Corporation 213 (M)	Lewington, Harold Hill (N) 5/74, wdn 7/74, storeshed until c9/76
214 SC	1332	"	(1172/70)	"	" 214 (M)	Foster, Ellesmere Port (C) 6/72 wdn 9/73
215 SC	1294	"	(1172/68)	"	" 215 (M)	-?-, Cotebrook (XC) for conversion to transporter by 3/78
216 SC	1293	"	(1172/69)	"	" 216 (M)	East Moors Bluebirds Jazz Band (XG) by 4/79, sold for scr c2/83
217 SC	1335	"	(1172/71)	"	" 217 (M)	Drewery, Woodford Bridge (N) 4/77, scr 10/78
218 SC	1337	"	(1172/66)	"	" 218 (M)	Carnegie, London SE13 (N) 8/77 destroyed in depot fire 3/82
9583 SM	1006	Du C52F	(1158/6)	/63	Little, Annan (M)	Watt & Allan, Spittal (L) 9/74, wdn by 3/78
4220 TE	1024	"	(1158/7)	4/63	Robinson, Great Harwood (C)	Karunaratne, Sri Lanka, registered 29-Sri-5726 2/81
4221 TE	1041	"	(1158/8)	5/63	"	Saxton, Heanor (E) 7/72, wdn 11/75
8193 TE	1094	Pn C52F	(632620)	"	Wood, Ashton-under-Lyne (C)	Spiral Showgroup, Hope, Wrexham (XC) 2/76 sold by 12/76
419 TF	1017	"	(632414)	3/63	Tatlock, Whitefield (C)	Wilfreda, Ranskill (E) 7/65
1461 TF	1055	Pn C49F	(632410)	4/63	Monks, Leigh (C)	Bott, Abergynolwyn (C) 5/77 wdn 6/80
1462 TF	1061	"	(632411)	"	"	Bairne, Kilcock (I) as VZL 179, 8/69
1463 TF	1086	"	(632412)	5/63	"	Abbey, Selby (ZB) 2/77, sold for scr 2/77
2895 TF	1045	Pn C52F	(632415)	"	Battersby, Morecambe (C)	McLennan, Spittalfield (L) 1/70
5399 TF	1007	Du C52F	(1158/20)	4/63	Bold, Melling (C)	Tor Coaches, Street (ZH) for spares 11/74, scr by 4/78
8178 TF	1147	Pn C52F	(632416)	5/63	Battersby, Morecambe (C)	Amcron Ltd (transporter) (X?) by 9/81
129 TU	1165	Du C52F	(1158/92)	9/63	Pride of Sale, Sale (C)	Taylor (transporter), Ringwood (XK) by 12/82
9800 UK	1035	Pn C52F	(632429)	4/63	Everall, Wolverhampton (D)	Read, Ryde (K) 8/71 wdn 10/73
9801 UK	1030	"	(632427)	"	"	Leach, Cheltenham (H) 10/69, wdn and sold 1/74
9802 UK	1070	"	(632428)	5/63	"	Garforth Coachways, Allerton Bywater (B) 4/72, sold 9/74
9803 UK	1073	"	(632539)	6/63	"	Dougall, Dundee (L) 8/74
9804 UK	1057	Du C52F	(1158/21)	5/63	"	Sunshine Line (caravan), London SW15 (XN) by 1/79
9805 UK	1071	"	(1158/46)	6/63	"	Shaw, Maxey (F) 3/73, wdn 7/73

7104 UP	1053	Du C52F	(1158/43)	6/63	Scarlet Band, West Cornforth (A)	Cafe on A64 near Tadcaster (XB) by 8/82
2090 VM	1106	Pn C52F	(632547)	4/63	North Manchester Cs, Manchester (C)	Maroner, Linwood (M) 10/79
5105 VU	1388	Du C52F	(1172/75)	3/64	Makinson, Manchester (C)	Johnson, Snodland (XK) 6/80
518 XJ	1256	Pn C49F	(642871)	4/64	Fingland, Rusholme (C)	Rosetta, Nottingham (E) 7/70, wdn 5/77
800 ACA	1371	Du C52F	(1172/53)	"	Royal Red, Llandudno (C)	Ellis, Llangefni (C) 6/76 wdn 5/81
633 BAN	1318	"	(1172/26)	1/64	Clarke, London E16 (N)	Chazon, St Leonards (K) 5/76
52 BDL	1175	Pn C52F	(632659)	6/63	Moss, Sandown (K)	Mauler, Winkfield (K) 9/80 (12/80)
288 BDL	1200	"	(632685)	"	Shotter, Brighstone (K)	Cole, Bexleyheath (N) 8/81
300 BRK	1290	Du C52F	(1172/12)	2/64	Margo, London SW16 (N)	Nicholls, Garway (D) wdn 11/76
100 BRU	1325	Hn C52F	(2913)	3/64	Shamrock & Rambler, Bournemouth (K)	Crompton, Dunbury (caravan) (XC) 2/78
9 BRV	1101	Pn C52F	(632656)	6/63	Byng, Southsea (K)	Blanshard, Barrow (transporter) (XA) r/reg BWH 586A 6/82
942 BWC	1223	"	(632678)	7/63	Airborne, Ramsden Heath (N)	Darrenettes Morris Troupe, Oldham (XC) 6/76, sold c3/79
574 BWF	1198	"	(642856)	4/64	Bailey, Fangfoss (B)	Frankish, Brandesburton (B) 9/73 wdn 5/80
426 CEL	1352	Du C52F	(1172/64)	3/64	Tex, Bournemouth (K)	Unknown owner (transporter), Hail Weston (XF) by 2/81
179 CNR	1126	Ys C52F	(002063)	5/63	Gibson, Barlestone 54 (E)	Waddon, Senghenydd (G) 3/75
700 CVJ	1154	Du C52F	(1158/61)	7/63	Yeomans, Canon Pyon (D)	Smith, Sacriston (ZA) for spares 12/78
222 CYG	1022	"	(1158/25)	5/63	Wilson, Stainforth (B)	Denys Fisher, Thorp Arch (XB) 8/73, wdn by 10/77
111 DAY	1091	Pn C49F	(632423)	"	N & S, Leicester (E)	Buggy, Castlecomer (I) as NIR 53 3/81 used for spares
333 DAY	1188	"	(632681)	6/63	"	Alfa Romeo Dealers Club Team (transporter) (X?) by 4/77
981 DAY	1040	Du C52F	(1158/58)	"	Robinson, Burbage (E)	Robinson, Burbage (E) wdn 2/74 sold 2/74
90 DBD	1099	Du C51F	(1158/27)	4/63	York, Northampton 90 (E)	Hooper (transporter), Budleigh Salterton (XH) by 1/80
649 DCE	1150	Du C52F	(1158/80)	6/63	Harris, Cambridge 55 (F)	Clancy & Carew, Sligo (I) as CZO 890, 3/70
750 DCJ	1110	"	(1158/62)	"	Wye Valley, Hereford (D)	Hutchinson, Husthwaite (B) 9/72 wdn 12/72
63 DFR	1075	"	(1158/55)	5/63	Enterprise, Blackpool (C)	Barnson, Ilford (N) 12/74, wdn 6/75, scr 3/76
64 DFR	1144	"	(1158/71)	"	"	Franks, Haswell Plough (A) 10/71, wdn 3/76
639 DJU	1120	"	(1158/89)	6/63	Lester, Long Whatton (E)	Hanks & Briggs (motorcycle transporter) (X?) -/80
772 DWW	1087	Pn C50F	(632424)	4/63	Mosley, Barugh Green (B)	A G Dean Ltd (XB) racing car transporter c3/68
773 DWW	1088	Pn C51F	(632548)	"	Ward, Lepton (B)	Smith, Linthwaite (B) 5/74 sold 7/75, to transporter, scr c3/78
486 DWY	1108	Pn C52F	(632617)	5/63	Guiseley Tours, Yeadon (B)	Dipton & Sunniside Sundowners Jazz Band (XA) 7/76
779 DYG	1023	Du C52F	(1158/33)	4/63	Billies, Mexborough (B)	Highland Fabricators, Nigg (XL) by 6/78
407 EAY	1195	Ys C51F	(002163)	10/63	Gibson, Barlestone 58 (E)	Lavery, Dublin (I) -/77
504 EBL	1059	Du C52F	(1158/44)	6/63	Reliance, Newbury 87 (K)	Reliance, Newbury (K) from new, still there 12/80
849 EBL	1186	Pn C52F	(632624)	"	Carter, Maidenhead (K)	Haughton Telstars Juvenile Jazz Band (XA) by 10/78
808 ECE	1341	"	(642858)	7/64	Fison, Cambridge (XF)	Trailer Centre (caravan), Kings Lynn (XF) 11/79
947 ECE	1273	"	(642043)	1/64	Harris, Cambridge (F)	Munden, Bristol (H) 5/77, wdn 10/79
948 ECE	1282	"	(642059)	"	Harvey, Cambridge (F)	Kearns, -?- (XI) 3/78
22 EFW	1160	"	(632558)	6/63	Daisy, Broughton (E)	Enfield Drum & Trumpet Corps (XN) 3/80
140 EJW	1305	"	(632030)	2/64	Everall, Wolverhampton (D)	Caravan by 11/80
141 EJW	1309	"	(632031)	"	"	Clarke, Thurston (F) 5/73, wdn 7/79
142 EJW	1311	"	(632032)	"	"	Monty, Halstead (F) 6/76, wdn 7/77
143 EJW	1331	"	(642033)	"	"	Under conversion to transporter, Poole (XK) 7/82
144 EJW	1324	"	(642034)	"	"	Jones, Flint (C) 9/75 (8/77)
153 EJW	1344	"	(642035)	"	"	Maroner, Linwood (M) 12/79
44 EMO	1025	Du C52F	(1158/77)	7/63	Eagle Line, Swindon (H)	Brice, Four Marks (K) 7/73 sold 7/78
4 ERP	1123	"	(1158/88)	"	KW, Daventry A44 (E)	Ellis (racing car transporter), Coppull (XC) by 4/79
695 ETH	1254	Pn C52F	(??2867)	/63	Eynon, Trimsaran (G)	S S & B E Smith, Pylle (H) 10/79 (12/82)
665 EWR	1100	"	(632616)	6/63	Larrett Pepper, Thurnscoe (B)	Caravan, noted Leicester (XE) by 6/79
65 EWT	1113	Du C49F	(1158/53)	"	Baddeley, Holmfirth 73 (B)	Pollen, Dawley (D) 10/76 wdn 9/80
134 EWW	1129	Pn C52F	(632657)	"	Gray, Hoyland Newton (B)	Hood, Wold Newton (B) 7/75, sold 9/76
933 FJB	1272	"	(632872)	11/63	Brimblecombe, Wokingham (K)	Unknown school, Reading (XK) 2/76, sold -/78
132 FUA	1014	"	(632621)	6/63	Wallace Arnold, Leeds (B)	Joyce, Ballynahown (I) as VZL 192 by 7/73
133 FUA	1136	"	(632622)	"	"	Rosetta, Nottingham (E) 3/75, wdn 5/77
134 FUA	1138	"	(632623)	"	"	Pentland, Loanhead (M) 12/64, wdn 6/76

73 FUM	1179	Pn C52F	(632662)	7/63	Heaps Tours, Leeds (B)	Crown, Cramlington (A) wdn 11/74
371 FVA	1090	"	(632549)	4/63	Park, Hamilton (M)	Ryland, Gloucester (H) 7/77, wdn 8/79, sold 7/80
727 GAA	1046	Du C52F	(1158/26)	5/63	Taylor, Caterham 62 (N)	Abingdon & Caldicott, Abingdon (K) sold 9/78
644 GBU	1350	Pn C52F	(642049)	1/64	Southsea Royal Blue, Portsmouth (K)	Kenny Ireland Racing Team (transporter) (X?) by 5/75
700 GBU	1320	"	(642869)	"	Thornton, Shaw (C)	Caravan, Burnley (XC) by 10/77, sold by 6/79, seen in Burnley 7/83
856 GBU	1249	"	(632851)	2/64	Ivory Coaches, Tetbury (H)	Maybury, Cranborne (H) 9/76; to static rest room, London (ZN) 9/81
390 GEW	1060	Ys C52F	(001963)	5/63	Whippet, Hilton (F)	James, Aberdare (G) by 11/70, sold -/75, to breaker by 5/76
935 GFR	1389	Du C52F	(1172/49)	3/64	Murray, Blackpool (C)	Devonways, Newton Abbot (H) 7/77
63 GOU	1020	"	(1158/24)	5/63	Parlane, Aldershot (K)	Murchison, Kyle (L) 2/75
521 GOU	1044	Du C49F	(1158/30)	"	Coliseum, Southampton (K)	Croft, Cardiff (G) 8/70, wdn by 3/75
522 GOU	1190	"	(1158/90)	6/63	"	Seat store at Everall (dealer) Wolverhampton 1/74
230 GWR	1241	Du C52F	(1172/4)	12/63	Morgan, Armthorpe (B)	Morgan, Great Bedwyn (H) 6/73, wdn 10/74
694 GWU	1298	Pn C49F	(642036)	1/64	Anderton, Keighley (B)	Sherman, Warwick (D) 8/72, wdn 4/78
27 GWX	1271	DM B54F	(CF825)	2/64	Wigmore, Dinnington (B)	Muir (contractor), Kilmarnock (XM) by 1/78
351 GYG	1276	Wk B54F	(CF826)	/64	Ford, Fairburn (B)	Butter, Childs Ercall (D) 11/71, wdn 2/76
448 GYR	1268	Du C51F	(1172/32)	12/63	Grey-Green, London N16 (N)	Unknown owner (caravan), Gloucester (XH) by 9/80
555 HEW	1152	Pn C52F	(632658)	7/63	Odell, Great Haughton (F)	Tally Ho!, Kingsbridge (ZH) 5/78
898 HHO	1173	Du C52F	(1158/87)	6/63	Creamline, Bordon (K)	Baird, Stubbington (XK) by 5/78
550 HLE	1289	"	(1172/11)	2/64	Harling, London SE1 (N)	Harling, London SE1 (N) wdn 4/76
450 HLW	1338	Du C51F	(1172/34)	"	Orange, London N16 (N)	Caravan (X?) 6/78
883 HMJ	1201	Du C52F	(1158/1)	2/63	Vauxhall, Luton (demonstrator) (XN)	Mobile caravan, Newcastle (XA) 3/77
100 HOR	1157	"	(1158/81)	6/63	Liss and District, Bordon (K)	Fox, Hayes (N) 9/77, wdn 10/78
300 HOR	1141	"	(1158/70)	7/63	Creamline, Bordon (K)	Denning, Newport (G) 11/71 wdn 3/74
221 HUM	1269	Pn C49F	(632859)	/64	Wallace Arnold, Leeds (B)	Wilding (racing car transporter), Blackpool (XC) by 10/78
222 HUM	1270	"	(632860)	/64	"	Barking Angling Club (XN) 5/77
223 HUM	1284	"	(632861)	/64	"	Manor Legion Angling Society, London E12 (XN) 3/77
224 HUM	1285	"	(632862)	/64	"	Cathedral, Gloucester (B) 5/78, wdn 1/79, office/store 3/81
225 HUM	1286	"	(632863)	/64	"	Watt & Allan, Spittal (L) 4/78, wdn by 5/80
226 HUM	1327	"	(642039)	/64	Wallace Arnold (Feather), Leeds (B)	Hayfield Mills, Glusburn (XB) 3/74
227 HUM	1287	"	(642037)	/64	Wallace Arnold (Kitchin), Leeds (B)	Pentland, Loanhead (M) 3/70, wdn 6/76
228 HUM	1321	"	(642038)	/64	"	Pentland, Loanhead (M) 6/70, wdn by 3/71
229 HUM	1408	"	(642179)	/64	Wallace Arnold, Leeds (B)	Gill & Munden, Wadebridge (H) 2/79 wdn by 6/82 and used as office
230 HUM	1409	"	(642180)	/64	"	Williamsons of Gauldry, Gauldry (L) 5/74, wdn by 10/76
231 HUM	1410	"	(642181)	/64	"	Hodgson, Millom (A) 8/67, wdn 1/70
232 HUM	1351	"	(642182)	/64	"	Henderson, Carstairs (M) 4/71, wdn by 11/78
233 HUM	1443	"	(642174)	/64	"	Unknown non-PSV owner, Scunthorpe (XE) 7/80
234 HUM	1455	"	(642175)	/64	"	Bancroft & Powers, Coalville (E) 12/73, wdn 12/74
235 HUM	1422	"	(642176)	/64	"	O'Neill, Glasgow (M) 8/71, sold by 4/75
236 HUM	1424	"	(642177)	/64	"	Bingley, Kinsley (B) 7/67, wdn 5/76
237 HUM	1442	"	(642178)	/64	"	Smith, Linthwaite (B) 5/74
290 HWN	1185	Pn C52F	(??2853)	4/64	Demery, Morriston (G)	Independent Upholsterers, Ilkeston (XE) by 5/81 later derelict
255 JCG	1221	"	(632661)	9/63	Elm Park, Romford (N)	Indigo, London SW1 (XN) 10/73, wdn 11/74 when operations ceased
350 JEA	1128	Du C52F	(1158/18)	6/63	Hill, West Bromwich (D)	Gloucester Guides and Scouts Band (XH) -/79
777 JKA	1417	"	(1172/41)	4/64	Topping, Liverpool (C)	Topping, Liverpool (C) from new, wdn 5/72
51 JMJ	1002	"	(1158/17)	4/63	Stringer, Ampthill (F)	Rosehill Royals Jazz Band, Gateshead (XA) by 8/77
6 JNM	1114	Pn C52F	(632417)	/63	Finchley Coaches, London N12 (N)	Ivy, Linthwaite (B) 8/72
7 JNM	1143	"	(632418)	/63	"	Ward Street Garage, Walsall (XD) 12/75, derelict 3/77
22 JOC	1033	Du C52F	(1158/5)	4/63	Stockland, Birmingham (D)	Ulsterbus 1275 (NI) 4/74
23 JOC	1047	"	(1158/40)	5/63	"	Ulsterbus 1276 (NI) 4/74
24 JOC	1127	"	(1158/64)	6/63	"	Montgomery, Bromley (N) 10/75, wdn 10/76
648 JOC	1037	"	(1158/11)	4/63	Allenways, Birmingham (D)	Willis, Bodmin (H) 11/73 wdn 8/80
246 JTM	1010	"	(1158/13)	"	Taylor, Meppershall (E)	Adkins, Upper Boddington (E) 2/77, engineless at depot 8/80
770 JUA	1399	Du C44F	(1172/65)	6/64	Heaps Tours, Leeds (B)	Conroy, Benfleet (F) 6/73, wdn 10/75

Reg	No	Body	Chassis	Date	Operator	History
166 JWA	1257	Hn C52F	(2847)	2/64	Gill, Sheffield (B)	D Lee-Davey (transporter) (X?) by 4/82
16 JWO	1192	Pn C52F	(632663)	/64	Davies, Tredegar 35 (G)	Everest, Swanley (N) 7/76, wdn 7/79
823 JWP	1034	"	(632413)	4/63	Price, Romsley (D)	Marsh, Wincanton (ZH) acquired for spares by 7/80
402 KAO	1026	Du C52F	(1158/41)	5/63	Hamilton, Workington (A)	Garrill & Wright, Lincoln (E) 7/75, wdn by 1/78
901 KHO	1356	"	(1172/47)	2/64	Southcott, Loughton (N)	Bridge St Garage (car transporter), Downham Market (XF) by 5/77
31 KNM	1105	"	(1158/47)	6/63	Seamark, Westoning (F)	Powell, Lapford (H) 2/77, wdn 8/78
361 KNM	1072	"	(1158/66)	"	Costin, Dunstable (N)	Cass, Hull (B) 11/76, sold 4/78
246 KOT	1310	"	(1172/23)	3/64	Budden, West Tytherley (K)	Budden, Woodfalls (H) 1/73 (2/82)
878 KOU	1288	Du C49F	(1172/10)	4/64	Coliseum, Southampton (K)	Scout group, Sherston (XH) c2/82
141 KUY	1001	Du C52F	(1158/37)	6/63	Black and White, Harvington (D)	North Cheshire Historic Vehicle Group (PC) by 4/80
151 KUY	1031	"	(1158/38)	5/63	"	Mitchell, Perranporth (H) 8/72 wdn 9/73
45 KWD	1322	"	(1172/52)	4/64	Marvin, Rugby (D)	Bavister & Perry, Luton (N) 6/69 burnt out 6/69
525 LMJ	1246	Wk B53F	(CF673)	11/63	Vauxhall, Luton (demonstrator) (N)	Transporter (X?) by 5/81
358 LOR	1504	Pn C52F	(642283)	5/64	Cooke, Stoughton (N)	Brophy, Bracknell (K) 4/74 wdn 4/76
531 LOR	1470	Hn C49F	(2973)	"	Richmond, Epsom (N)	Margo, London SE19 (N) 5/69, scr 5/71
532 LOR	1487	"	(2975)	"	"	Lord & Sims, Rugby (ZD) 2/74
533 LOR	1479	"	(2974)	"	"	Red Arrows Jazz Band, Blaina (XG) by 10/78, sold 10/81
535 LOR	1545	Hn C52F	(3004)	8/64	"	Reneeus, Den Haag, Holland 5/75
536 LOR	1546	"	(3005)	"	"	Bradford-Lahore Transport, Bradford (B) 12/74
388 MBM	1274	Du C52F	(1172/28)	1/64	Cook, Biggleswade (F)	Blair, Guthrie (L) 7/72
72 MMJ	1349	Hn C52F	(2918)	3/64	Taylor, Meppershall 72 (F)	Unknown non-PSV operator, Branston (XD) by 4/83
91 MMJ	1381	Du C48F	(1172/50)	"	Stringer, Ampthill (F)	Wing, Sleaford (E) 3/72 sold 3/79
956 MNM	1397	Pn C52F	(642183)	"	Hillside, Luton (N)	Welshways, Caernarfon (C) 10/74, wdn 3/76
25 MTM	1464	"	(642167)	"	Buckmaster, Leighton Buzzard (E)	Smith, Wishaw (M) by 10/74
26 MTM	1447	"	(642168)	4/64	"	Smith, Attleborough (F) 1/74, operations ceased 9/80
535 MUP	1411	Du C52F	(1172/87)	7/64	Wilson (Economic), Whitburn 7 (A)	Shephardson, Barton-on-Humber (E) 5/75, wdn by 12/77
908 NBM	1431	"	(1172/79)	"	Ementon, Cranfield (F)	Easey, March (F) 6/74, sold 2/79
307 NOF	1516	Pn C52F	(642350)	"	Newton, Birmingham (D)	Head, Lutton (E) 12/73, wdn 3/80, sold by 1/81, later derelict
225 PMJ	1573	Du C52F	(1185/20)	12/64	Cook, Biggleswade (F)	Caravan, Skirbeck (XE) by 3/83
226 PMJ	1584	Du C39F	(1185/21)	"	"	Willis, Bodmin (H) 2/73, wdn 5/77
592 PUR	1003	Du C52F	(1158/3)	4/63	Premier, Watford (N)	Harding, Bagborough (H) 1/71, wdn 11/77
593 PUR	1018	"	(1158/29)	5/63	"	Tea bar on A505 at Royston (XN) 12/81
985 ROO	1102	"	(1158/51)	6/63	Pathfinder, Chadwell Heath (N)	Barton (racing car transporter), Chelford (XC) by 8/76
375 RVO	1081	Pn C49F	(632551)	4/63	Moxon, Oldcotes (E)	Caravan, Coulsdon (XN) by 5/81
963 RVO	1016	Ys C50D	(001063)	6/63	Barton, Chilwell 963 (E)	Rannoch, Haughley (XF) 1/74
964 RVO	1104	"	(001163)	"	" 964 (E)	Sayer, Ipswich (F) 9/74, scr after accident 11/74
965 RVO	1111	"	(001263)	7/63	" 965 (E)	Rannoch, Haughley (XF) by 4/74
966 RVO	1115	"	(001363)	"	" 966 (E)	Phillips, Shiptonthorpe (B) 5/75
967 RVO	1145	Ys DP56D	(001563)	"	" 967 (E)	Liversidge, Doncaster (B) 1/73, wdn 8/76
968 RVO	1146	"	(001463)	"	" 968 (E)	Meller, Goxhill (E) 10/73, wdn by 12/77
969 RVO	1167	"	(001663)	"	" 969 (E)	S Stockdale, Selby (B) 6/75
516 RWL	1058	Du C52F	(1158/36)	5/63	Higgins, Marcham (K)	Marston, Kennington (K) wdn 9/78
41 SAU	1004	"	(1158/22)	"	Skill, Nottingham 41 (E)	Barwell, Swavesey (XF) 7/75
42 SAU	1019	"	(1158/23)	"	" 42 (E)	Pollard, St Ives (H) 6/74 wdn 8/74
43 SAU	1052	Du C49F	(1158/39)	"	" 43 (E)	St Thomas School, London SE15 (XN) 1/75, sold 12/75
44 SAU	1122	"	(1158/63)	6/63	" 44 (E)	Caine, Askam (A) 9/77, sold 8/79
45 SAU	1148	"	(1158/72)	"	" 45 (E)	Mellor, Goxhill (E) 5/76, wdn 5/78
46 SAU	1180	"	(1158/73)	5/63	" 46 (E)	Watts, Lye (D) 2/67, wdn 4/75, still on site derelict 7/77
47 SAU	1176	"	(1158/74)	6/63	" 47 (E)	Crusader, Thornhill (B) 4/71 wdn 10/72
48 SAU	1187	"		7/63	" 48 (E)	Threlfall, Failsworth (C) 6/66 wdn 6/69
414 SRR	1117	Pn C52F	(632618)	5/63	Barton, Chilwell 970 (E)	McSorley, Eardington (ZD) 12/76
971 SRR	1028	"	(632611)	"	" 971 (E)	"
650 SVO	1125	"	(632619)	"	" 972 (E)	Phillips, Shiptonthorpe (B) 9/73

Reg	No	Body	Chassis	Date	Operator	History
433 TAL	1133	Pn C52F	(632665)	6/63	Barton, Chilwell 973 (E)	Prospect, Lye (D) 4/73, wdn 4/76
223 THU	1193	"	(632550)	5/63	Western Roadways, Patchway (H)	Brice, Chartham (K) 9/72 wdn 5/74
365 TTT	1330	Du C51F	(1172/78)	5/64	Blue Coaches, Ilfracombe (H)	Phillips, North Tawton (H) 1/73 wdn 1/79
1 VAL	1336	Du C52F	(1172/14)	4/64	Wilfreda Luxury Cs, Ranskill (B)	Wilfreda, Ranskill (B) from new, disused by 2/81
100 VAL	1376	"	(1172/54)	3/64	Brumpton, Dunham (E)	Swanbrook, Staverton (ZH) by 2/79, sold 9/79
440 VAL	1255	Pn C52F	(642870)	1/64	Sherwood, Worksop (E)	Overstone, Sywell (E) wdn 5/75
448 VAL	1316	Du C52F	(1172/37)	2/64	Leon, Finningley 64 (B)	Leon, Finningley 64 (B) from new, wdn 7/81
101 VRL	1427	"	(1172/40)	5/64	Jennings, Bude (H)	Anglian Builders, Lenwade (XF) 7/77
900 VRO	1342	Pn C52F	(642184)	2/64	Street, Hertford (N)	Redbourn Junior School (XN) by 5/76, sold 10/79
989 VRR	1391	Hn C52F	(2949)	4/64	Barton, Chilwell 989 (E)	Prospect, Lye (D) 11/73, wdn 4/76
990 VRR	1401	"	(2950)	"	" " 990 (E)	Phillips, Shiptonthorpe (B) 9/73
991 VRR	1429	"	(2948)	"	" " 991 (E)	Palmer, Carlisle (A) 11/72, wdn 11/77
992 VRR	1437	"	(2951)	"	" " 992 (E)	Prospect, Lye (D) 8/73, wdn 10/76
993 VRR	1392	"	(2952)	5/64	" " 993 (E)	Ricroft Racing, Eardington (XD) by 9/80, sold for scr by 11/81
994 VRR	1407	"	(2953)	"	" " 994 (E)	Cafe near Scarborough (XB) by 9/82
995 VRR	1435	"	(2954)	"	" " 995 (E)	Smith, Slaithwaite (B) 10/73, sold 2/75
996 VRR	1440	"	(2955)	"	" " 996 (E)	Caravan, Brighouse (XB) by 3/78
658 WKJ	1107	Pn C52F	(632625)	5/63	Margo, Bexleyheath (N)	Carlton & Bullen (transporter), Fulbourn (XF) -/76
395 WTG	1357	Du C47F	(1172/44)	/64	Rhondda Transport 395 (G)	Watts, Stourbridge (D) 4/73, wdn 6/75, derelict 2/76
396 WTG	1358	"	(1172/45)	/64	" 396 (G)	Watts, Stourbridge (D) 4/73, burnt out 9/73, remains on site 7/77
397 WTG	1359	"	(1172/46)	4/64	" 397 (G)	Prospect, Lye (D) 5/73, wdn 10/76
561 WYA	1164	Du C52F	(1172/18)	2/64	Wake, Sparkford (H)	Austerfield, London SE20 (N) broken up for spares 10/77
978 WYB	1253	"	(1172/3)	3/64	West Somerset Co-op (H)	Price, Newcastle (D) 5/70
814 XAF	1077	Pn C52F	(632546)	4/63	Clue, Menheniot (H) (Note 1)	Millman, Buckfastleigh (H) 2/81 (7/82)
931 XBF	1168	"	(632679)	6/63	Berresford, Cheddleton (D)	Converted to horsebox 12/76
166 XHN	1508	"	(642346)	6/64	Scotts Greys, Darlington (A)	Kinsman, Bodmin (H) 9/77 (7/82)
52 XNN	1474	"	(642340)	"	Thomas, North Muskham (E)	Tours, Douglas (IOM) as BMN 111 1/72; to Lavery, Dublin (I) 4/78
704 XYA	1460	"	(642189)	5/64	Crown Tours, Frome (H)	Crown, Frome (H) from new, still there 2/82
792 XYB	1501	"	(642335)	7/64	Chivers, Midsomer Norton (H)	Boyd, Eden (NI) 12/74
332 YBF	1149	Du C52F	(1158/78)	7/63	James, Tamworth (D)	Jenkins, Llanelli (G) 1/78, sold for scr by 5/79
461 YMA	1074	Pn C51F	(632421)	/63	Niddrie, Middlewich (C)	Brown, Aldbourne (H) 1/76, wdn 1/77
800 YTU	1085	Pn C52F	(632609)	4/63	Jackson, Altrincham (C)	Sportsman, Whiston (C) 6/72 wdn 6/73 sold by 7/73
AME 719A	1093	"	(632556)	"	J A Brown, Crawley (N)	Tally Ho!, Kingsbridge (H) 3/77 (12/82)
AME 720A	1097	"	(632557)	6/63	"	Stock car transporter, London SW18 (XN) 7/75, derelict by 3/77
AML 148A	1079	"	(632419)	4/63	Janes, Wembley (N)	Wilde, Heage (E) 3/71 wdn 8/74
AMY 440A	1080	"	(632553)	/63	Whitehall Motorways, London N7 (N)	Miller, Foxton (ZF) for spares 1/75
BMK 345A	1183	Wn C49F	(M504)	7/63	Rowson, Hayes (N)	Glevum, Gloucester (ZH) for spares 8/73
BML 870A	1112	Pn C52F	(632612)	5/63	Conway Hunt, Ottershaw (N)	Rosetta, Nottingham (E) 6/74, wdn 5/77
BMM 19A	1036	Du C52F	(1158/16)	"	Wilder, Feltham (N)	Shephardson, Barton-on-Humber (E) 10/73, wdn 12/75
BMX 296A	1156	Pn C52F	(632627)	6/63	Hume, Hockley (F)	Ward, Hognaston (E) 4/75, wdn after accident 8/78
BMY 7A	1139	Du C52F	(1158/82)	7/63	Wilder, Feltham (N)	Holvey, Bristol (H) 11/73, wdn 6/76
CMD 204A	1068	"	(1158/67)	"	Banfield, London SE17 (N)	Hehir, Kilkenny (I) -/75
CMD 205A	1069	"	(1158/84)	"	Empire's Best, London SE17 (N)	Merseyside, Liverpool (C) 7/71, licence expired 7/75
CMD 206A	1066	"	(1158/86)	"	" "	Barlow, Lichfield (D) 2/73
DME 976A	1260	"	(1172/9)	11/63	Martin, Hillingdon (N)	Chesterfield Toppers Carnival Band (XB) 3/78, sold 5/79
DME 999A	1225	Du C49F	(1172/2)	10/63	Shaw and Kilburn, London W3 (N)	Sabelis, Bugbrooke (E) 1/73, wdn 10/75
AAD 991B	1323	Du C52F	(1172/51)	3/64	Pulham, Bourton-on-the-Water (H)	Green, Brierley Hill (D) 7/72, wdn 7/76
AAW 320B	1261	"	(1172/19)	"	Whittle, Highley (D)	Tierney, Liverpool (C) 3/72, exported to Eire 5/76
AAY 400B	1414	Pn C52F	(642169)	2/64	Wheildon, Castle Donington (E)	Wheildon, St Austell (H) 6/78 (12/82)
ABD 91B	1390	Du C52F	(1172/63)	4/64	York, Northampton 91 (E)	Brown, Gloucester (ZH) by 5/80
ABD 310B	1428	Pn C52F	(642187)	"	Orsborn, Wollaston (E)	Pilning Garage (XH) as low-loading recovery vehicle by 8/82
ABE 300B	1466	"	(642243)	6/64	Daisy, Broughton (E)	Hyke, Lincoln (E) 10/68, wdn by 1/78
ABE 641B	1512	"	(642343)	"	Hornsby, Ashby (E)	Worksop Descaling (transporter), Clowne (XE) by 8/78, wdn by 7/81

Reg	No.	Body	(No.)	Date	Operator	History
ABT 966B	1528	Du C52F	(1172/109)	7/64	Boddy, Bridlington (B)	Roots, Puttenham (N) 9/79, wdn 7/80 (licensed in SETA until 5/80)
ADC 195B	1329	"		3/64	Begg, Thornaby (A)	Quondam, Enfield (N) 5/74, wdn 5/75
ADF 557B	1308	"	(1172/13)	5/64	Perrett, Shipton Olliffe (H)	Warren, Neath (G) 4/82 wdn by 1/83
ADG 479B	1458	"	(1172/82)	"	Grindle, Cinderford (H)	Prospect, Lye (D) 7/79 wdn -/82
ADL 109B	1493	"	(1172/72)	6/64	Southern Vectis 401 (K)	Rising Sun Legionnaires Jazz Band (XA) by 5/79
ADL 110B	1434	"	(1172/73)	4/64	" 402 (K)	Thorntree Garage (caravan), Leyland (XC) 3/82
ADL 252B	1334	Pn C52F	(642334)	5/64	Moss, Sandown (K)	Bagshaw, Bracknell (ZK) 10/80 exported to Eire 4/81
ADL 321B	1306	DM B54F	(CF831)	4/64	Seaview Services, Seaview (K)	Seaview Services, Seaview (K) sold 4/80
ADP 555B	1517	Du C52F	(1172/11)	7/64	Smith, Reading (K)	Page, Penryn (H) 5/77, wdn 1/79
ADY 724B	1541	"	(1185/5)	10/64	Leighton, Barking (N)	Easton, Brandiston (F) 2/79, dismantled at Cromer 6/79
ADY 926B	1587	Du C51F	(1185/12)	12/64	Ellis, Barking (N)	Burgess, Hemel Hempstead (XN) for conversion to caravan 9/82
AES 339B	1251	Pn C52F	(632857)	2/64	King, Dunblane (L)	Shanahan, Waterford (I) as SIY 920 8/76
AEX 6B	1277	Du C52F	(1172/38)	4/64	Seagull, Great Yarmouth (F)	Palace Bingo, Lowestoft (XF) 2/76
AEX 750B	1461	"	(1172/98)	6/64	Haylett, Great Yarmouth (F)	Mascot-Seagull, Great Yarmouth (F) wdn 12/75
AEX 850B	1489	"	(1172/106)	7/64	"	Cobholm, Great Yarmouth (F) 5/77 (4/80)
AFD 199B	1482	"	(1172/108)	"	Kendrick, Dudley (D)	Gould, Pilton (H) 9/73 wdn 5/80
AFR 17B	1452	Hn C52F	(2990)	6/64	Abbott, Blackpool (C)	Holvey, Bristol (H) 12/74, wdn 10/76
AFR 27B	1453	"	(2991)	"	"	Parsons, Harrow Weald (N) 8/74, sold 6/75
AGV 235B	1562	Pn C49F	(652502)	10/64	Morley, West Row (F)	P Kavanagh, Urlingford (I) 2/79
AJA 130B	1423	Sn B52F	(52130)	7/64	North Western Road Car Co 130 (C)	Tanner & Allpress, Sibford Gower (E) 9/73
AJA 131B	1497	"	(52131)	"	" 131 (C)	GAA Club, Hilltown (XNI) ?/??
AJA 132B	1498	"	(52132)	8/64	" 132 (C)	Tanner & Allpress, Sibford Gower (E) 9/72 sold as caravan by 7/81
AJA 133B	1513	"	(52133)	"	" 133 (C)	Jameson et al (preservationists), Manchester (PC) 11/81
AJA 134B	1509	"	(52134)	"	" 134 (C)	Tanner & Allpress, Sibford Gower (E) wdn by 7/78
AJA 135B	1524	"	(52135)	"	" 135 (C)	Ulster Defence Association (XNI) ?/??
AJA 136B	1525	"	(52136)	"	" 136 (C)	Grimshaw, Brackley (E) 3/72
AJA 137B	1519	"	(52137)	"	" 137 (C)	Wdn by North Western -/71
AJA 138B	1518	"	(52138)	"	" 138 (C)	Derelict in car park at Urmston, Manchester (XC) 4/74
AJA 139B	1523	"	(52139)	"	" 139 (C)	Jones, Flint (C) 6/74 (8/77)
AJS 110B	1459	DM B51F	(CF838)	6/64	Mitchell, Stornoway (L)	Morris, Swansea (G) 1/72, wdn 1/77, sold for scr 3/78
AJU 670B	1451	Du C52F	(1172/83)	5/64	Boyden, Castle Donington (E)	Swindon Village, Cheltenham (XH) c2/80
ALR 451B	1245	Hn C51F	(2849)	4/64	Grey-Green, London N16 (N)	Muldoon, London N17 (N) 7/73, wdn and sold for scr 7/74
ALR 452B	1283	Du C51F	(1172/94)	5/64	Orange, London N16 (N)	Caravan, Ferryhill (XA) by 9/76
ALR 453B	1370	Hn C52F	(2979)	"	Batten, London N16 (N)	Crows Nest Hotel (transporter), Anstruther (XL) by 9/81
AMB 300B	1360	Du C52F	(1172/29)	1/64	Bullock, Cheadle (C)	Watson, Runcorn (C) 12/76
AMB 461B	1450	Pn C51F	(642247)	4/64	Niddrie, Middlewich (C)	Watts, Warrington (B) 7/72
AMB 666B	1404	Pn C52F	(642166)	3/64	Jackson, Altrincham (C)	Grenville, Camborne (H) 5/73 (3/83)
AMB 888B	1383	Du C52F	(1172/48)	2/64	Abbott, Timperley (C)	Heard, Hartland (H) out of use by 9/78
ANK 399B	1162	Pn C52F	(632683)	3/64	Harpenden Motor Co, Harpenden (N)	Ferry & Simpson, Glasgow (M) 10/68, wdn by 1/71
ANN 700B	1551	Du C52F	(1185/8)	10/64	Barton, Chilwell 1000 (E)	Crown, Frome (H) 6/75, wdn 8/75
ANT 929B	1448	Pn C52F	(642060)	4/64	McSorley, Eardington (D)	Wilkinson (stock car transporter), Salford (XC) 6/82
ANY 135B	1177	"	(??2852)	5/64	Brewer, Caerau (G)	Jones, Login (ZG) for spares c3/82
AOO 759B	1281	Du C52F	(1172/36)	1/64	Leach, Harold Wood (N)	Leach, Harold Wood (N) wdn 9/79
APW 344B	1387	Pn C52F	(642188)	3/64	Towler, Emneth (F)	G & G, Leamington (D) 4/67 sold for scr 12/79
ARR 720B	1557	DM B53F	(CF1008)	12/64	Leon, Finningley 65 (B)	Leon, Finningley (B) disused by 6/79
ARY 693B	1467	Pn C52F	(642337)	6/64	Provincial, Leicester B8 (E)	Mellor, Ashbourne (XE) by 5/77
ATV 49B	1483	"	(642245)	5/64	Skill, Nottingham 49 (E)	B Kavanagh, Urlingford (I) 6/70, re-registered 3124 IP by 8/76
ATV 50B	1446	"	(642246)	"	" 50 (E)	Hallums, Prittlewell (F) 7/78, wdn 3/80
AUE 857B	1515	"	(642347)	7/64	De Luxe, Mancetter (D)	Cormorant A S, Cheshunt (XN) c2/79
AUP 650B	1415	Du C52F	(1172/15)	3/64	Cooper, Gilesgate Moor (A)	G Lees (racing car transporter), (X?) 7/77
AWD 217B	1430	Hn C52F	(2998)	6/64	Aston, Marton (D)	Cass, Hull (B) 6/73 wdn 11/76 loaned to Hull preservationists -/81
AWH 371B	1348	Hn C48F	(2924)	3/64	Leigh, Bolton (C)	Titterington, Blencowe (A) 4/66, wdn 5/77, sold by 8/79
AWT 351B	1259	Du C52F	(1172/7)	"	Store, Stainforth (B) (note 2)	Keenan, Bellurgan Point (I) by 3/76

Reg	No.	Body	(No.)	Date	Operator	History
AXD 525B	1473	Du C52F	(1172/88)	5/64	Seamark, Westoning (F)	Piper, Sheerness (K) 9/79, reinstated by 9/81
AXD 526B	1463	"	(1172/89)	"	"	Church group, Crayford (XN) by 10/78, wdn 7/79, no further user
AXD 527B	1488	"	(1172/90)	6/64	"	Chalfont, Greenford (N) 9/77, sold 1/78
AXD 528B	1481	"		"	Seamark, Westoning (F)	Swinard, Ashford (K) 5/66; burnt out 7/67
AXD 529B	1462	"	(1172/92)	"	"	Swanbrook, Cheltenham (H) 6/67 wdn 12/79 scr 2/80
AXD 530B	1472	"	(1172/93)	5/64	"	Brayford, Blackburn (C) 4/73, wdn 4/76
AYL 463B	1444	Du C51F	(1172/103)	"	Fallowfield & Britten, London N16(N)	Cornish Tartan Majorettes (XH) c2/81
AYL 464B	1445	"	(1172/102)	"	"	Caravan, Shotley, Suffolk (XF) by 8/82
AYV 92B	1181	Ys C52F	(002964)	4/64	Rickards, London W2 (N)	Leach, Harold Wood (N) 6/69 wdn 11/73
BDL 214B	1514	Pn C52F	(642336)	6/64	Seaview Services, Seaview (K)	Seaview Services, Seaview (K) sold 2/80
BDR 256B	1363	Du C52F	(1172/101)	"	Embankment, Plymouth (H)	Clark & Herrington, Flushing (H) by 4/82
BFU 431B	1549	Pn C52F	(652499)	11/64	Atkins, Skegness (E)	Greenwood, Chelmsford (F) 12/78, ceased operations by 9/82
BHK 519B	1292	Du C52F	(1172/31)	1/64	West, London E18 (N)	TS Explorer, West Leigh (XK) by 5/78
BJU 468B	1505	"	(1172/99)	6/64	Hart, Donisthorpe (E)	Grayscroft, Mablethorpe (E) 4/69 wdn c1/78 sold by 10/80, derelict
BMB 199B	1191	"	(1172/5)	4/64	Lingley, Sale (C)	Caravan, Balsall Common (XD) by 6/78
BMB 680B	1457	Pn C52F	(642280)	3/64	Bostock, Congleton (C)	King, West Bridgford (E) 9/77
BNG 888B	1480	"	(642345)	6/64	Babbage, Cromer (F)	Harris, Hillingdon (N) 5/78, broken up for spares 10/79
BNL 762B	1226	"	(??2854)	4/64	Craiggs, Amble (A)	Caravan, Grangetown (XA) by 3/79
BOO 165B	1343	"	(642040)	2/64	Thorpe, Dagenham (N)	Porter, Dummer (K) 11/76, wdn 7/79
BPL 920B	1300	Du C52F	(1172/24)	5/64	White, Camberley 12 (K)	Crosson, Drogheda (ZI) by 10/77
BPR 70B	1588	Pn C52F	(652721)	12/64	Bluebird, Weymouth (H)	Norris, Hawkhurst 66 (K) 1/78 (12/80)
BRX 539B	1494	Du C52F	(1172/110)	8/64	Eagle, Swindon (H)	42nd Leicester Scouts (XE) 3/78
BUJ 909B	1534	Pn C52F	(642339)	10/64	Jones, Market Drayton (D)	Sanders, Holt (ZF) for spares, broken up 9/79
BUP 148B	1307	DM B54F	(CF836)	5/64	Jolly, South Hylton (A)	Groocock, Rothwell (XE) 4/72
BUP 396B	1405	Du C52F	(1172/74)	"	Graham (Primrose), Winlaton Mill (A)	Campbell, East Kilbride (M) 5/72 wdn by 8/73
BWE 755B	1426	Du C49F	(1172/86)	6/64	E H Sims, Sheffield (B)	Ulsterbus 1272 (NI) 4/74
BWY 709B	1438	Du C52F	(1172/96)	"	Baddeley, Holmfirth 81 (B)	Butter & Managh, Childs Ercall (D) 1/72 wdn 10/79
BWY 710B	1465	"	(1172/97)	"	" 82 (B)	Baddeley, Holmfirth (B) delicensed by 2/81
BYU 338B	1560	"	(1185/9)	10/64	Ward, London E11 (N)	Team Eaton (transporter) (X?) by 12/82
CAB 583B	1485	Pn C52F	(642342)	6/64	Black and White, Harvington (D)	Thomas, Huddersfield (B) 11/76
CAB 593B	1490	"	(642344)	"	"	Abacus Racing, Cinderford (XH) for spares 9/79, sold by 2/83
CHP 329B	1538	Du C52F	(1185/4)	11/64	Shaw, Coventry (D)	Lakelin, Felindre (G) 4/76 (9/81)
CLK 700B	1530	Du C49F	(1185/1)	12/64	Grey-Green, London N16 (N)	Caravan, Downham Market (XF) 8/79
CMA 298B	1418	Du C52F	(1172/76)	5/64	Pride of Sale, Sale (C)	Hambridge, Kidlington (E) 6/70 wdn 5/74
CNV 698B	1576	Pn C52F	(652713)	11/64	Johnson, Rushden (E)	Garratt, Leicester (E) 10/75, wdn 2/76
CPT 333B	1354	Du C52F	(1172/81)	5/64	Derwent, Swalwell (A)	Robinson (transporter) (X?) by 4/77
CTC 856B	1319	Pn C52F	(642047)	1/64	Mitton, Colne (C)	Lucas, Ipstone (D) 10/74, wdn 12/75
CTD 322B	1275	Du C52F	(1172/59)	4/64	Robinson, Great Harwood 122 (C)	Tinlic (Tinsley Foods), Holbeach St Matthews (XF) 3/76
CTD 323B	1339	"	(1172/60)	"	" 123 (C)	Barlow, Lichfield (D) 10/73, wdn 1/76
CTD 324B	1347	"	"	"	" 124 (C)	John Rea (Rea Racing) (transporter), Temple Patrick (XNI) -/78
CTD 325B	1353	"	(1172/62)	"	" 125 (C)	Thomsett, Deal (K) 6/80
CTD 576B	1314	Pn C49F	(642048)	1/64	Monks, Leigh (C)	Price, Celbridge (I) as VZL 191, 6/70
CTJ 706B	1377	Hn C49F	(2925)	3/64	Jackson, Chorley (C)	Outten, Westcliff (F) 9/75, wdn 3/77
CTU 888B	1496	Pn C52F	(642338)	6/64	Jackson, Altrincham (C)	Easton, Brandiston (F) 2/79, sold 2/80
CUP 250B	1511	"	(642348)	7/64	Smith, Murton (A)	Begg, Middlesbrough (A) 6/76, wdn after accident damage 10/78
CUP 347B	1425	Du C52F	(1172/95)	6/64	Martindale, Ferryhill (A)	Thomsett, Deal (K) 5/72, wdn 6/78, being used for spares 1/81
CVW 928B	1326	Hn C49F	(2931)	4/64	Harris, Grays (N)	Wiggins, Thundersley (XF) 11/74
DEV 66B	1345	"	(2932)	"	"	Pollard, Hayle (H) 1/75, wdn 2/76
DMA 280B	1412	Du C52F	(1172/105)	7/64	Bullock, Cheadle (C)	O'Sullivan, Hospital (I) as 101 AIU, 5/75
DPP 777B	1577	Pn C52F	(652709)	12/64	Jeffways & Pilot, High Wycombe (N)	Bates, Rothwell (E) 8/76, wdn 10/79
DRF 990B	1262	Du C52F	(1172/16)	1/64	Gee and Harrison, Whittington (D)	Quinton, Sheffield (B) 3/76
DRF 991B	1291	"	(1172/17)	4/64	"	Sanders, Holt (F) 11/75, shed on premises 5/82, still there 8/83
DTC 563B	1346	Pn C52F	(642171)	/64	Tatlock, Whitefield (C)	Hayball, Warminster (H) 6/76, wdn 2/79

DTC 564B	1395	Pn C52F	(642865)	3/64	Davies & Mawson, Little Hulton (C)	Helms, Eastham (C) 12/69, wdn 4/76
DTE 723B	1252	"	(642868)	4/64	Shipley, Ashton-under-Lyne (C)	Kinsley, Stocksbridge (B) 5/72 wdn 3/79
DWW 838B	1554	DM B56F	(CF1006)	12/64	Wigmore, Dinnington (B)	Joseph, Stratford (XD) 5/69
EMH 811B	1248	Du C52F	(1172/21)	1/64	Banfield, London SE15 (N)	St John's Ambulance Brigade (first aid unit), Weybridge (XN) 11/76
EMH 820B	1299	"	(1172/33)	"	Biss, Bishops Stortford (N)	Gay, Northlew (H) 5/76 wdn by 6/82
EMH 821B	1293	"	(1172/35)	"	"	Sudbury Coaches, Sudbury (F) 3/76, sold 2/78
EMK 396B	1340	"	(1172/43)	4/64	Rutherford, London E11 (N)	Dance (transporter), Graveley (XK) by 3/80
EMP 798B	1379	"	(1172/58)	"	Empire's Best, London SE15 (N)	Hussars Jazz Band, Pelaw (XA) by 9/81
EMP 799B	1373	"	(1172/22)	"	Banfield, London SE15 (N)	Cafe on A500 (XD) 4/83
EMP 800B	1367	"	(1172/85)	6/64	"	Industrial Linen, London E15 (XN) 10/77, wdn 9/78, no further user
EMP 804B	1364	Pn C52F	(642185)	3/64	Sapphire, London WC2 (N)	McSorley, Eardington (ZD) 12/76
EMP 808B	1368	Du C52F	(1172/84)	6/64	Banfield, London SE15 (N)	Unknown non-PSV operator, Havant (XK) by 6/76
ERE 878B	1313	Pn C52F	(642173)	2/64	Mills, Gornal Wood (D)	Kendall & Newton, Guildford (N) 9/77, sold 9/79
ETF 330B	1355	Du C52F	(1172/77)	5/64	Hadwin, Ulverston (A)	Mullaney (transporter), Leicester (XE) 2/83
ETJ 778B	1372	"	(1172/80)	6/64	"	Butcher, Manchester (C) 7/77 wdn 7/78
FMG 984B	1317	"	(1172/25)	/64	Stevenage Travel, Stevenage (N)	Franks, Haswell (A) 7/71, wdn 3/75
FML 126B	1406	Pn C52F	(642190)	3/64	Janes, Wembley (N)	P Kavanagh, Urlingford (I) by 9/72
FML 127B	1421	Pn C44F	(642186)	4/64	"	Halfway Service Stn (recovery vehicle), Congresbury (XH) by 6/77
FMV 126B	1132	Du C52F	(1172/20)	2/64	Leighton, Barking (N)	Garforth Coachways, Garforth (B) 1/71 scr 10/74
FTB 231B	1491	Pn C49F	(642349)	6/64	Monks, Leigh (C)	Caravan, noted Rugby (XD) by 5/77
HMK 142B	1531	"	(642351)	7/64	JM Coaches, London WC2 (N)	Heywood, Langwith (B) 10/73
KRF 875B	1386	Du C52F	(1172/100)	6/64	Harper, Heath Hayes 75 (D)	Rowson, Hayes (N) 1/75
KRF 876B	1502	"	(1172/107)	7/64	" 76 (D)	Transporter, Leamington (XD) by 4/82
ABM 802C	1617	Pn C52F	(652500)	3/65	Cook, Biggleswade (F)	Goodwin Racing (racing car transporter), Bottesford (XE) by 6/81
ABY 300C	1580	"	(652715)	1/65	Margo, London SW16 40 (N)	King, Ilkeston (E) 3/77
ACG 77C	1600	Du C52F	(1185/32)	2/65	Creamline, Bordon (K)	'The Family' (caravan), Scotforth (X?) by 6/78
ACG 401C	1599	Pn C51F	(652853)	1/65	Coliseum, Southampton (K)	Clarke, Pailton (D) 5/76, wdn 9/77
ACG 992C	1631	"	(652856)	"	Banstead Coaches, Banstead (N)	Fisher & Redford (horsebox), Chichester (XK) by 3/81
AHB 928C	1607	Pn C52F	(652714)	"	Morlais, Merthyr (G)	Heard, Hartland 11 (H) 7/67 (7/82)
AHO 345C	1579	"	(652710)	"	Barfoot, Southampton (K)	BAC Tug-of-War Club, Weybridge (XN) by 7/75
AJM 555C	1674	Du C52F	(1185/73)	3/65	Brown, Ambleside (A)	Semmence, Wymondham (F) 6/72, wdn on premises by 4/83
AJP 95C	1618	"	(1185/40)	1/65	Liptrot, Bamfurlong (C)	Jackson, Beith (M) 12/75
AJP 377C	1689	"	(1185/63)	4/65	Unsworth, Wigan (C)	White (motorcycle transporter), Rossington (XB) 4/79
AMJ 333C	1602	"	(1185/42)	5/65	Baxter, Moggerhanger (F)	Peel Green Majorettes Morris Troupe, Liverpool (XC) by 6/78
AMJ 828C	1767	"	(1185/108)	6/65	Sproat, Bedford (F)	Ashroy, Newport (XG) 3/79
ANM 574C	1667	Pn C49F	(652990)	4/65	Taylor, Meppershall 74 (F)	Carter, Foulden (F) 8/70 (4/80)
ANM 575C	1746	Pn C45F	(653002)	7/65	" 75 (F)	Ardcavan, New Ross (I) as VMI 950, ?/??
AOR 378C	1623	Pn C52F	(652516)	4/65	Glider & Blue, Bishops Waltham (K)	Linfield, Thakeham (XK) by 9/78
AOR 379C	1639	"	(652517)	"	"	Cuff, Piddlehinton (H) 1/76, wdn 12/80
BAA 659C	1675	Du C52F	(1185/43)	"	Hearn, Edgware (N)	Brough, Wimborne (ZH) for spares 4/79, broken up by 9/79
BAF 836C	1572	"	(1185/19)	2/65	Brown and Davies, Truro (H)	Page, Penryn (H) 8/76, wdn 12/76
BCC 1C	1787	Du C49F	(1185/87)	6/65	Creams, Llandudno (C)	Jones, Rhosgadfan (C) 6/79
BCC 6C	1788	"	(1185/88)	"	"	Jones, Llandudno (C) 6/82
BCC 795C	1810	Du C52F	(1185/114)	"	Royal Red, Llandudno (C)	Jones, Flint (C) 11/76 wdn 5/81
BCN 633C	1792	"	(1185/85)	"	Thirlwell, Swalwell (A)	Hood, Wold Newton (B) 4/77, wdn 6/79
BCU 281C	1853	"	(1185/126)	7/65	Hall, South Shields (A)	Jim Price (transporter), Nottingham (XE) by 7/79
BCU 282C	1854	"	(1185/127)	"	"	Williams, Porthcawl (G) by 1/74, wdn 9/78
BDH 401C	1622	Pn C52F	(652498)	1/65	Everall, Walsall (D)	Holden, Lower Darwen (C) 4/76 (7/78)
BDH 510C	1736	Du C52F	(1185/17)	3/65	Central, Walsall (D)	Jenkins, Newport (G) 4/70 sold to breaker -/76
BDH 511C	1738	"	(1185/22)	4/65	"	Weeks, Sutton Valence (K) 3/78, broken up 10/78
BED 366C	1561	Hn C52F	(3033)	3/65	Shadwell, Warrington (C)	Frost, Eaton Socon (F) 6/72, wdn 1/73, sold 7/73
BEK 98C	1815	Pn C49F	(652839)	6/65	Smith, Wigan (C)	Caravan, Wellsborough (X?) by 5/81
BEK 316C	1852	Pn C52F	(653045)	"	"	Taylor (stock car transporter), Aveley (XN) by 5/78

Reg	No.	Body	Serial	Date	Operator	History
BET 530C	1777	Du C52F	(1185/113)	5/65	Riley, Rotherham (B)	Gogarth School, Llandudno (XC) 3/80
BHD 440C	1859	Pn C52F	(652842)	6/65	Gath, Dewsbury (B)	Baxendale, Bredbury (C) 9/80
BJE 474C	1646	Du C52F	(1185/66)	5/65	Morley, Whittlesey (F)	Morley, Whittlesey (F) sold 7/79
BKM 91C	1591	Pn C52F	(652724)	1/65	Bexleyheath Tpt, Bexleyheath (N)	Smith, Swanley (N) 4/77, wdn 7/80
BMJ 259C	1825	"	(653046)	10/65	Stringer, Ampthill (F)	Swanbrook, Staverton (H) 9/79, wdn 5/80, sold for scr 11/80
BMW 398C	1529	"	(652493)	1/65	Rimes, Swindon (H)	Water ski transporter (X?) c6/82
BND 156C	1728	"	(652496)	4/65	North Manchester Cs, Manchester (C)	Chandler, North Bradley (H) 6/68
BNF 490C	1527	"	(652505)	2/65	Mayne, Manchester (C)	Murray, Farnworth (C) 1/78 wdn 12/78
BNF 491C	1670	"	(652518)	3/65	"	Smith (stock car transporter), Bradford (XB) by 4/82
BNF 492C	1654	"	(652519)	5/65	"	Hodgson, Chatburn (C) 10/74 (7/78)
BNN 105C	1603	"	(652730)	1/65	Wright, Newark (E)	Wright, Newark (E) from new, sold 7/73
BNW 615C	1765	Pn C49F	(653104)	/65	Wallace Arnold (Feather), Leeds (B)	Lloyd, Maghull (C) 5/71, wdn 8/75
BNW 616C	1779	"	(653105)	/65	"	Woodhouse, Bolsover (B) 6/72, wdn 2/79
BNW 617C	1783	"	(653106)	/65	"	Exported to Eire 7/74
BNW 618C	1811	"	(653111)	/65	Wallace Arnold, Leeds (B)	Don Corning Cavaliers Jazz Band, Barry (XG) by 4/80
BNW 619C	1836	"	(653110)	/65	Wallace Arnold (Wardways), Leeds (B)	Murray, St Helens (C) 4/71, wdn 9/74
BNW 620C	1837	"	(653109)	/65	"	Mountain Management (showroom), London W1 (XN) -/77, sold by 2/79
BNW 621C	1870	"	(653107)	/65	"	Walshema Jazz Band, Walsall (XD) by 5/80
BNW 622C	1857	"	(652515)	/65	"	Pettigrew, Mauchline (M) 12/70, wdn 3/74 but still owned -/78
BNW 623C	1864	"	(653108)	/65	"	Hehir, Kilkenny (I) 6/76
BNW 636C	1706	Pn C51F	(652512)	/65	"	Wiggins, Thundersley (XF) 6/79
BNW 637C	1647	"	(652513)	/65	"	Aspey, Upholland (C) 1/76, wdn 6/77
BNW 638C	1734	"	(652514)	/65	"	Easton, Brandiston (F) 9/74, wdn 5/80 and broken up on premises
BNW 639C	1750	"	(652716)	/65	"	Sealand Sapphires Morris Troupe (XC) 9/81
BNW 640C	1753	"	(652718)	/65	"	Crantours, Romford (N) 7/75, wdn 8/77
BNW 641C	1749	"	(652717)	/65	Wallace Arnold (Kitchin), Leeds (B)	Salford Caravelles Morris Troupe (XC) 1/81
BNW 643C	1733	Du C52F	(1187/74)	/65	Wallace Arnold, Leeds (B)	Holder, Coppull (C) 5/77, wdn 12/77
BOP 505C	1633	Pn C52F	(652992)	3/65	H Brown, Birmingham (D)	Huby, Willerby (B) 1/74
BOR 237C	1794	Du C52F	(1185/102)	5/65	Martin, West End (K)	Cowdrey, Gosport (K) 10/75, wdn 10/75
BOT 371C	1820	"	(1185/109)	6/65	Blunt, Mitcham (N)	Kennyland School, Reading (XK) 5/76
BOT 544C	1822	"	(1185/117)	"	Richmond, Epsom (N)	Stoneman & Brown, Nanpean (H) 9/78, wdn 10/79
BOU 634C	1842	"	(1185/116)	7/65	Warren, Alton (K)	Warren, Alton (K) wdn 7/79, sold to contractor's site hut by 8/81
BSD 13C	1592	Pn C52F	(652708)	4/65	Garnock Valley, Kilbirnie (M)	Cowdrey, Gosport (ZK) c6/79, broken up for spares by 8/79
BSN 700C	1606	Du C52F	(1185/69)	"	Cunningham, Drymen Station (M)	Littlesea Racing (transporter), Weymouth (XH) by 2/78
BTH 987C	1683	"	(1185/105)	5/65	Eynon, Trimsaran (G)	Coastal Continental, Barry (G) wdn 7/78, burnt out 8/79
BTK 397C	1693	"	(1185/47)	4/65	Rendell, Parkstone (K)	Bland, Cottesmore (E) 6/70, wdn by 9/77, scr 11/78
BTK 399C	1657	"	(1185/37)	"	"	Gear, London SE13 (N) 8/77 wdn 5/79
BVD 828C	1540	Wk B54F	(CF972)	/65	Irvine, Salsburgh (M)	Meffan, Kirriemuir (L) wdn by 12/79 scr at depot by 11/81
BVD 829C	1563	"	(CF1009)	/65	"	Keenan, Bellurgan (I) as YIY 684 by 8/79
BVO 464C	1558	Pn C52F	(652509)	3/65	Lindrick, Langold (E)	Willis, Bodmin (H) 9/77 (12/82)
CAL 227C	1731	"	(652504)	4/65	Moxon, Oldcotes (E)	Lavery, Dublin (I) as 1129 ZB 3/81
CBK 501C	1642	"	(652857)	2/65	Byng, Portsmouth (K)	Jones, Bontnewydd (C) 2/78 exported to Eire by -/81
CBU 901C	1704	"	(652993)	5/65	Stott, Oldham (C)	Jones, Llanfaethlu (C) 5/70 (8/77)
CBV 223C	1601	"	(652837)	4/65	Aspden, Blackburn (C)	Portonians Morris Troupe, Ellesmere Port (XC) 2/81
CCB 621C	1776	Du C52F	(1185/86)	5/65	Ribblesdale, Blackburn (C)	Jones & Hughes, Buckley (C) 11/72, wdn 12/74
CCE 949C	1581	Pn C52F	(652720)	2/65	Harris, Cambridge (F)	Hughes, Buckley (C) 5/75, wdn ?/??
CCE 950C	1626	"	(652731)	"	"	Hughes, Widnes (C) 11/73, wdn 10/74
CCF 468C	1732	Pn C49F	(653179)	5/65	Morley, West Row (F)	Caravan, Soham (XF) by 9/82
CCG 704C	1819	"	(652492)	7/65	Chisnell, Winchester (K)	White, Weaverham (C) 1/77
CCR 963C	1665	Hn C52F	(3091)	4/65	Summerbee, Southampton (K)	Caravan, Llangennech (G) 10/81
CCT 732C	1717	Pn C52F	(653190)	6/65	Simmons, Great Gonerby (E)	Greenwood (racing car transporter) by 9/80
CCV 835C	1661	Du C52F	(1185/60)	5/65	Stevens, St Ives (H)	Stevens, St Ives (H) from new, wdn 7/74
CCW 257C	1691	"	(1185/68)	"	Shutt, Burnley (C)	Ackroyd & Abbott, Sheffield (XB) by 12/77, wdn -/80

CCW 582C	1697	Pn C52F	(653003)	5/65	Sandown, Padiham (C)	Lloyd, Maghull (C) 8/72
CDC 495C	1668	Du C52F	(1185/59)	"	Begg, Thornaby (A)	Hayfield Riding Stables (horsebox), Aberdeen (XL) 1/82
CDK 408C	1649	Pn C52F	(653112)	/65	Yelloway, Rochdale (C)	Lucas, Hollington (D) 8/74, wdn 12/75
CDK 409C	1681	Hn C49F	(3104)	/65	"	Baker, Weston-super-Mare (H) 5/81 (9/82)
CDK 410C	1690	"	(3105)	/65	"	Wooley & Beecham, Loughborough (E) 9/74 wdn 1/76 scr 10/80
CDK 411C	1719	"	(3106)	5/65	Creams, Rochdale (C)	Penmaenmawr Motor Co, Penmaenmawr (C) 7/77
CDK 412C	1740	"	(3107)	"	"	Prospect, Lye (D) 10/75, wdn 5/77
CDW 722C	1760	Pn C52F	(653178)	"	Gulley, Newport (G)	Smith, Ingham (E) 8/74 (5/80)
CEB 124C	1786	Du C52F	(1185/107)	8/65	Miller, Foxton (F)	Cafe on A1 at Sawtry (XF) by 10/80; later caravan by 6/81
CED 764C	1851	Pn C52F	(653193)	7/65	Cooper, Warrington (C)	Farm at Honiton (XH) -/80 gone by 10/81
CEX 705C	1791	Du C52F	(1185/120)	6/65	Cobholm, Great Yarmouth (F)	Palace Bingo, Gorleston (XF) 11/76, sold 1/80
CFA 645C	1799	Du C49F	(1185/79)	5/65	Viking, Burton (D)	Transporter, Kegworth (XE) by 5/81
CFA 646C	1828	Du C52F	(1185/80)	6/65	" 6 (D)	Swanbrook, Staverton (H) 2/79 to breakdown tender 6/80
CFG 824C	1798	Pn C52F	(653175)	5/65	Rennie, Dunfermline (L)	Wellock, Scarborough (B) 9/73 wdn 3/80
CFV 189C	1643	Du C52F	(1185/33)	4/65	Enterprise, Blackpool (C)	Holden, Lower Darwen (C) 6/76 (7/78)
CFY 956C	1645	Pn C49F	(652840)	"	Smith, Wigan (C)	Simms (transporter), Horbury (XB) by 4/81
CFY 957C	1650	"	(652841)	"	"	Fletcher, Skelmersdale (C) 1/71 wdn 9/78
CHA 495C	1702	Du C52F	(1185/94)	5/65	Mann, Smethwick (D)	Flanagan, Corby (E) 5/71, wdn 5/76
CHY 490C	1724	"	(1185/97)	"	Monarch, Bristol (H)	Gwalia, Llanbyther (ZG) by 7/81
CND 9C	1742	Pn C52F	(653013)	4/65	Fingland, Rusholme (C)	Swanbrook, Staverton (H) 9/78, wdn 9/80, sold 2/81
CNW 154C	1653	Hn C44F	(3113)	5/65	Heaps Tours, Leeds (B)	Sumner (dealer), Crook (ZA) as storeshed 3/77
CNW 155C	1694	"	(3114)	"	"	Hood, Wold Newton (B) 4/72 wdn 6/80
COD 925C	1768	Ml B52F	(B3489)	6/65	Burton, Brixham (H)	Tally Ho!, Kingsbridge (H) 2/78, sold for scr 8/82
COH 25C	1685	Du C52F	(1185/38)	3/65	Stockland, Birmingham (D)	Queensway, Bootle (C) 5/76 (6/76)
COH 26C	1621	"	(1185/39)	"	"	Britton, Yate (H) 3/77, wdn 3/78
COP 500C	1745	Pn C52F	(653010)	4/65	Smith, Birmingham (D)	Hubber, Newquay (H) 11/75, wdn 11/80
COP 600C	1781	"	(653011)	"	"	Redditch Association Football Club (XD) 10/77
COR 970C	1877	Du C52F	(1185/118)	9/65	Hodge, Sandhurst (K)	Harwood, Weybridge (N) 2/70 sold by 2/83
COR 980C	1909	Pn C49F	(669311)	"	Coliseum, Southampton (K)	Caravan, Gloucester (XH) 10/82
CRW 229C	1658	Pn C52F	(652996)	3/65	Bonas, Coventry (D)	Caravan, Eastbourne (XK) 4/83
CUJ 309C	1619	Du C52F	(1185/10)	1/65	Whittle, Highley (D)	Easey, March (F) 12/75, wdn 10/81
CUJ 313C	1586	"	(1185/11)	2/65	" 13 (D)	Ardcavan, Wexford (I) as UMI 890, 6/72
CUJ 492C	1663	Pn C52F	(653103)	4/65	Jones, Market Drayton (D)	Paulrich, Hull (B) 11/73 sold 9/74
CUK 501C	1748	"	(652727)	"	Everall, Wolverhampton (D)	Hughes, Rhyl (C) 7/77, wdn 2/79
CUK 502C	1570	"	(652725)	1/65	"	Circus Hoffman (X?) by 3/79
CUK 503C	1604	"	(652726)	"	"	Fussell, Swansea (G) 3/72, wdn by 3/78, scr -/78
CUK 504C	1771	"	(652844)	5/65	"	Kronprinsens & Guards Jazz Band, Washington (XA) by 7/81
CUK 505C	1775	"	(652845)	6/65	"	Baker, Hopton (F) 5/77, wdn 4/79, dismantled on premises 12/79
CUK 506C	1796	"	(652846)	5/65	"	Martin, Corlough (I) as 933 ID, by 8/79
CUK 526C	1797	Du C52F	(1185/46)	6/65	"	-?-, Walsall (XD) 10/76
CUM 494C	1439	Wn C52F	(M1569)	7/65	Wallace Arnold, Leeds (B)	Horsfall, Glusburn (XB) 7/69 wdn 3/74 after accident, sold for scr
CVC 2C	1906	Pn C52F	(669308)	10/65	McGhie, Coventry (D)	Matthews, Cwmbran (G) 1/81 sold 5/81
CVD 68C	1743	"	(653001)	4/65	Gorman, Rutherglen (M)	Davidson, Forfar (L) -/71 wdn by 7/73
CVE 666C	1722	"	(653000)	"	Kenzie, Shepreth (F)	Fussell, Fforestfach (G) 6/69, wdn by 3/78
CVJ 500C	1614	"	(652497)	1/65	Yeomans, Canon Pyon 19 (D)	-?-, Leamington (XD) by 7/77
CVJ 800C	1568	DM B54F	(CF1074)	"	" 9 (D)	Cleverly, Cwmbran (G) 6/79 sold 8/82
CYC 943C	1679	Pn C52F	(652511)	4/65	Baker, Weston (H)	Sing, Cardiff (G) by 3/83
DAC 195C	1640	Du C52F	(1185/49)	2/65	Smith, Long Itchington (D)	Warnes (stock car transporter), Kings Lynn (XF) by 6/79
DAO 986C	1636	Pn C49F	(652855)	3/65	Hamilton, Workington (A)	David Turner (transporter), Soham (XF) 6/78
DAW 825C	1812	Pn C52F	(653176)	6/65	Cooper, Oakengates (D)	City of Coventry Drum Corps (XD) 2/81
DAW 826C	1785	"	(653177)	"	"	Jones, Bontnewydd (C) 5/80, exported to Eire by -/81
DBE 921C	1778	Pn C49F	(653191)	5/65	Appleby, Conisholme (E)	Appleby, Conisholme (E) wdn by 7/78
DBN 642C	1648	Hn C49F	(3092)	4/65	Leigh, Bolton (C)	Parker (horsebox), Winfarthing (XF) 10/76

DCG 66C	1882	Du C52F	(1202/2)	11/65	Creamline, Bordon (K)	Castle, Horndean (K) 8/67, wdn 2/76
DCG 160C	6804349	Pn C49F	(669319)	"	Coliseum, Southampton (K)	Jones, Gloucester (H) by 1/82
DDP 636C	1856	Du C52F	(1185/115)	6/65	Smith, Reading (K)	Brown, Millbrook (XH) 8/81
DES 398C	1873	Pn C52F	(653194)	7/65	King, Dunblane (L)	Graham & Davies, Lennoxtown (M) 8/75
DEX 22C	1867	"	(653066)	9/65	Seagull, Great Yarmouth (F)	Mobile caravan, Thorney (XF) 11/81, to scrapyard c2/83
DJB 919C	1880	"	(663180)	"	Bryan, Didcot (K)	Glider & Blue, Bishops Waltham (K) 2/75, wdn 12/77, scr by 8/79
DJJ 779C	1605	Du C52F	(1185/18)	1/65	Empress, London E2 (N)	Brophy, Bracknell (K) 9/75, wdn 5/76
DJU 705C	1585	"	(1185/29)	3/65	Gibson, Barlestone 61 (E)	Lewington, Harold Hill (N) 9/74, sold 12/76
DJU 706C	1756	"	(1185/67)	4/65	" 62 (E)	Compass, Wakefield (B) sold by 3/79
DKF 444C	1772	"	(1185/77)	"	Pearsons, Liverpool (C)	Intercity, London E4 (XN) 3/76, wdn 2/77, sold, derelict by 3/78
DRT 745C	1809	"	(1185/121)	8/65	Classic, Lowestoft (F)	Shreeve, Lowestoft (F) 8/71, to staff rest room 7/78
DUE 511C	1559	"	(1185/16)	4/65	Cotton, Bilton (D)	Derby Midshipmans Band (XE) by 1/81
DUJ 771C	1800	"	(1185/89)	6/65	Brown, Donnington Wood (D)	Reece (transporter) (X?) by 7/81
DUT 456C	1735	Pn C52F	(652847)	4/65	Howlett, Quorn 23 (E)	Baker, Hopton (F) 11/76, wdn 9/80, kept for preservation by 8/83
DVJ 600C	1801	"	(653173)	6/65	Wye Valley, Hereford (D)	Open Air Campaigners (XH) 9/81
DWF 50C	1894	"	(669304)	8/65	Abbey, Selby (B)	Chalk, Coombe Bissett (H) 12/76 (2/82)
DWF 51C	1897	"	(669306)	"	"	Baker, Weston-super-Mare (H) 5/81 (2/82)
DXE 531C	1630	Du C52F	(1185/48)	1/65	Seamarks, Westoning (F)	West Ham Garage Freshwater Angling Club, London E13 (XN) 7/79
DXE 532C	1634	"	(1185/56)	3/65	"	Landliner, Birkenhead (C) 6/72 wdn 4/74
DXE 533C	1651	"	(1185/57)	"	"	Smith, Linthwaite (B) 2/76, wdn 9/78
DXE 534C	1641	"	(1185/58)	"	"	Hayball, Warminster (H) 1/77, wdn 4/78
EAC 881C	1711	"	(1185/91)	4/65	Moreton, Nuneaton (D)	Parker, Derby (E) 9/75, wdn by 5/77
EAP 474C	1803	"	(1185/84)	7/65	Bradley, London E17 (N)	Short, Wingland (XF) 6/78
EAX 888C	1737	"	(1185/76)	3/65	Davies, Tredegar 44 (G)	Llanylltyd Troupers Jazz Band (XG) by 8/81
EAY 191C	1773	"	(1185/90)	5/65	Robinson, Burbage (E)	Horton, Ripley (E) 6/78, wdn c11/78
EDD 373C	1813	Pn C52F	(653192)	6/65	Say, Gloucester (H)	Abergavenny Tornadoes Jazz Band (XG) 2/81
EDD 883C	1816	Du C52F	(1185/100)	"	Western Roadways, Patchway 21 (H)	Hamilton (transporter), Burton (XD) by 7/77
EGD 160C	1556	"	(1185/6)	4/65	Gorman, Rutherglen (M)	Crosson, Drogheda (I) 4/75
EJU 133C	1695	Pn C52F	(653189)	6/65	Caldwell, Loughborough (E)	Outten, Westcliff-on-Sea (F) 5/76, wdn 6/78
EKD 240C	1761	Du C52F	(1185/95)	7/65	James, Liverpool (C)	Graviner, Colnbrook (XN) 10/77, sold c8/78, no further user
EKL 732C	1814	"	(1185/128)	10/65	Clubb, Wilmington (N)	Tea bar, Stockley, Kent (XK) by 11/80
ELL 386C	1729	"	(1185/72)	6/65	Latham, Kenton (N)	Clark & Herrington, Flushing (H) 5/79, wdn 8/80
ENV 1C	1766	"	(1185/101)	5/65	KW, Daventry (E)	Shephardson, Barton-on-Humber (E) 5/75, wdn and used as store 5/77
ENV 310C	1806	Pn C52F	(652719)	5/65	Orsborn, Wollaston (E)	Cooper & Hochrath, Rothwell (E) 12/76, wdn 11/79
EPM 950C	1843	Du C52F	(1185/103)	6/65	Clubb, Wilmington (N)	Whitstable Majorettes Jazz Band (XK) 7/80
ERM 103C	1725	Pn C51F	(653197)	"	Hamilton, Workington (A)	Theakston's Brewery, Masham (XB) by 8/82
ERM 210C	1821	Du C52F	(1185/123)	7/65	Kirkpatrick, Brigham (A)	Kirkpatrick, Brigham (A) wdn 4/77
ERP 434C	1710	Pn C52F	(652995)	6/65	Basford, Greens Norton (E)	Basford, Greens Norton (E) wdn by -/81
ETY 996C	1795	Du C52F	(1185/111)	"	Wansbeck, Ashington (A)	Humphries, Bridgend (G) 8/79, sold by 9/80
EWD 674C	1826	"	(1185/122)	"	Shirley, Meriden (D)	David, Pontycymmer (G) 11/78, wdn by 8/80
EWU 587C	1590	Pn C52F	(652495)	2/65	Davison, Brighouse 30 (B)	White Heather, Southsea (K) 6/79 wdn 5/81 being scr 8/82
EWU 980C	1741	Du C52F	(1185/99)	5/65	Anderton, Keighley (B)	Featherstone & District ?Angling? Association (XB) 5/83
EWY 577C	1655	Pn C52F	(652860)	2/65	Furness, Sheffield (B)	Symeade Race Rally Team (transporter), Beech Hill (XK) by 6/81
FAC 101C	1712	Hn C52F	(3165)	7/65	Lloyd, Nuneaton (D)	Lloyd, Nuneaton (D) wdn 7/77
FAX 8C	1416	Wn C52F	(M1567)	5/65	Davies, Tredegar 50 (G)	Vanstone, London N1 (N) 8/71 sold 12/72
FAX 88C	1730	Du C52F	(1185/75)	/65	Howells & Withers, Pontllanfraith(G)	Bethesda Church, Bury (XC) by 4/78
FAX 314C	1420	Wn C52F	(M1568)	5/65	Jones, Aberbeeg 122 (G)	Transporter, Shifnal (XD) by 5/83
FAX 697C	1762	Pn C49F	(653188)	"	Davies, Tredegar (G)	Autofair, Burton-on-Trent (ZD) by 6/77
FBW 206C	1610	Du C52F	(1185/15)	6/65	Spiers, Henley (E)	Tor Coaches, Street (H) 4/75, wdn 4/78
FBW 207C	1793	"	(1185/98)	"	"	Chivers, Midsomer Norton (H) 9/75, wdn 10/77
FBW 657C	1817	Du C52F	(1185/110)	"	Maybury, Souldern (E)	Godding, Cwm (G) 1/76 wdn -/82
FGJ 303C	1862	Du C52F	(1185/119)	"	Costin, Dunstable (N)	John, Tonypandy (G) 9/71 wdn by 4/74
FGJ 304C	1863	Pn C52F	(653194)	7/65	Fox, Hayes (N)	Dougall, Dundee (L) 9/74, sold 10/76, exported to Ireland

Reg	No.	Body	(No.)	Date	Operator	History
FNP 965C	1565	Du C52F	(1185/14)	3/65	Coaches, Bromsgrove (D)	Brown, Swindon (H) 2/71 wdn 11/71
FPL 12C	1555	Pn C52F	(652501)	"	Conway Hunt, Ottershaw (N)	Platt, London SW19 (XN) c-/76, sold by 2/80
FPP 626C	1673	Du C52F	(1185/35)	4/65	Dell, Chesham (N)	Hookway, Meeth (H) for spares 2/77
FPT 440C	1533	"	(1185/2)	1/65	Wilson (Economic), Whitburn 10 (A)	Shephardson, Barton-on-Humber (E) 9/75, wdn by 12/77
FRM 618C	6808136	"	(1202/24)	12/65	Cumberland Motor Services 300 (A)	Adamson, Edinburgh (M) -/75, sold -/75
FTX 946C	1876	"	(1185/104)	8/65	Davies, Glyn Neath (G)	Fochriw Miniparaders Jazz Band (XG) by 4/76, sold by 6/77
FWA 611C	1611	"	(1185/41)	3/65	Sims, Sheffield (B)	Morley, Whittlesey (F) 3/73, wdn 7/75
FWB 778C	1754	Pn C49F	(653007)	4/65	Littlewood, Sheffield (B)	-?-, Swansea (G) by 12/76
FWJ 444C	1764	Pn C51F	(653174)	"	Anderson, Sheffield (B)	Clark & Herrington, Flushing (H) 3/79, wdn 9/80
FWR 666C	1542	Pn C52F	(652507)	3/65	Mosley, Barugh Green (B)	Robertson, Harthill (M) 8/69
FWT 323C	1707	"	(652997)	4/65	"	Porter, Little Weighton (ZB) sold by 5/78
FWT 444C	1571	"	(652712)	"	"	D Coaches, Morriston (G) wdn by 11/77
FWU 222C	1553	Du C52F	(1185/13)	"	Wilson, Stainforth (B)	Mobile caravan, Newport (XG) 7/80
FWU 243C	1532	Pn C52F	(652506)	3/65	Revill and Broadbent, Deepcar (B)	Grant, Glasgow (M) 12/68, sold 8/75
FWW 301C	1770	Du C52F	(1185/81)	4/65	Stringer, Pontefract (B)	Dane-Line, Petersfield (K) 11/78 sold for scr 4/80
FWW 302C	1769	"	(1185/82)	"	"	Langston & Tasker, Steeple Claydon (E) 9/73 wdn 2/81
FWW 809C	1441	Wn C52F	(M1570)	5/65	Billies, Mexborough (B)	Millward, Sheffield (B) 5/76, sold by 6/79
FYG 918C	1708	Pn C52F	(653004)	4/65	Baddeley, Holmfirth 83 (B)	Evans, Sunderland (XA) by 10/78
FYG 920C	1739	"	(653005)	"	84 (B)	Edmond, Hemyock (H) 5/74 wdn 4/80
FYH 957C	1861	"	(653008)	7/65	Bushnell, Hanworth (N)	Tunbridge Wells Majorettes (XK) 1/81
FYN 100C	1879	"	(652843)	9/65	Rowson, Hayes (N)	Gould, Pilton (H) 5/73, sold for conversion to caravan by 7/82
GAR 401C	1597	Du C52F	(1185/26)	5/65	Premier-Albanian, St Albans (N)	Exported to Dacca, Bangladesh 3/77
GAR 402C	1656	"	(1185/27)	"	"	Williams, Chirk (C) 6/80
GAR 403C	1669	"	(1185/28)	"	"	Elliott & Potter, Wimborne (H) 3/74, wdn 8/76
GMB 111C	1564	Pn C52F	(652838)	1/65	Jackson, Altrincham (C)	Magor, Carharrack (H) 5/74 wdn 1/79
GMB 112C	1594	"	(652490)	"	Shearing, Altrincham (C)	Evans, Shifnal (D) 5/73 wdn 9/82
GMB 200C	1569	Du C52F		1/65	Bullock, Cheadle (C)	Pugsley, Yeo Vale (H) 9/77, wdn 3/80
GMB 300C	1703	Pn C52F	(652503)	2/65	"	Justice, Daventry (E) 5/77, wdn by 3/80
GMB 746C	1676	Du C52F	(1185/36)	1/65	Yates, Runcorn (C)	Timewell, Maghull (C) 7/71, wdn 12/74
GMB 749C	1747	"	(1185/45)	4/65	"	Crosson, Drogheda (I) 6/76
GNK 328C	1628	Pn C52F	(652858)	3/65	Lea Valley, Hertford (N)	Eyres, Cippenham (N) 1/76, sold 10/76
GNP 140C	1784	"	(653014)	5/65	Price, Halesowen (D)	Roberts, Douglas (IOM) as MAN 72D, 2/75 (1/80)
GPC 58C	1612	"	(652836)	1/65	Cooke, Stoughton (A)	Watkins, Brighton (K) 8/76, sold for scr by 5/78
GPC 340C	1671	Du C52F	(1185/50)	3/65	Stanley, Hersham (N)	Hillingdon Assocn of Voluntary Social Service (XN) 10/78, wdn 9/80
GPL 260C	1672	"	(1185/55)	4/65	White, Camberley 6 (K)	Pandora, St Leonards (K) 3/77, wdn 3/78
GUP 245C	1755	"	(1185/83)	"	Cosy, Meadowfield (A)	Daneline, Petersfield (K) wdn 5/79
GUP 703C	1620	Pn C52F	(652711)	"	Emmerson (OK), Bishop Auckland (A)	Brewer, Sparham (F) 6/76, disused by 1/80
GUP 743C	1698	"	(653006)	"	Carr, New Silksworth (A)	Kenzie, Shepreth (PF) for preservation by 1/81
GWJ 920C	1818	"	(653195)	7/65	Law, Sheffield (B)	Fullarton, Falkirk (M) 4/76, used for spares -/80
GXE 996C	1908	Du C49F	(1202/11)	1/66	Vauxhall Motors, Luton (N)	Ementon, Cranfield (F) sold for caravan conversion, Bicester 10/81
HAR 203C	1616	Pn C44F	(652854)	4/65	Sapphire, London WC2 (N)	MacArthur, Strathpeffer (L) 8/76
HMA 577C	1718	Pn C52F	(652581)	"	Jackson, Altrincham (C)	Moore, Ashby (XE) by 4/79
HMA 588C	1713	Pn C51F	(652852)	"	Shearing, Altrincham (C)	Nisbet, Kirknewton (XM) 6/79
HMA 597C	1699	Du C52F		3/65	Abbott, Timperley (C)	Jimmy Robertson Racing (transporter) (X?) by 8/80
HMA 598C	1763	"	(1185/93)	4/65	"	Guest, Runcorn (C) 1/75
HPB 951C	1582	Pn C52F	(652728)	3/65	Safeguard, Guildford (N)	MacKnight, South Mimms (N) 7/77, wdn 6/80
HPT 942C	1701	Du C52F	(1185/96)	5/65	Graham (Primrose), Winlaton Mill (A)	Watson, Annfield Plain (A) 6/70 reinstated by 4/81
HRO 510C	1652	Hn C52F	(3134)	"	Brunt, Hatfield (N)	Abbey, Selby (ZB) 2/77, sold 2/77
HTU 881C	1615	Du C52F	(1185/24)	6/65	Jackson, Altrincham (C)	Mellers, Goxhill (E) 8/78 wdn 8/81, scr 3/82
HTU 882C	1757	"	(1185/92)	5/65	"	British Airways Club, Heathrow (XN) 8/78, wdn 7/82
HTU 883C	1744	Pn C52F	(652849)	4/65	Shearing, Altrincham (C)	Frater (car transporter), Stockton (XA) by 5/78, **wdn 10/78**
HTU 884C	1660	"	(652850)	5/65	"	Wrigglesworth, Carlton (E) 5/76 wdn 9/80
HUP 876C	1849	Du C52F	(1185/124)	/65	Jewitt, Spennymoor (A)	Sault & Roff, London SE15 (N) 3/76, wdn 3/77

HWJ 719C	1869	Pn C52F	(653067)	7/65	Gill, Sheffield (B)	Smith, Linthwaite (B) 6/76, wdn 8/77
HWU 402C	1858	DM B56F	(CF1166)	8/65	Wigmore, Dinnington (B)	D Coaches, Morriston (G) by 5/75, wdn by 11/79
HWU 403C	1874	"	(CF1171)	"	"	Hearson, Arnold (E) 9/75 (5/80)
JLG 326C	1613	Pn C49F	(652491)	4/65	Bostock, Congleton (C)	Terrier, Choppington (A) 5/68 burnt out 7/70
JNK 248C	1677	Du C52F	(1185/106)	5/65	Clubb, Wilmington (N)	Everest, Swanley (N) 8/77, wdn 8/79
JNK 686C	1471	Wn C52F	(M1571)	6/65	Fox, Hayes (N)	Jones, Login (G) 11/68, body scr, chassis derelict by 7/81
JPT 643C	1752	Pn C52F	(653182)	"	Scarlet Band, West Cornforth 61 (A)	Dickson (transporter), Perth (XL) by 4/76
JTW 969C	1578	Du C52F	(1185/31)	1/65	West, London E18 (N)	Welsh, Fethard (I) by 10/82
JWT 925C	6801135	"	(1202/13)	12/65	Morgan, Armthorpe (B)	Warnes (stock car transporter), Sheffield (XB) 7/80, wdn by 8/81
KHK 997C	1638	Pn C52F	(652859)	3/65	Pathfinder, Chadwell Heath (N)	Sudbury Coaches, Sudbury (F) 5/76, wdn 1/77
KMB 900C	1850	Du C52F	(1185/125)	/65	Jackson, Altrincham (C)	Ball, Plymouth (H) 4/78, wdn 10/79
KMC 628C	1552	Pn C52F	(652508)	2/65	Neale, Teddington (N)	Carnell, Sutton Bridge (F) 2/77 to scrapyard 7/81
KRO 544C	1878	"	(653068)	9/65	Blackford, Isleworth (N)	Jenkins (stock-car racing support unit), Bishops Cleeve (XH) c10/80
KRO 545C	1280	Wn C52F	(M1566)	10/65	Clarke, London SE20 (N)	Leonard, London SE24 (N) 3/73 burnt out 4/74
KTC 126C	1635	Du C52F	(1185/54)	3/65	Ashlunds, Great Harwood 126 (C)	Fenn, March (F) 3/78 sold 4/80
KTC 127C	1593	"	(1185/51)	"	Robinson, Great Harwood 127 (C)	Lockbray, London SE1 (N) 6/76, sold 6/76
KTC 128C	1637	"	(1185/52)	"	" 128 (C)	Karunaratne, Sri Lanka, registered 29-Sri-5726 2/81
KTC 129C	1662	"	(1185/53)	3/65	" 129 (C)	Riverway, Harlow (N) 8/71 wdn 8/72
KTC 661C	1598	Pn C52F	(652723)	2/65	Eaves, Ashton-in-Makerfield (C)	Prentice, West Calder (M) 3/78, wdn by 11/78
KTC 662C	1696	"	(652729)	3/65	"	DPL Racing (transporter) (X?) by 5/80
KTF 909C	1537	Du C52F		1/65	Battersby, Walkden (C)	Teece, Stockport (C) 10/72, wdn 10/75
KTJ 403C	1575	Pn C49F	(652494)	2/65	Overland, Preston (C)	Stone, Edenbridge (N) 10/79, wdn by 6/81
KTJ 669C	1574	Pn C52F	(652510)	"	Bracewell, Colne (C)	DiLusso Kitchens, Chadderton (XC) 2/76, sold c6/80
LHX 510C	1543	Hn C52F	(3017)	1/65	Brunt, Hatfield (N)	Norton Canes Greystones Jazz Band (XD) by 4/81, sold for scr 9/82
LMG 155C	1627	Ml B40C	(B3492)	10/65	BEA, Northolt 6548 (XN)	British Airports Authority, Stansted (XF) 11/78
LMG 156C	1664	"	(B3491)	"	" 6549 (XN)	Grand Prix Midget (transporter), London (XN) c7/82
LMG 157C	1789	"	(B3493)	"	" 6550 (XN)	Air Anglia, Norwich (XF) 12/78
LMG 158C	1790	"	(B3500)	11/65	" 6551 (XN)	Barnard, Welwyn Garden City (N) 3/79
LMG 159C	1804	"	(B3494)	10/65	" 6552 (XN)	Island Records, London W6 (XN) 1/79, wdn 1/80, no further user
LMG 160C	1805	"	(B3495)	"	" 6553 (XN)	North Denes Aerodrome, Great Yarmouth (XF) 12/79
LMG 161C	1844	"	(B3497)	11/65	" 6554 (XN)	Webb Machine Tools, Basingstoke (XK) 1/79 wdn 4/79
LMG 162C	1845	"	(B3498)	10/65	" 6555 (XN)	Exported to Oda, Ghana, 1/80
LMG 163C	1846	"	(B3499)	"	" 6556 (XN)	Caravan, Stoke Mandeville (XE) by 12/78
LMG 164C	1823	"	(B3496)	"	" 6557 (XN)	British Airways, Heathrow (XN) wdn 8/80
LMG 951C	1595	Hn C50F	(3078)	2/65	Interline, London WC2 (N)	Bovis (contractor's site mess hut) by 7/80
LMG 952C	1596	"	(3079)	/65	"	Green, Aston Ingham (D) 5/75 (8/80)
LMK 397C	1589	Pn C52F	(652722)	2/65	Ward, Epping (N)	Tally Ho!, Kingsbridge (H) 6/75, wdn 11/79
LTJ 306C	1666	Du C52F	(1185/70)	/65	Hadwin, Ulverston (A)	Easey, March (F) 5/78, wdn 8/79
LTJ 596C	1659	Pn C52F	(652991)	5/65	Rambler, Morecambe (C)	Williams, Deiniolen (C) 8/80
LTJ 900C	1624	"	(652732)	4/65	Tatlock, Whitefield (C)	Red Car, Norwich (F) 5/68, wdn 5/78
LVX 320C	1644	Hn C49F	(3117)	"	Harris, Grays (N)	Crosson, Drogheda (I) as KIA 1777 7/78; broken up
MMC 308C	1608	Du C52F	(1185/34)	"	RACS, London SE18 118 (N)	Wilding, Clayton-le-Moors (C) 4/77
MMC 309C	1782	"	(1185/71)	5/65	" 119 (N)	Palmglade, Long Buckby (E) 10/75, burnt out by 4/81
MMC 400C	1678	"	(1185/44)	4/65	Rutherford, London E11 (N)	Roberts, Aylesham (K) 6/78, wdn 7/79, scr -/80
MMD 687C	1682	"	(1185/61)	"	Fox, Hayes (N)	Mellers, Goxhill (E) 11/78 (5/80)
MMF 162C	1609	Pn C44F	(652848)	3/65	Janes, Wembley (N)	Lyco Engineering (caravan), London SW6 (XN) -/79
MMH 832C	1547	Du C52F		4/65	Thorpe, London NW10 (N)	Hayward, Coventry (D) 7/75, scr 7/76
MMT 144C	1583	"	(1185/30)	"	Wilmott, Southall (N)	Lewis, Rhydlewis (G) wdn by 4/81 reinstated by 4/82
MTB 402C	1684	Du C52F	(1185/64)	"	C & H, Fleetwood (C)	Transporter, noted Driffield (XB) 5/80
MTC 180C	1726	Du C52F	(1185/78)	"	Hadwin, Ulverston (A)	Karun & Raja, Bradford (B) 9/75, wdn 9/76
MTC 330C	1692	Pn C52F	(653009)	5/65	Bold, Melling (C)	Breadner, Queensferry (C) 10/76 wdn 1/78
MTF 900C	1680	"	(652994)	"	Tatlock, Whitefield (C)	Baker, Weston-super-Mare (H) 5/81 (2/82)
NTB 286C	1827	Du C52F	(1185/112)	6/65	Monks, Leigh (C)	Moore, Morley (E) 4/75, wdn 1/77

Reg	Chassis	Body	Body No	Date	Operator	History
PTB 921C	1759	Pn C50F	(653196)	7/65	Holmeswood, Rufford (C)	Moore, Ashby (XE) by 4/79
PTC 716C	1758	Pn C52F	(653181)	"	Bracewell, Colne (C)	Heywood & Stokes (stock car transporter), Heywood (XC) by 4/82
TRF 217C	1686	"	(652998)	3/65	Hazeldine, Bilston (D)	Littleton Startones Jazz Band (XD) -/77
TRF 218C	1751	"	(652999)	6/65	"	Rogers, Southampton (K) 3/79 wdn for scr 9/80
BFT 942D	1885	"	(669301)	4/66	Priory, North Shields 50 (A)	Nuttall, Modbury (H) 9/76 (7/82)
CCU 276D	6813940	Du C52F	(1202/46)	"	Hall, South Shields (A)	Budd, Taffs Well (G) 5/74, wdn by 6/79
CCU 277D	6813988	"	(1202/47)	"	"	Red Sharks PA, Cardiff (XG) by -/82
CCU 768D	6810795	"	(1202/43)	"	"	Atkinson, Mattersey (E) 4/74 wdn 10/74 reinstated 12/75
CCU 769D	6811310	"		7/66	"	Wood & Platt, Liverpool (C) 3/75, wdn 10/75
CEK 53D	6807477	Pn C44F	(669337)	4/66	Smith, Wigan (C)	Clancy & Carew, Sligo (I) 4/72
CEK 54D	6809003	Pn C49F	(669342)	"	"	Knowles, Culcheth (C) 9/73
CEK 55D	6813756	"	(669348)	"	"	Swanbrook, Staverton (H) 11/76, wdn 11/78
CEK 56D	6806806	"	(669340)	"	"	Kemp, Clacton (F) 11/74, wdn 1/78
CEK 57D	6807512	"	(669341)	"	"	Joyce, Ballinahown (I) as MLI 220 by 8/76
CFP 973D	6838708	Du C52F	(1202/137)	7/66	Ward, Oakham (E)	Easey, March (F) 5/77, wdn 5/78
CHB 213D	6816608	"		4/66	Morlais, Merthyr (G)	Morlais, Merthyr (G) from new, wrecked in accident 5/72
CKV 890D	6826486	"	(1202/120)	5/66	Shaw, Coventry (D)	Cass, Hull (B) 6/76
CRN 946D	6827125	Pn C49F	(669407)	3/66	Majestic (Ferguson), Preston (C)	Transporter (X?) by 11/81
DBM 144D	6821727	"	(1202/126)	4/66	Stringer, Ampthill (F)	Mundus, London W2 (N) wdn 2/78
DCU 584D	6830205	"	(1202/132)	8/66	Hall, South Shields (A)	Berriman, Langtoft (B) 4/75
DCU 585D	6830084	"	(1202/134)	"	"	Blatchly, Stevenage (N) 9/77, wdn 2/78
DET 772D	6805148	Pn C52F	(669338)	4/66	Gouid, Rotherham (B)	Flatt, Dunnington 3 (B) 8/77 (2/81)
DET 909D	6827495	Wk B54F	(CF1317)	5/66	Maltby Miners, Maltby (B)	Collins, Worthing (K) 5/79 wdn 6/80
DFP 158D	6808900	Du C52F	(1202/49)	10/66	Back, Uppingham (E)	Shephardson, Barton-on-Humber (E) 12/75
DHG 286D	6811905	Pn C52F	(669351)	5/66	Bracewell, Padiham (C)	Yarm Black & Gold Jazz Band (XA) by 6/81
DSN 860D	6818241	"	(669382)	2/66	Stewart, Dalmuir (M)	Unknown Jazz Band, Newcastle (XA) -/81
DTK 245D	6818507	"	(669386)	"	Rendell, Parkstone (K)	Nesbit, Somerby (E) 4/72, wdn 7/76
DTK 246D	6824829	"	(669387)	3/66	"	Holt, Newport (B) 7/76, wdn 5/77
DTL 341D	6811727	"	(669350)	1/66	Blankley, Colsterworth (E)	Caravan, Boston (XE) by 8/81
ECE 536D	6802119	"	(669318)	"	Harris, Cambridge (F)	Skill, Nottingham (ZE) -/79
ECE 891D	6821397	"	(669389)	3/66	"	Turner & Butcher, Kenninghall (F) 6/78
ECE 892D	6802852	"	(669390)	1/66	"	Berresford, Cheddleton (D) 6/71, sold 7/78
ECG 429D	6815827	Du C52F	(1202/64)	4/66	Hutchinson, London SE25 (N)	Mellor, Goxhill (E) 8/76, wdn by 12/78
ECG 796D	1912	"	(1202/6)	2/66	Elm Park, Romford (N)	Enniscorthy Coach Tours, Enniscorthy (I) by 3/75
ECG 797D	1883	"	(1202/5)	"	"	Sillan, Shercock (I) 12/75
ECW 259D	6822147	"	(1202/98)	4/66	Shutt, Burnley (C)	Peyton & Noonan, Standish (C) sold by 2/78
EDC 315D	6824260	"	(1202/51)	3/66	Begg, Thornaby (A)	Kime, Folkingham (E) 4/70 wdn by 4/81
EDK 389D	6810582	Pn C52F	(669373)	1/66	Yelloway, Rochdale (C)	Collingwood, Wheatley Hill (A) 3/77 wdn 6/80
EDK 390D	6823886	"	(669374)	3/66	"	Art Forma, Castle Donington (XE) 6/77
EDK 391D	6829248	"	(669375)	"	"	Huxley, Malpas (C) 4/75 wdn 3/80
EDK 392D	6823661	"	(669379)	"	Creams, Rochdale (C)	Miller, Foxton (F) 3/71, wdn 8/80
EDK 393D	6824522	"	(669378)	"	"	Smith, Attleborough (F) 5/73, operations ceased 9/80
EDL 783D	1279	Du C49F	(1172/30)	"	Moss, Sandown (K) (Note 3)	Ewells (transporter), Canterbury (XK) by 4/81
EDL 992D	6822165	Du C52F	(1202/103)	5/66	Southern Vectis 403 (K)	Quay Coronets Dance Troupe, Deeside (XC) 10/81 (7/83)
EDL 993D	6822981	"	(1202/104)	"	" 404 (K)	'Ivy-Lee' (caravan), Burnley (XC) 2/83 (7/83)
EDL 994D	6826468	"	(1202/105)	"	" 405 (K)	Southern Vectis 405 (K) wdn 9/80
EFA 494D	6827452	Du C49F	(1202/81)	4/66	Viking, Burton 4 (E)	Fitton, Leigh (C) 6/77 (6/78)
EHL 470D	6812778	Pn C52F	(669344)	3/66	West Riding 1 (B)	Cockerton Comets, Darlington (XA) by 10/80
EHL 471D	6820225	"	(669345)	"	" 2 (B)	Unity Brass Band, Leicester (XE) 12/81
EHL 472D	6819997	"	(669346)	"	" 3 (B)	Smith, Blofield (F) 5/74 (9/80)
EJY 328D	1911	"	(669307)	7/66	Embankment, Plymouth (H)	Greenwoods Jazz Band, Edwinstowe (XE) by 6/81
ENA 150D	6804796	"	(669328)	2/66	Mayfair, Wythenshawe (C)	White, Easthouses (M) 9/69
ENE 454D	6825332	"	(669391)	4/66	Mayne, Manchester (C)	Mobile café on A43 at Silverstone (XE) 6/83

Reg	Chassis	Body	Body No	Date	Operator	History
ENE 455D	6826599	Pn C52F	(669392)	4/66	Mayne, Manchester (C)	Jones, Birmingham (D) 11/75, wdn 3/79
ENM 951D	6852610	Du C52F	(1209/7)	10/66	Ementon, Cranfield (F)	Sowerby, Gilsland (A) 3/70 wdn 9/72
EOT 721D	6826863	Pn C52F	(669420)	4/66	Queens Park (Margo), Croydon (N)	Eagle Line, Faringdon (K) 2/71 sold 3/82
EOT 974D	6829254	"	(669418)	"	Williams, Emsworth (K)	Jackson, Beith (M) 4/78
EOU 703D	1907	Pn C49F	(669309)	3/66	Chisnell, Winchester (K)	Wright, Connahs Quay (C) 1/77 (8/77)
ERD 301D	1889	Du C52F	(1202/4)	1/66	Smith, Reading (K)	Barrett, Deal (K) 7/75 wdn 7/81
ETH 260D	6824783	"	(1202/136)	8/66	Eynon, Trimsaran (G)	Smith, Greenslade & Mabey, Blandford (H) 6/76, wdn 6/78
ETL 726D	6837758	"	(1202/138)	6/66	Delaine, Bourne 61 (E)	Gilley Law Cavaliers Jazz Band (XA) by -/80
ETL 899D	6846817	"	(1202/14)	"	Wing, Sleaford (E)	Wing, Sleaford (E) from new, still there 5/80
EUG 904D	6828468	Pn C49F	(669323)	3/66	Wallace Arnold (Feather), Leeds (B)	Transporter (X?) by 4/79
EUG 905D	6828199	"	(669320)	"	Wallace Arnold, Leeds (B)	Caravan, Holbeach St John (XE) -/77
EUG 906D	6805094	"	(669321)	"	"	Caravan, Northampton (XE) by 5/82
EUG 907D	6806264	"	(669322)	"	"	Tiffen, Abbots Langley (N) 5/74, wdn 3/77
EUG 908D	6815933	"	(669324)	"	Wallace Arnold (Kitchin), Leeds (B)	Sykes, Blackpool (C) 10/78, sold by 4/82
EUG 909D	6816393	"	(669325)	"	"	Newton, Dingwall (L) 4/72, sold for scr by 1/75
EUG 910D	6831537	"	(669326)	"	"	Bett (contractor), Dundee (XL) 7/74
EUG 911D	6836129	"	(669327)	"	"	Ian Stirling Racing Team (racing car transporter) (X?) by **4/79**
EUG 912D	6805305	"	(669331)	"	"	Costain (contractor) exported to Saudi Arabia ?/??
EUG 913D	6805625	"	(669332)	"	"	Pratt, Leeds (B) 7/77, wdn by 1/78
EUG 914D	6805968	"	(669333)	"	"	Go-kart transporter, Woodlesford (XB) by 3/82
EUG 915D	6805687	"	(669334)	"	"	B Kavanagh, Urlingford (I) 6/74, re-registered 3276 IP by 8/76
EUG 916D	6806574	"	(669336)	"	Wallace Arnold (Feather), Leeds (B)	Stubbington, Thundersley (F) 7/75
EUG 919D	6805618	"	(669335)	"	Wallace Arnold (Wardways), Leeds (B)	Embling, Guyhirn (F) 5/77 sold 11/82
EUG 921D	6816709	"	(669381)	"	Wallace Arnold, Leeds (B)	Sweetin, Crosshouse (M) 8/73, believed wdn by 10/79
EUG 926D	6811855	"	(669353)	"	"	Shropshire Farmers & Prepackers, Barway (XF) 7/83
EUG 927D	6817684	"	(669383)	"	"	Alpine, Dublin (I) 3/77
EUM 242D	6810746	Du C44F	(1202/50)	2/66	Heaps Tours, Leeds (B)	Williams, Hornchurch (N) 5/74, wdn 5/79
EUM 401D	6822228	Pn C52F	(669412)	3/66	Wallace Arnold, Leeds (B)	Plant, Rishton (C) 12/71 sold by 7/73
EVP 369D	6818854	"	(669369)	"	Allenways, Birmingham (D)	Tattersall, Hawkswick (B) 2/75
EVP 370D	6816768	"	(669370)	"	"	Emerald Isle, Altrincham (C) 4/70 wdn 11/72
FAA 435D	6828263	Du C52F	(1202/130)	5/66	Elm Park, Romford (N)	Stock car transporter, Cambridge (XF) by 4/83
FAW 100D	1893	"	(1202/22)	1/66	Corvedale, Ludlow (D)	Embling, Guyhirn (ZF) for spares 2/81, dismantled
FAW 118D	1904	"	(1202/15)	2/66	Whittle, Highley (D)	White Heather, Southsea (K) 2/79, wdn 5/81, scr by 6/82
FCF 602D	1881	"	(1202/7)	6/66	Mulley, Ixworth (F)	Crosson, Drogheda (I) 10/77
FCY 815D	6819535	Pn C52F	(669377)	1/66	Demery, Morriston (G)	Travelways, Barry (G) 2/77, wdn -/77, sold for scr by 2/81
FDL 585D	6825058	"	(669424)	6/66	Seaview Services, Seaview (K)	Kerr, Dungannon (NI) as FJI 1262 11/80, sold c8/81
FEA 430D	6834414	Du C52F	(1202/95)	4/66	Hill, West Bromwich (D)	Moreton, Birmingham (XD) 10/75 for Birmingham - Istanbul service
FEA 440D	6834481	"	(1202/108)	"	"	Transporter (X?) by 1/79
FFL 86D	6818930	"	(1202/127)	6/66	Whippet, Hilton (F)	Rebuilt to showman's living van, Lincolnshire (XE) c3/82
FHA 148D	6819194	"	(1202/66)	4/66	Mann, Smethwick (D)	Dow-Mac, Tallington (XE) 10/78
FHA 601D	6846158	Pn C52F	(669398)	5/66	Morris, Bearwood (D)	Payne, Croydon (N) 3/75, wdn 11/76
FHO 422D	6824533	Du C52F	(1202/124)	"	Hodge, Sandhurst (K)	Shephardson, Barton-on-Humber (E) 5/77
FHO 900D	6824314	"		"	Creamline, Bordon (K)	Castle, Horndean (K) 8/67, wdn 12/74
FJA 990D	6829765	Du C49F	(1205/56)	/66	North Western Road Car Co 990 (C)	Priory, Christchurch (K) 1/73, wdn 2/78
FJA 991D	6824545	"	(1205/57)	/66	" 991 (C)	Bridger, Bishops Waltham (K) 9/77
FNW 718D	1890	Du C52F	(1202/1)	4/66	Tetley, Leeds (B)	Davis, Hull (B) 1/77
FOC 1D	6811642	"	(1202/37)	5/66	Stockland, Birmingham (D)	Astill & Jordan, Ratby (E) 1/70, wdn by 1/79
FOC 2D	6811361	"	(1202/40)	"	"	Hepworth (transporter), Rastrick (XB) 8/72, destroyed by fire 4/73
FOC 3D	6817034	"	(1202/39)	"	"	Wood, Earl Shilton (XE) 8/77
FOC 4D	6811261	"	(1202/38)	"	"	Field, Blackheath (D) 6/77 (12/82)
FOC 32D	1913	Pn C52F	(669310)	2/66	Lees, Birmingham (D)	Multiple Sclerosis Association, Atherstone (XD) by 5/78
FRH 586D	6814509	"	(669330)	"	Danby, Hull 16 (B)	Reid, Bedford (F) 10/75, wdn 5/79
FRU 420D	6817566	Du C52F	(1202/61)	4/66	Shamrock & Rambler, Bournemouth (K)	Beardsmore & Mills, Northwich (C) 2/76, operations ceased 9/77

FTA 797D	6810118	Du C52F	(1202/62)	3/66	Trathen, Yelverton (H)	Gower, Hayes (N) 5/76, wdn 7/77
FWH 354D	6812897	Pn C52F	(669360)	6/66	Leigh, Bolton (C)	Barron, Dublin (I) as 284 HZC by 8/81
GAO 38D	6808189	Du C52F	(1202/23)	1/66	Cumberland Motor Services 301 (A)	Carson, Deiniolen (C) 6/79
GBE 300D	6828533	"	(1202/109)	4/66	Daisy, Broughton (E)	Reed, Guildford (N) 1/76, wdn 9/76
GBU 1D	6813119	"	(1202/59)	3/66	Pleasureways, Oldham (C)	Lea Valley, Bishops Stortford (N) 8/79 (1/81)
GBU 461D	6809553	"	(1202/64)	"	Schofield, Ashton-under-Lyne (C)	Plaskow & Margo, Uxbridge (N) 10/74, sold 11/76
GBU 462D	6819254	"	(1202/65)	4/66	Stott, Oldham (C)	Wythenshawe Community Trust (XC) 5/79, vandalised and scr 11/81
GBU 950D	6824214	Pn C52F	(669410)	"	Southsea Royal Blue, Southsea (K)	Fuell (mobile caravan), Redditch (XD) 1/80
GDD 324D	6811022	Du C52F	(1202/41)	2/66	Ivory Coaches, Tetbury (H)	Shaw, Silverdale (C) 7/77, wdn 1/80
GDG 467D	6807163	"	(1202/80)	4/66	Western Roadways, Patchway 24 (H)	Britton, Yate (H) 6/77, wdn 3/79
GDH 303D	6806838	"	(1202/29)	1/66	Mason, Darlaston (D)	Dawson, Walsall (D) wdn 9/80 sold for scr 4/81
GEW 786D	6829893	"	(1202/100)	5/66	Edwards, Huntingdon (F)	Ementon, Cranfield (F) 4/78, disused on premises 4/83
GFU 444D	6807843	Pn C52F	(669314)	6/66	Hudson, Horncastle (E)	Transporter, Epworth (XE) c-/80
GJN 501D	6822962	"	(669358)	3/66	Airborne, Leigh-on-Sea (F)	Burns (stock car transporter), Ilford (XN) by 4/82
GJU 945D	6806890	Du C52F	(1202/74)	"	Gibson, Barlestone 64 (E)	Smith, Attleborough (F) 5/73, operations ceased 9/80
GJU 946D	6817910	"	(1202/73)	"	" 63 (E)	Light, Shaftesbury (H) wdn 1/81 sold 12/81
GLV 1D	6815207	"	(1202/72)	4/66	Queensway, Liverpool (C)	Lockbray, London SE1 (N) 6/76, wdn 9/79
GNB 516D	6876806	Pn C47F	(672506)	12/66	Manchester City Transport 201 (C)	M Kavanagh, Tipperary (I) 8/74
GNB 517D	7812038	"	(672508)	"	" 203 (C)	Hyke, Lincoln (E) 6/75 wdn 6/80
GNB 518D	7806015	"	(672515)	"	" 205 (C)	Axon, Chertsey (N) 3/77 (8/80)
GNN 333D	6823551	Pn C52F	(669406)	4/66	Thomas, North Muskham (E)	Powell (caravan), Malvern (XD) by 3/80
GOA 100D	6821659	"	(669394)	"	Smith, Birmingham (D)	Caravan, Winterbourne Zelston (XH) by 4/82
GOR 181D	6873280	Pn C49F	(672497)	10/66	Coliseum, Southampton (K)	Eagle, Faringdon (K) wdn 2/76
GOR 182D	6877012	"	(672496)	"	"	Eagle, Faringdon (K) -/71, broken up for spares 1/76
GPM 817D	6812198	Du C52F	(1202/34)	3/66	Essex Coachways, London E12 (N)	Semmence, Wymondham (F) 7/73, disused on premises 5/80
GRX 89D	6823031	"	(1202/84)	5/66	Windsorian, Windsor (K)	Prout, Port Isaac (H) 9/74 wdn 10/80
GSM 84D	6827208	"	(1202/82)	"	Turnbull, Lockerbie (M)	Prospect, Lye (D) 5/76, wdn 7/77
GTA 828D	6822678	"	(1202/129)	"	Salaman, Hockworthy (H)	Baker, Weston-super-Mare (H) 5/81 (2/82)
GUD 402D	6813702	Pn C52F	(669352)	1/66	Smith, Upper Heyford (E)	Swanbrook, Staverton (H) 10/77, wdn 10/80, sold 3/81
GVA 91D	6815768	Du C52F	(1202/69)	3/66	Galloway, Harthill (M)	Silverstone (transporter) (X?) 3/78
GVJ 275D	6838042	Pn C52F	(669036)	6/66	Wye Valley, Hereford (D)	Philip, Arbroath (XL) 10/77
GVO 266D	6825077	Du C52F	(1202/111)	5/66	Lindrick, Langold (E)	Danesmoor Daybreakers Junior Jazz Band (XB) 5/82 sold for scr 2/83
GVO 267D	6840519	Pn C52F	(669408)	"	"	Transporter (X?) by 7/79
GVT 362D	6821047	Du C52F	(1202/104)	4/66	Procter, Hanley (D)	Mattersey Coaches, Mattersey (E) 8/72, wdn 6/75
GWN 8D	6810632	Pn C52F	(669313)	"	Demery, Morriston (G)	D Coaches, Morriston (G) wdn by 11/77
GYD 57D	6811806	Du C52F	(1202/16)	"	Crown Tours, Frome (H)	Crown, Frome (H) from new, still there 2/82
HAC 322D	6820908	"	(1202/60)	3/66	Bermuda, Nuneaton (D)	Baker, Hopton (F) 4/79, wdn 12/82, retained for spares for DUT 456C
HAO 86D	6819630	Du C51F	(1202/67)	8/66	Hamilton, Workington (A)	Aviators Jazz Band (XA) -/81
HAY 400D	6812249	Pn C52F	(669316)	5/66	N & S, Oadby (E)	Bridge House Garage (recovery vehicle), Barlborough (XB) by 6/82
HBW 120D	6817359	"	(669315)	2/66	Back, Witney (E)	Cooke, Porchfield (K) 6/81
HDH 947D	6827516	Du C52F	(1202/118)	5/66	Hayes, Walsall (D)	Turner & Butcher, Kenninghall (F) 11/80
HJB 823D	6828135	Pn C52F	(669405)	2/66	Eagle, Faringdon (K)	Circle Line, Cheltenham (H) 7/81
HJU 499D	6804773	Du C52F	(1202/45)	5/66	Howlett, Quorn 26 (E)	Stephenson, Hull (B) 2/77
HKF 683D	6809029	"	(1202/122)	4/66	Walker, Liverpool (C)	Owen, Llandudno (C) by 9/82
HNX 187D	6804061	"	(1202/17)	"	Lloyd, Nuneaton (D)	Lloyd, Nuneaton (D) wdn 3/81
JAC 25D	6821640	"	(1202/117)	5/66	Smith, Long Itchington (D)	Bush & Martin (preservationists), London (PN) by 5/82
JAE 927D	6867820	"	(1209/13)	12/66	Wessex, Bristol (H)	Greenhalgh & Pennington, Longton (C) 6/76, wdn 6/77
JAE 928D	6866953	"	(1209/14)	"	"	Kaye (stock car transporter), Huddersfield (XB) 1/80
JAX 384D	6814860	"	(1202/58)	4/66	Jones, Aberbeeg 10 (G)	Lavery, Dublin (I) 9/79
JAX 444D	6823211	Pn C52F	(669419)	"	Davies, Tredegar (G)	Phillips, Penrhiwceiber (G) by 6/71 written off 1/73
JAX 634D	6812844	"	(669368)	6/66	" 62 (G)	Burry & Read, Canvey (F) 9/74, wdn 12/78
JAX 898D	6838089	Du C52F	(1202/131)	"	Jones, Aberbeeg 11 (G)	Lavery, Dublin (I) 10/79
JAX 932D	6818571	"	(1202/125)	5/66	Davies, Tredegar 52 (G)	Swanbrook, Staverton (H) 12/76, wdn 5/80, scr 5/81

JBF 670D	6808849	Pn C52F	(669354)	1/66	Hazeldine, Bilston (D)	Thurcroft Garage, Thurcroft (B) 4/75
JBF 671D	6812147	"	(669357)	"	"	Lavery, Dublin (I) ex MAN 618, 5/76
JJR 153D	1892	"	(669302)	6/66	Craiggs, Amble (A)	Caswell, Bolton (C) 8/76 (6/78)
JKA 607D	6823970	Du C52F	(1202/121)	"	James, Liverpool (C)	Astill & Jordan, Ratby (E) 5/72
JLB 272D	6826803	"	(1202/105)	5/66	Empress, London E2 (N)	Dorset County Council (school bus) (XH) 3/72 wdn 8/80
JNG 190D	6823929	"	(1202/133)	6/66	Culling, Claxton (F)	Culling, Norwich (F) sold 6/80
JWO 794D	6848903	Pn C52F	(669037)	7/66	Jones, Aberbeeg 115 (G)	Lavery, Dublin (I) as 858 AZE, 8/78
JWU 401D	6810683	"	(669343)	2/66	Rowe, Cudworth (B)	Cobholm, Great Yarmouth (F) 6/74, wdn 12/80
JWX 235D	6807897	Pn C49F	(669312)	"	Guiseley Tours, Yeadon (B)	Assemblies of God, Dundonald (XNI) c-/76
JXD 541D	6821935	Du C52F	(1202/70)	5/66	Seamarks, Westoning (F)	Sherrin, Carhampton (H) 12/71, wdn 10/75
JXD 542D	6830459	"	(1202/85)	4/66	"	D Warwick (transporter) (X?) by 10/77
JXD 543D	6838411	"	(1202/113)	"	"	Tally Ho!, Kingsbridge (H) 10/74 (12/82)
JXD 544D	6832775	"	(1202/110)	"	"	Bell, Springhead (C) 4/75, wdn 4/76
JXD 545D	6834091	"	(1202/114)	"	"	Shephardson, Barton-on-Humber (E) 5/77
JXD 546D	6828798	"	(1202/99)	"	"	Thornes, Bubwith (B) 8/68 wdn 6/72
JXD 547D	6832188	Pn C52F	(669417)	7/66	"	Abridge, Hadleigh (F) 1/77, dismantled on premises 1/82
JXD 548D	6831579	"	(669416)	"	"	Brown & Preddy, Gloucester (H) 6/77, wdn 8/78
JXD 549D	6834161	"	(669411)	5/66	"	Lainchbury, Bishops Itchington (D) 11/75, wdn 1/78
JXD 550D	6835809	"	(669415)	7/66	"	Warren, Alton (K) 4/69 wdn for spares 10/79
JXE 307D	6840654	Du C52F	(1202/112)	12/66	Vauxhall Motors, Luton (N)	Pathfinders Display Team, Northampton (XE) by 10/80
JYC 600D	6804400	"	(1202/20)	7/66	Wake, Sparkford (H)	Budden, Woodfalls (H) 9/78 wdn 2/79, seat store, sold for scr 7/81
KBD 666D	6852901	"	(1209/1)	12/66	Head, Lutton (E)	Toxteth Team Ministry, Liverpool (XC) 5/79
KDM 792D	6829185	Pn C52F	(669413)	6/66	Lloyd, Bagillt (C)	Welshways, Caernarfon (C) 3/80
KHM 21D	6824192	Du C49F	(1202/53)	5/66	Birch Brothers, London NW5 K21 (N)	Norris, Hawkhurst 65 (K) 10/77 (12/80)
KHM 22D	6826822	"	(1202/52)	"	" K22 (N)	Gibbs (caravan), Frensham (XK) 6/80
KHM 23D	6827886	"	(1202/54)	"	" K23 (N)	Luna Tours, Dublin (I) as 419 MZD, -/81
KHM 24D	6829120	"	(1202/55)	"	" K24 (N)	Technograph & Telegraph, Bracknell (XK) by 12/74
KNX 537D	6852340	Pn C52F	(669039)	9/66	Smith, Tysoe (D)	Gastonia, Cranleigh (K) by 5/72, wdn 9/78
KRB 426D	6827558	Du C52F	(1202/83)	5/66	Tailby and George, Willington (E)	Derby Corporation 38 (E) 12/73, destroyed in depot fire 1/76
KVK 131D	6820691	"	(1202/128)	7/66	McIver, Newcastle upon Tyne (A)	Magor, Redruth (H) 2/79, wdn 11/79
KWJ 393D	6822525	"	(1202/77)	4/66	Bradway, Sheffield (B)	Chisholm, Swanley (N) 9/77, wdn 7/79
KWW 554D	6805191	"	(1202/35)	3/66	Morgan, Armthorpe (B)	Transporter, Felixstowe (XF) c4/83
LBY 169D	6845219	Du C48F	(1202/86)	5/66	Rickard, Brentford (N)	Fox, Hayes (N) 9/72, wdn 2/78
LBY 170D	6837139	"	(1202/87)	"	"	Breadner, Buckley (C) 1/78
LBY 171D	6841654	"	(1202/88)	6/66	"	Roberts, Cove (K) 9/72 wdn 7/78
LBY 172D	6844201	"	(1202/89)	"	"	Mitchell (caravan), Pogmoor (XB) by 7/81
LBY 173D	6816158	"	(1202/90)	5/66	"	Poole Sea Cadet Corps (XK) by 5/82
LBY 174D	6822615	"	(1202/91)	"	"	Fox, Hayes (N) 9/72, broken up 3/78
LBY 175D	6837387	"	(1202/92)	"	"	Williams, Garnant (G) 1/76, sold 9/78
LBY 176D	6845202	"	(1202/93)	"	"	Fox, Hayes (N) 9/72 wdn 10/78
LBY 177D	6851343	"	(1202/94)	"	"	Deacon, Watford (N) 5/78, wdn 10/78
LGK 461D	1905	Du C52F		2/66	County, Brentwood (N)	Edwards, Hayes (N) burnt out 6/70
LGT 801D	6819838	"	(1202/75)	4/66	Banfield, London SE15 (N)	Carter (mobile caravan), Reading (XK) c-/77
LGT 802D	6821362	"	(1202/76)	"	"	Burton, London N3 (N) 5/75, wdn 5/77
LGT 803D	6831108	"	(1202/106)	"	"	Holmewood Heatherbelles (XB) by 4/82
LGT 804D	6830812	"	(1202/115)	"	"	Collettes & Cresta Troupe, Failsworth (XC) 1/79 (7/83)
LHM 24D	6808244	Pn C52F	(669339)	1/66	Hall, Hounslow (N)	Moore, Thorp Arch (XB) by 8/82
LHM 25D	6840377	"	(669349)	5/66	"	Heywood, Langwith (B) 6/79
LLY 600D	6824334	"	(669409)	"	Rutherford, London E11 (N)	Easton, Brandiston (F) 6/76 wdn 6/82 sold 12/82
LPB 239D	6804860	Du C52F	(1202/36)	4/66	White, Camberley 14 (K)	Tally Ho!, Kingsbridge (H) 9/76 (3/83)
LUP 418D	6809930	"	(1202/33)	1/66	Roberts, Wingate (A)	Kinsley, Stockbridge (B) 2/76, wdn 11/79
LUP 478D	1486	"	(1172/104)	2/66	Cooper, Gilesgate Moor (A)	Rothbury Mobile Veterinary Surgery, Rothbury (XA) 7/80
LUP 846D	6807562	"		"	Martindale, Ferryhill (A)	Martindale, Ferryhill (A) from new, wdn 11/72

LWW 926D	6826547	Pn C52F	(669423)	5/66	Furness, High Green (B)	Moore, Thorp Arch (XB) by 4/74
LWY 820D	1687	Wk B53F	(CF1111)	6/66	Phillipson, Shiptonthorpe(B)(Note 4)	Whittle, Highley (D) as JNT 252E (q.v.)
LYE 800D	6827924	Pn C52F	(669038)	7/66	Hanworth-Acorn, Hounslow (N)	Davies, Letterston (G) 2/75, wdn by 8/81
LYG 892D	6836448	"	(669422)	6/66	Bingley, Kinsley (B)	West Yorkshire PTE (Metro Bingley) (XB) delicensed by 2/81
MJJ 943D	1891	Du C52F	(1202/3)	3/66	Popular, London E16 (N)	Lempriere, Witham (XF) 11/78
MNK 924D	6813651	Pn C52F	(669329)	1/66	Don, Bishops Stortford (N)	Stanstead Secondary School, Stanstead (XF) 10/75
MRO 144D	6814274	"	(669355)	3/66	Frames Tours, London WC2 141 (N)	Travelwell, Luton (N) wdn 4/82
MRO 145D	6814570	"	(669359)	"	" 142 (N)	Arthur (transporter), North Anston (XB) c9/79
MRO 148D	1899	Du C52F	(1202/8)	2/66	Davis, London SW16 (N)	Bell, Hayes (N) 11/73, wdn 10/77
MRO 149D	1898	"	(1202/10)	5/66	"	Williams, London SW15 (N) 7/76 wdn 7/79 kept as caravan (XN) c9/82
MUU 157D	6849812	Pn C52F	(669040)	8/66	Safeway, Hornchurch (N)	Safeway, Hornchurch (N) wdn by 8/81
MYU 1D	1910	Du C52F	(1202/21)	3/66	Claremont, Worcester Park (N)	Cooper, Warlingham (N) 2/79 wdn by 9/81
MYY 99D	6831179	Pn C52F	(669385)	5/66	Clarke, London E16 (N)	Miller, Foxton (F) 2/71, wdn 7/80
NBF 836D	6837714	"	(669376)	3/66	Green, Brierley Hill (D)	Jones, Bancyfelin (G) by 6/76
NJH 814D	6822918	"	(669393)	2/66	Knightswood, Watford (N)	Brophy, Bracknell (K) 7/76, sold 12/76
NMB 301D	6814801	"	(669361)	1/66	Shearing, Altrincham (C)	Ellis, Llangefni (C) 6/79
NMB 302D	6814223	"	(669362)	"	"	Upton-on-Severn Youth Band (XD) 9/82
NMB 304D	6820345	"	(669363)	"	Jackson, Altrincham (C)	Hitchen, Sheffield (B) 6/71, wdn 11/75
NMB 305D	6821706	"	(669364)	"	"	Puttock, Wokingham (K) 4/76, wdn 1/78
NMB 501D	6821301	Pn C49F	(669371)	"	Yates, Runcorn (C)	Moore, Sleaford (E) 3/75, wdn by 1/78
NMB 502D	6822634	"	(669372)	"	"	Viking Jazz Band (XA) by 10/78
NPT 761D	6821027	Du C52F	(1202/68)	4/66	Scarlet Band, West Cornforth (A)	Heworth Dragoons Jazz Band (XA) by 1/83
NRO 158D	1896	Pn C52F	(669305)	"	West Herts, Garston (N)	Guildford Drum & Trumpet Corps (XN) 11/78
NUR 888D	6808799	Du C52F	(1202/31)	1/66	Shirley, Meriden (D)	Sheppard, Broad Town (H) 10/73, broken up on premises 8/82
NUR 999D	6807793	"	(1202/25)	3/66	"	Rowson, Hayes (N) 1/75
NWR 788D	6868971	DM B56F	(CF1422)	11/66	Wigmore, Dinnington (B)	O'Brien, Horizon Racing Team (transporter), Warrington (XC) 3/82
OJH 304D	6824761	Pn C49F	(669402)	4/66	Capital, London W1 (N)	Chelmsford Corps of Drums (XF) by 9/80
OJH 305D	6826527	"	(669403)	"	"	Tunbridge Wells Radio Taxis (K) 5/79 believed sold by 1/83
OJH 310D	6838458	Pn C44F	(669404)	8/66	"	David, Pontycymmer (G) 7/70, wdn by 6/79, being scr by 8/80
OMA 501D	6823329	Pn C52F	(669365)	4/66	Shearing, Altrincham (C)	Gill & Munden, Wadebridge (H) 1/82
OMA 502D	6830397	"	(669366)	"	"	Smith, Rainhill (C) 10/71, exported to Ireland 7/75
OMA 503D	6833235	"	(669367)	"	Jackson, Altrincham (C)	Unknown owner, Trimdon (A) by 4/81
OMA 504D	1871	Du C52F	(1202/27)	3/66	"	Dickson, Stoke Mandeville (E) 11/73
OMA 505D	6807213	"	(1202/30)	6/66	"	Crane Engineering, Moulton Pk (XE) c3/78 sold c1/80 derelict c1/81
OPT 888D	6803992	"	(1202/19)	"	Smith, Murton (A)	Claireaux, Hadleigh (ZF) for spares 8/78, dismantled by 8/83
ORO 968D	1895	Pn C52F	(669303)	5/66	Bellamy, London N15 (N)	Beynon, Bexley (N) 5/80 (8/80)
ORO 977D	6843556	"	(669032)	"	Sapphire, London W1 (N)	Hehir, Kilkenny (I) 11/78
ORO 978D	6842961	"	(669034)	"	"	Lewis, Llanerchymedd (C) 2/76 (8/77)
ORO 979D	6841129	"	(669033)	"	"	Parish, Hawarden (C) 4/73, wdn 4/76
OTU 602D	6823593	Pn C49F	(669400)	3/66	Bostock, Congleton (C)	Kinsley, Stocksbridge (B) 11/79 (5/81)
OVW 569D	6822207	"	(669395)	"	Harris, Grays (N)	Hammond, St Margaret's Bay (K) 6/80, sold 10/80
PLG 782D	6815265	Du C52F	(1202/71)	4/66	Watson, Winsford (C)	Mainwaring (motorcycle transporter), Northwich (XC) 12/82
PMA 246D	6816098	"	(1202/79)	3/66	Bostock, Congleton (C)	Meon Valley, Moreton (H) 3/75, wdn 1/78
PNO 634D	6814176	"	(1202/48)	"	Roydonian, Roydon (N)	Tinsley, Holbeach (XF) 6/76
PPT 615D	6848245	Pn C52F	(669041)	7/66	Chandler, Seaham (A)	Selston Royals Junior Jazz Band (XE) c1/82
PTW 67D	1884	"	(669300)	5/66	Salmons, Corringham (N)	Greenhalgh, Staining (C) 6/78, out of use by -/81
PVX 171D	1824	Pn C45F	(653012)	"	Kirby, Rayleigh (F)	Cole, Bexleyheath (N) 10/77 wdn 1/80
RAR 264D	1901	Du C52F	(1202/9)	8/66	Thomas, Ewell (N)	Nationwide, Lanark (M) 4/80 (4/81)
RAR 267D	6846478	Ml B40C	(B3906)	/66	Interline, London WC2 (N)	Whyte, Colnbrook 45 (XN) 2/75 (10/81)
RAR 268D	6847639	"	(B3908)	/66	"	" 47 " wdn by 11/82, to seat store 4/83
RAR 269D	6845533	"	(B3907)	/66	"	" 48 " (10/81)
RAR 270D	6850674	"	(B3945)	/66	"	" 46 " (10/81)
RMA 326D	6836770	Pn C52F	(669401)	5/66	Bostock, Congleton 16 (C)	'Mobile Chef' snack bar on A30 near South Zeal (XH) by 8/82

STJ 440D	6820985	Pn C52F	(669380)	2/66	Kirkham, Oswaldtwistle (C)	Highland Fabricators, Nigg (XL) by 6/80
SUR 898D	6826926	"	(669421)	12/66	Kirby, Busheyheath (N)	Regent, Whitstable (K) 10/73, wdn 8/78, sold (scr?) by 3/81
TTJ 338D	6804448	Pn C49F	(669356)	2/66	Jackson, Chorley (C)	Baker, Weston-super-Mare (H) 5/81 (2/82)
TTJ 845D	6825351	"	(669396)	5/66	Eavesway, Ashton-in-Makerfield (C)	Holbrook, Dublin (I) 4/77
TTJ 846D	6831479	"	(669397)	"	"	Harris, Cheadle (C) 6/74, operations ceased 6/77
UTB 129D	6803199	Du C51F	(1202/26)	2/66	Walls, Wigan (C)	Unknown Jazz Band, Stockton (XA) by -/82
UTB 130D	6828862	"		5/66	"	Jones & James, Caerphilly (G) wdn 3/78
UTC 388D	1900	Du C52F	(1202/12)	2/66	Ireland, Lancaster (C)	Caine, Askam (A) 8/79, sold for scr by 5/82
UTD 934D	6827865	"	(1202/96)	5/66	Battersby-Silver Grey, Morecambe (C)	Robson, Wolsingham (XA) by 1/80
UTD 935D	6828925	"	(1202/107)	"	"	Greenwood, Chelmsford (F) 5/79, wdn 8/79 after accident
UTD 936D	6828595	"	(1202/116)	"	"	Embling, Guyhirn (F) 1/79 sold 11/82
UTF 100D	6818014	Pn C52F	(669384)	3/66	Tatlock, Whitefield (C)	Goodsir, Holyhead (C) 3/82
UTJ 88D	6810016	Du C52F	(1202/42)	4/66	Bold, Melling (C)	Ellis, Llangefni (C) 2/80
UTJ 100D	6810066	Pn C52F	(669347)	"	Tatlock, Whitefield (C)	Sweet, Llanvihangel Gobion (XG) 8/81
VTB 557D	6830754	"	(669399)	"	Davies & Mawson, Little Hulton (C)	Unknown Jazz Band, Penygraig (XG) by 7/80
VTB 568D	6817257	Du C52F	(1202/78)	7/66	Hadwin, Ulverston (A)	G Smith, Leicester (E) 4/78, scr 4/78
VTC 830D	6823531	Pn C52F	(669414)	5/66	Benson, Oswaldtwistle (C)	Graham (transporter), Bromley (XN) 8/80
WTC 112D	6827285	Du C51F	(1202/19)	"	Walls, Wigan (C)	Turner & Butcher, Kenninghall (F) 5/73 (9/80)
WTC 432D	6830146	Du C52F	(1202/135)	"	Harrison (Favourite), Morecambe (C)	Transporter (X?) by 9/81
ATE 891E	6866196	"	(1209/27)	2/67	Battersby-Silver Grey, Morecambe (C)	Ronnetts Morris Troupe, Hindley Green (XC) 6/82 (6/83)
ATE 894E	6870344	"	(1209/28)	"	"	Tanner & Allpress, Sibford Gower (E) 11/80
ATF 740E	6875955	DN C52F	(179/8)	"	Hadwin, Ulverston (A)	Brown, Hundred House (ZG) 12/82
ATJ 143E	7816411	Pn C52F	(672537)	3/67	Robinson, Great Harwood 143 (C)	Lynch, St Helens (C) 10/77 wdn 10/80
ATJ 144E	7815911	"	(672538)	2/67	" 144 (C)	Piranha Swimming Club, Preston (XC) 10/80, sold 4/82
BTE 714E	6865701	Du C52F	(1209/26)	"	Griffiths, Walkden (C)	Watson, Annfield Plain (A) 6/78
CHB 959E	7807647	DN C52F	(179/15)	"	Morlais, Merthyr (G)	Rice, Woodbury Salterton (H) 7/77, wdn 2/79
CTB 400E	7816665	Pn C52F	(672551)	3/67	Tatlock, Whitefield (C)	Butler, Loughborough (E) 11/76, sold 11/78
CTB 995E	7811325	"	(672528)	"	Eavesway, Ashton-in-Makerfield (C)	Brice, Four Marks (K) 11/76 (9/79)
DJC 886E	7822572	DN C52F	(179/40)	4/67	Royal Red, Llandudno (C)	Red Garage, Llandudno (C) from new, still there 8/77
DJM 138E	7833571	DN C49F	(179/17)	"	Robinson, Appleby (A)	Jackson, Beith (M) by 3/78
DJM 450E	6820967	Pn C52F	(672511)	3/67	Brown, Ambleside (A)	Mobile cafe on A30 at Nyland, Dorset (XH) by 7/82
DTB 988E	7814412	"	(672560)	7/67	Eaves, Ashton-in-Makerfield (C)	Carnegie, London SE13 (N) 9/78 destroyed in depot fire 3/82
DTD 154E	7832874	DN C52F	(179/61)	6/67	Hadwin, Ulverston (A)	Lyles, Batley (B) 8/78, sold 9/78
ECC 770E	7836103	"	(179/68)	"	Creams, Llandudno (C)	Owen, Llandudno (C) 11/77
ECK 946E	6874165	Pn C52F	(672495)	"	Overland, Preston (C)	Believed to Ebert Silva, Colombo, Sri Lanka (29-Sri-5555?) 9/79
ECU 583E	6876967	DN C52F	(179/14)	4/67	Mallam, South Shields (A)	Biggs, St Albans (N) 11/78 wdn 2/81
EFB 69E	6870610	DN C49F	(179/1)	2/67	Roman City, Bath (H)	Densley & Bennett, Bath (H) 11/76, wdn 5/79
EMJ 632E	7813978	Pn C49F	(672540)	1/67	Buckmaster, Leighton Buzzard (E)	Whybrow, Kelvedon (F) 8/74 sold 10/80
ERF 301E	7827953	DN C52F	(179/49)	5/67	Eyre, Rushton (D)	Williams, Chirk (C) 7/72 (8/77)
FBM 706E	7809364	DN C46F	(179/7)	3/67	Cook, Biggleswade (F)	Mulholland, Carrickfergus (NI) as GIA 9946, 2/75
FCP 745E	7822274	DN C52F	(179/45)	"	Sheard, Halifax (B)	Saunders (mobile caravan), Buckfastleigh (XH) 11/81
FHG 177E	7817328	Pn C52F	(672543)	"	Sandown, Padiham 70 (C)	Camm, Nottingham (E) 11/81
FNM 768E	7801686	"	(672562)	5/67	Taylor, Meppershall (F)	Moore, Saffron Walden (F) 7/71, wdn by 10/82 and offered for sale
FPR 701E	6829830	"	(669035)	3/67	Rendell, Parkstone (K)	Baker, Weston-super-Mare (ZH) by 1/80
FPR 702E	6844753	"	(669388)	"	"	Hetherington, Stocksfield (A) 10/76, wdn 3/81, to caravan -/81
FTM 989E	6862280	Du C52F	(1209/8)	5/67	Eynon, Trimsaran (G)	White Marines Jazz Band, Wolverhampton (XD) by 7/81
FXG 85E	7816430	DN C52F	(179/18)	3/67	Begg, Thornaby (A)	Adamson, Edinburgh (ZM) 3/79, sold for scr 3/81
GBK 995E	6853239	Pn C52F	(672477)	1/67	Byng, Portsmouth (K)	Young, Rampton (F) 7/73, sold 5/78
GBK 996E	6866845	"	(672479)	3/67	Southsea Royal Blue, Portsmouth (K)	Spratt, Wreningham (F) 4/77, wdn 8/81
GBM 304E	7836367	DN C52F	(179/66)	7/67	Eayrs, Goldington (F)	Hogg, Benington (E) 1/73, wdn by 7/78
GCE 999E	7815215	Pn C52F	(672510)	2/67	Kenzie, Shepreth (F)	Caravan, Peterborough (XF) 11/82
GFA 601E	7828976	Pn C49F	(672555)	3/67	Viking, Woodville 1 (E)	Williams, Mold (C) 8/73 (8/77)
GJT 877E	7832001	DN C52F	(179/57)	6/67	Sheasby, Corfe Castle (H)	Sheasby, Corfe Castle (H) from new, still there 12/82

GND 111E	7813407	Pn C47F	(672507)	/67	Manchester City Transport 202 (C)	B Kavanagh, Urlingford (I) 8/71, re-registered 3277 IP by 8/76
GND 112E	7813140	"	(672509)	/67	" 204 (C)	House, Hilton (H) 3/80 (7/82)
GND 113E	7810430	"	(672516)	/67	" 206 (C)	Milbourn, Westcliff (F) 9/74, wdn 5/79
GND 328E	7808950	"	(672487)	1/67	Mayfair, Wythenshawe (C)	Ogden, Haydock (C) 3/77, wdn 3/79, scr ?/??
GSN 710E	7810968	DN C52F	(179/31)	/67	Cunningham, Drymen Station (M)	Southern, Barrhead (M) 8/67 sold by 10/72
GSN 724E	7817033	"	(672547)	4/67	Stewart, Dalmuir (M)	Pentland, Loanhead (M) by 5/72, derelict by 9/77
GTL 825E	6848629	Du C52F	(1202/140)	5/67	Delaine, Bourne 62 (E)	Eady, Washington (A) 11/75, sold 1/78
GVM 237E	6850405	"	(1209/4)	4/67	Mostonian, Manchester (C)	Hot-rod transporter (X?) 7/82
GVM 238E	6871165	DN C52F	(179/4)	"	Mancunian, Manchester (C)	Richard Jones (racing car transporter) (X?) by 4/79
GVM 239E	6873343	"	(179/3)	5/67	"	Grimethorpe Majorettes (XB) by 7/83
HDK 44E	6866016	Pn C49F	(672475)	/67	Yelloway, Rochdale (C)	Moreton, Birmingham (XD) 12/76 for Birmingham – Istanbul service
HDK 45E	7812635	"	(672517)	/67	"	Turner, Luton (N) 6/76, exported to Eire 12/76
HDK 46E	7812894	"	(672518)	/67	"	Cliff Hotel, Trearddur Bay (XC) 4/81, out of use by 9/82
HDL 228E	7822846	DN C52F	(179/21)	3/67	Southern Vectis 406 (K)	Sold for conversion to caravan, West Cowes (XK) 9/80
HDL 229E	7822537	"	(179/22)	"	" 407 (K)	Under conversion to caravan, Squires Gate (XC) by 4/81
HDL 230E	7822910	"	(179/23)	"	" 408 (K)	Southern Vectis 428 (K) from new, wdn 7/80
HDL 231E	7822879	"	(179/24)	"	" 409 (K)	Westmacott, Weymouth (H) 3/81 (12/82)
HDL 454E	6851001	Pn C52F	(672476)	4/67	Seaview Services, Seaview (K)	Kim, Sandown (K) 2/80
HDL 793E	7827066	DN C52F	(179/56)	6/67	Shotter, Brighstone (K)	Hallam & Smith, Ilkeston (E) 11/78 (12/79)
HDL 794E	7828456	Pn C52F	(672564)	"	"	Wren, London NW9 (N) 6/82
HOD 691E	7807952	DN C52F	(179/27)	2/67	Trathen, Yelverton (H)	Clarke, Elmswell (F) 11/78
HOR 358E	7810604	Pn C52F	(672552)	4/67	Parker, London NW10 (N)	On Reflection, Rainham (XN) 12/80
HOR 883E	6859825	Du C52F	(1209/5)	2/67	Cowdrey, Gosport (K)	Huntley, Luton (N) 8/72 wdn 4/82
HOV 224E	7817278	Pn C52F	(672542)	"	Allenways, Birmingham (D)	Hasemore, Snodland (K) 6/75 wdn 6/80
HUB 542E	6862719	Pn C49F	(672480)	4/67	Heaps Tours, Leeds (B)	Moore, Thorp Arch (XB) by 12/82
HUB 543E	7814893	"	(672531)	"	"	Berger, London N7 (N) 6/77, sold 9/78
HUJ 506E	6869624	Du C52F	(1209/3)	1/67	Whittle, Highley (D)	B Kavanagh, Urlingford (I) by 9/74
HUJ 507E	6872786	"	(1209/23)	"	"	Watkins, Meliden (C) 3/73 (8/77)
HUJ 508E	6868493	"	(1209/24)	"	"	AFMP Euroracing (transporter) (X?) by 6/77
HUJ 515E	6868608	"	(1209/22)	"	"	Street, Bickington (H) 5/80 (12/82)
HWF 420E	6847916	"	(1202/139)	3/67	Bailey, Fangfoss (B)	Bailey, Fangfoss (B) from new, still there 2/81
HWH 984E	7813706	Pn C52F	(672544)	1/67	Leigh, Bolton (C)	Palmer & Coombe, Dunstable (N) 2/78, scr 11/78
JAA 339E	6868858	Du C52F	(1209/17)	3/67	Hutchinson, London SE25 (N)	George, Hare Street (N) 4/78, wdn 7/82, kept for poss. preservation
JAA 350E	7811800	Pn C52F	(672557)	4/67	Glider and Blue, Fareham (K)	Foster, Glastonbury (H) 10/73 (2/82)
JAA 498E	6869039	Du C52F	(1209/16)	5/67	Hodge, Sandhurst (K)	Cropley, Fosdyke (E) 4/77 (11/81)
JAA 499E	7811615	DN C52F	(179/53)	6/67	"	Porter, Dummer (K) 1/76, wdn 9/79
JAF 353E	6867186	Pn C52F	(672482)	2/67	Kinsman, Bodmin (H)	Kinsman, Bodmin (H) from new, still there 7/82
JAJ 551E	7815182	"	(672539)	1/67	Eddie Brown, Helperby (B)	Burton, Fellbeck (B) 4/78, wdn 5/79
JBE 522E	6870840	"	(672481)	2/67	Daisy, Broughton (E)	Swanbrook, Staverton (H) 6/77, wdn 9/79, sold 10/79
JBN 150E	6873687	"	(672493)	5/67	Hargreaves, Bolton (C)	Jackson, Beith (M) 12/77
JDG 747E	7812089	Pn C48F	(672541)	2/67	Grindle, Cinderford (H)	Hall & Ashby, Cheltenham (H) 7/81 (7/82)
JED 181E	7835687	Pn C52F	(672569)	7/67	Cooper, Warrington (C)	Ayton, Nantwich (C) 4/77 wdn 1/79
JNT 252E	1687	Wk B53F	(CF1111)	4/67	Whittle, Highley (D) (note 4)	Thistle, Doncaster (B) 4/78, wdn 4/79
JNW 912E	7826119	Pn C52F	(672553)	3/67	Fallas, Leeds (B)	Caravan (X?) by 6/80
JOD 529E	7809921	"	(672565)	6/67	Burton, Brixham (H)	Hudson, Rowlands Castle (K) 4/78 (9/79)
JOK 10E	7826371	DN C52F	(179/41)	3/67	Stockland, Birmingham (D)	Beckett, Little Horwood (E) 4/78, wdn 3/79, to caravan by 9/81
JRL 101E	6874631	Pn C52F	(672485)	4/67	Jennings, Bude (H)	Hudson, Rowlands Castle (seat store) (ZK) c-/77
JSM 267E	6867018	"	(672491)	/67	Little, Annan (M)	Wren, London NW9 (N) 4/81 (10/81)
JUA 318E	6840320	"	(672524)	/67	Wallace Arnold, Leeds (B)	Racing car transporter (X?) by 7/79
JUA 319E	6808740	"	(672525)	"	"	Billing, Skipton (B) 3/79, wdn 4/80
JUA 320E	7808970	"	(672526)	"	"	Walker, Louth (E) 1/79 wdn by 1/82
JUA 321E	7809260	"	(672520)	"	"	Sinclair, South Hetton (A) 8/75 wdn by 7/81
JUA 322E	7817297	"	(672521)	"	"	Liddell, Auchinleck (M) 9/77 (3/81)

Reg	Chassis	Body	Body No	Date	Operator	History
KHA 329E	7815750	DN C52F	(179/34)	4/67	Mann, Smethwick (D)	Redfern, Sheffield (B) 5/76, wdn 3/77
KHP 602E	7820625	"	(179/37)	3/67	Shaw, Coventry (D)	Jones, Login (G) 4/78, wdn by 6/79, to seat store by 9/80
KHP 769E	7828785	Pn C52F	(672558)	"	Bonas, Coventry (D)	Kimber Smith (transporter), Allerton (X?) 6/78
KKF 913E	7809566	DN C52F	(179/16)	4/68	Georgeson, Liverpool (C)	Bryland, Beeston (E) 4/76
KNJ 716E	6875283	"	(179/2)	2/67	Leighton, Barking (N)	Elsey, Gosberton (E) 4/77 wdn c8/81
KRM 647E	7822240	DN C51F	(179/29)	3/67	Hamilton, Workington (A)	Trefaldwyn, Montgomery (C) wdn 9/81
KRP 52E	6861271	Du C52F	(1209/25)	2/67	Jeffs, Helmdon (E)	Sharifan Begum, Newport (XG) 5/79
KRP 310E	7815792	DN C52F	(179/19)	"	Coales, Wollaston 39 (E)	RPM Racing (transporter), Hutton (X?) by 2/81
KRW 466E	7832811	"	(179/66)	7/67	Shaw, Coventry (D)	Tidworth Coaches, Tidworth (H) 5/68 (12/82)
KWF 4E	7816995	"	(179/63)	6/67	Abbey, Selby (B)	Stock car transporter, Cambridge (XF) as WER 99, 8/79
KWN 827E	6861938	Du C52F	(1209/6)	"	Morris, St Thomas (G)	Carnell, Ash (K) 10/73 (9/79)
LAL 547E	7826570	Pn C52F	(672478)	4/67	Leon, Finningley 70 (B)	Able, Holbeach Drove (XF) as mobile kitchen-unit showroom 5/83
LAO 580E	7807930	DN C51F	(179/25)	5/67	Cumberland Motor Services 302 (A)	Campbell, Linlithgow (M) 4/78 sold for scr 11/81
LAO 581E	7807995	"	(179/26)	"	" 303 (A)	Wilson, Farnworth (C) 11/76, wdn 11/77
LBU 885E	7814608	Pn C52F	(672533)	"	Wood, Ashton-under-Lyne (C)	Rhodes, Guiseley (B) 6/75
LBW 868E	7827305	"	(672545)	3/67	Maybury, Souldern (E)	Robertson, Romford (N) 10/80 (10/81)
LBW 869E	7827586	"	(672546)	"	"	Jackson, Beith (M) by 9/78
LGE 427E	6876291	DN C52F	(179/30)	/67	Galloway, Harthill (M)	Deacon, Watford (N) 5/78, wdn 10/78
LNR 38E	7822630	"	(179/55)	7/67	Hart, Donisthorpe (E)	The Trevals, Stoke-on-Trent (XD) by 12/81
LNV 1E	7807347	"	(179/46)	5/67	KW, Daventry (E)	Elim Church, Pontypridd (XG) by 3/81
LRP 1E	7836640	Pn C52F	(672572)	"	Basford, Greens Norton (E)	Lavery, Dublin (I) 1/82
LUE 461E	7825543	Du C52F	(179/38)	3/67	Cotton, Bilton (D)	Victoria Starlights Jazz Band, Rowlands Gill (XA) 2/82
LVO 878E	7822329	DN C52F	(179/28)	4/67	Lindrick, Langold (E)	Angland, Boherbue (I) 5/77
LYD 351E	6877175	Du C52F	(1209/19)	"	R & S, London SW7 (N)	Woodhouse, Bolsover (B) 5/70
MBW 252E	7814783	DN C52F	(179/35)	5/67	Back, Witney (E)	O'Toole, London SE1 (N) 6/78, wdn 7/78
MFD 218E	7827809	"	(179/44)	3/67	Kendrick, Dudley (D)	McBrearty, Londonderry (NI) as SZP 117, 1/80
MFD 649E	7829404	"	(179/48)	5/67	Mills, Gornal Wood (D)	Camm, Nottingham (ZE) 9/82
MHN 386E	7820325	Pn C52F	(672532)	3/67	GNE, Darlington (A)	Sayer, Bellerby (B) 5/74 wdn 9/77
MTG 169E	7804651	DN C52F	(179/6)	"	Cream Line, Tonmawr (G)	Ementon, Cranfield (F) 1/79, wdn 4/80, disused on premises 10/82
MVT 115E	7833878	"	(179/51)	5/67	Procter, Hanley (D)	Kettlewell, Retford (E) 9/73, wdn 3/78
NDM 1E	7812390	Pn C52F	(672519)	1/67	Hollis, Shotton (A)	Costelloe, Barnoldswick (B) 6/78 (2/81)
NRT 773E	7837815	"	(179/50)	5/67	Classic, Lowestoft (F)	Shreeve, Lowestoft (F) 5/73 (9/80)
NTG 410E	7828303	"	(179/43)	"	Brewer, Caerau (G)	Jones, Login (ZG) for spares c3/82
NWW 60E	7807345	"	(179/5)	2/67	Anderton, Keighley (B)	Jopling, Birtley (A) 10/80
NYE 717E	6861635	Du C52F	(1209/29)	4/67	RACS, London SE18 120 (N)	Knill, Cross Gates (G) 4/82
NYE 718E	7816731	DN C52F	(179/42)	"	" 121 (N)	Unknown non-PSV owner, Pantydwr (XG) c9/82
ODM 100E	7829988	"	(179/52)	6/67	Davies (Voel), Dyserth (C)	Prestatyn Coachways, Prestatyn (ZC) 2/82
OGO 337E	7809052	M1 B40D	(B3976)	7/67	BEA, Ruislip 6560 (XN)	Whyte, Colnbrook 74 (XN) 9/80 (10/81)
OGO 340E	6870435	"	(B3975)	"	" 6563 (XN)	Babcock & Wilcox, London W6 (XN) 7/78, believed sold by 5/83
OHM 260E	6875458	Pn C52F	(672488)	2/67	Margo, London SE20 (N)	Cowley, Harthill (B) 1/76
OHM 300E	7815280	Pn C52F	(672529)	6/67	Hanworth-Acorn, Hounslow (N)	Curtis, Manchester (C) 2/77 (6/78)
OHM 301E	7820031	DN C52F	(179/20)	2/67	Claremont, North Cheam (N)	Austerfield, London SE20 (N) 6/78, wdn 8/78, sold by 9/78
OHM 400E	7835387	Pn C52F	(672535)	4/67	Hanworth-Acorn, Hounslow (N)	Easton, Brandiston (F) 2/79, wdn 2/81, broken up on premises -/81
OLM 400E	7835965	"	(672563)	"	Rutherford, London E11 (N)	Redcoat Corps, London E14 (XN) 5/80
OWJ 501E	6845866	"	(672550)	"	Law, Sheffield (B)	Barnard (mobile showroom), Melton Mowbray (XE) 7/81
OWU 379E	7809654	"	(672527)	3/67	Rowe, Cudworth (B)	Rowe, Cudworth (B) from new, wdn 7/77
OWW 686E	7807070	DM B56F	(CF1423)	"	Wigmore, Dinnington (B)	Leon, Finningley (B) 12/70, disused by 6/79
OWW 687E	7818034	"	(CF1424)	"	"	Crosson, Drogheda (I) 5/77
OYG 456E	7815153	Pn C52F	(672530)	5/67	Furness, High Green (B)	Moore, Thorp Arch (XB) by 4/74
PGO 303E	6870511	Du C52F	(1209/15)	4/67	Empress, London E2 (N)	Empress, London E2 (N) wdn 4/79
PPE 886E	6860961	Pn C52F	(672490)	"	Thomas, West Ewell (N)	Felixstowe Omnibuses, Ipswich (F) 3/83
PWT 732E	7815954	"	(672534)	5/67	Bingley, Kinsley (B)	West Yorkshire PTE (Metro Bingley) (XB), delicensed by 2/81
PWX 386E	7833633	DN C52F	(179/59)	6/67	Morgan, Armthorpe (B)	M & M, Braintree (F) 1/74, wdn 3/79

Reg	Chassis	Body	(Body no)	Date	Operator	History
RLD 96E *	7814475	DN C52F	(179/47)	6/67	Duval, London SE18 69 (N)	Everest, Swanley (N) 4/78, wdn 4/79
RLD 97E *	6850098	Du C52F	(1209/10)	4/67	" 70 (N)	Evans, Walsall (D) 9/76, wdn 9/77, sold by 5/78
RLO 196E*	7822668	DN C52F	(179/36)	7/67	Cannon, Kingston (N)	Alleycats Jazz Band, Church Warsop (XE) 7/82
RUW 990E*	6875971	Pn C52F	(672486)	4/67	Homerton, London E9 (N)	Davey (mobile caravan), Kingsthorpe (XE) as KBD 453Y, 6/81
RVB 996E*	6871836	Pn C51F	(672484)	5/67	Lacey, London E6 (N)	Curtis, Elm Park (N) 12/75, wdn 12/78
RWA 188E*	7829118	DN C52F	(179/58)	6/67	Sims, Sheffield (B)	Barrow Community Trust (XA) 11/81
RYO 412E*	7802912	Pn C52F	(672494)	"	Leighton, Barking (N)	Budden, Woodfalls (H) 9/78 sold for scr 1/82
SJH 783E*	7806787	"	(672536)	"	Lea Valley, Hertford (N)	Celtic, Holyhead (C) 9/82
SJH 789E*	6863207	Du C52F	(1209/9)	1/67	Grosvenor, Enfield (N)	Rose Cruisers, Hatfield (XN) 5/80
SNU 85E *	7835138	Pn C52F	(672568)	6/67	Briggs, Chesterfield (B)	Caribonnaires Jazz Band, Mansfield (XE) 7/80
SPT 196E*	7811109	DN C52F	(179/12)	2/67	General, Chester-le-Street (A)	Bishop, Oxhey (N) 7/79, sold 8/80, caravan in S Wales (XG) 7/81
SPT 197E*	7811034	"	(179/13)	"	"	Ede, Par (H) 6/78, wdn 8/79
TPT 800E*	7826039	Pn C52F	(672554)	4/67	Shaw Brothers, Byers Green (A)	Knight, Hazelbury Bryan (H) 6/77 (7/82)
TRO 706E*	7811555	"	(672499)	"	Frames, London WC2 150 (N)	Caravan (X?) c11/78
TRO 707E*	7811391	"	(672500)	"	" 151 (N)	Poynter, Wye (K) 2/74, wdn 1/76
TRO 711E*	6874364	DN C52F	(179/9)	3/67	Biss, Bishops Stortford (N)	Button, Hadleigh (F) 4/76, wdn 5/79
TRO 712E*	7811178	Du C52F	(179/10)	"	"	Falcon, Bathgate (M) 7/74
TRO 713E*	7807048	DN C52F	(179/11)	"	"	Hardie, Aberchirder (L) 4/72, sold 1/78
TRO 714E*	7810375	Pn C52F	(672512)	6/67	Thompson, London N18 (N)	Allenson (racing car transporter), Sale (XC) 11/81
TRO 718E*	6860456	Du C52F	(1209/2)	3/67	Capital, London W1 (N)	Green, Aston Ingham (ZD) for spares 6/79
TTU 776E*	6877303	"	(1209/20)	1/67	Bullock, Cheadle (C)	Caravan, Boston (XE) by 8/80
TUP 259E*	7816769	Pn C52F	(672549)	5/67	Smith, Murton (A)	Southwick Bluetonians Jazz Band (XA) 1/80
ULG 21E *	7810154	"	(672501)	4/67	Shearings, Altrincham 21 (C)	Jopling, Birtley (A) 4/80
ULG 22E *	7811866	"	(672502)	"	" 22 (C)	Fuell (transporter), Redditch (XD) 3/79, re-regd BUK 899T by 6/79
ULG 23E *	6874977	"	(672505)	"	" 23 (C)	Roberts, Douglas (IOM) as MN 8964, 3/74 sold for scr 7/81
ULG 27E *	7810672	"	(672504)	"	Jackson, Altrincham 27 (C)	Glensilver, London N12 (ZN) 5/77, wdn 1/80
ULG 30E *	7810099	"	(672503)	"	Pleasureways, Altrincham 30 (C)	Grouptravs, Luton (N) 5/80
ULG 31E *	6875322	"	(672498)	"	" 31 (C)	Excelsior, Dinnington (B) 10/78, wdn by 7/80
ULG 33E *	7814362	"	(672522)	"	" 33 (C)	Starlite Majorettes, Plymouth (XH) by 1/83
ULG 34E *	7815930	"	(672523)	"	" 34 (C)	Beegan, Doncaster (B) 7/77, sold for scr 3/79
ULG 35E *	7812104	"	(672489)	"	Jackson, Altrincham 35 (C)	Bishops Stortford Boys' High School (XN) 9/80
ULG 38E *	6876334	DN C52F	(179/32)	"	" 38 (C)	Thompson, London SW16 (N) 7/79 (10/81)
ULG 39E *	7832537	"	(179/33)	"	" 39 (C)	Fred Cowell Racing (transporter) (X?) by -/82
UMA 615E*	7805826	"	(179/31)	3/67	Pride of Sale, Sale (C)	Palmer, Carlisle (A) 11/77 sold for scr by 4/82
UNK 617E*	6870776	Du C52F	(1209/11)	4/67	T H Bruton, London SW11 (N)	Tor Coaches, Street (H) 5/78 (12/82)
UNK 618E*	6870673	"	(1209/12)	"	"	Ellis, Llangefni (C) 6/73 (8/77)
URO 913E*	6876646	Pn C52F	(672559)	6/67	Fox, Hayes (N)	Hand & Newey, Selsey (K) 2/79 reinstated 3/81
URO 914E*	6867122	"	(672483)	"	"	Taylor & Jenkins, Bracknell (K) 9/78, wdn 5/79
URO 925E*	7806725	"	(672566)	7/67	Crump, Pinner (N)	Grimes Racing Team (transporter) (X?) by 6/80
VBH 500E*	7816454	"	(672561)	5/67	Wingrove, Hazlemere (N)	Powell, Lapford (H) 9/76, wdn 10/79
VLG 76E *	7829639	"	(672556)	3/67	Bostock, Congleton 12 (C)	David, Pontycymmer (G) 11/74 wdn 12/82
VLG 739E*	6877136	Du C52F	(1209/18)	6/67	Lomas, Macclesfield (C)	Hampson, Macclesfield (C) 12/77 wdn 6/81
WJH 438E*	7832237	DN C52F	(179/64)	"	Smith, Rickmansworth (N)	Pollard, Hayle (H) 9/78, scr 6/80
WJH 510E*	7801258	Pn C52F	(672574)	3/67	Brunt, Hatfield (N)	Quaife (transporter), Tonbridge (XK) as EOL 83V 3/80
ARO 238F	7T450042	"	(688575)	1/68	Sworder, Walkern (N)	Spring Terrace Tabernacle, Swansea (XG) cut down to lorry by 8/80
ATU 50F	7T451322	"	(688566)	4/68	Shearing, Altrincham 50 (C)	Astill & Jordan, Ratby (E) 11/74 used for spares 10/80
ATU 51F	7T451638	"	(688567)	"	" 51 (C)	Smith, East Farleigh (K) 3/83
ATU 52F	7T451271	"	(688546)	"	" 52 (C)	Tiffen, Abbots Langley (N) 5/75, wdn after fire damage 7/77
ATU 53F	7T451186	"	(688547)	"	" 53 (C)	Freeman, Uffington (ZK) acquired for spares after accident 7/79
ATU 54F	7T451124	"	(688548)	"	" 54 (C)	G McLean, Harthill (M) 6/76, sold 10/78
ATU 55F	7T451207	"	(688549)	"	Jackson, Altrincham 55 (C)	Binks, Blackpool (C) by 4/82
ATU 56F	7T451225	"	(688550)	"	" 56 (C)	Alexanders Jazz Band, Barry (XG) 5/82
ATU 57F	7T451175	"	(688564)	"	Shearing, Altrincham 57 (C)	Jackson, Altrincham (C) wdn 10/70

ATU 58F	7T451137	Pn C52F	(688565)	4/68	Shearing, Altrincham 58 (C)	Jackson, Altrincham (C) wdn 10/70
AUP 401F	7T454286	DN C52F	(182/71)	5/68	Gardiner, Spennymoor (A)	Hinckley Festival Band (XE) –/82
AUP 402F	7T454303	"	(182/59)	"	"	Smith, Ashton-in-Makerfield (C) 2/75, wdn 4/78
AUP 403F	7T454327	"	(182/72)	"	"	Jackson, Beith (M) 3/77
AUP 404F	7T454351	"	(182/73)	"	"	Joyways, Bradford (B) 5/79, wdn 3/80
AUP 525F	7857624	"	(182/43)	"	Winter, Washington (A)	Private owner, Bordon (XK) by 1/83
AXF 379F	7T452183	Pn C52F	(688630)	6/68	Burton, Brixham (H)	Burton, Brixham (H) destroyed by fire 8/71
BAR 826F	7T451666	DN C52F	(182/20)	3/68	West, Woodford (N)	Deacon, Watford (N) 5/78, wdn 10/78
BAR 828F	7T453981	Pn C52F	(688628)	6/68	Universal Cream, London N9 (N)	Earnside, Glenfarg (L) 5/76, wdn 6/80
BAR 829F	7856721	"	(688533)	3/68	Barber, Mitcham (N)	Three Seas Caravan Accessories, Hull (XB) by 4/78
BAR 834F	7860473	DN C52F	(179/83)	4/68	C & H, Fleetwood (C)	Caravan, Stockport (XC) 6/79
BAR 837F	7T453535	Pn C52F	(688633)	6/68	Parsons, London N22 38 (N)	Draper, Bromley (N) 8/78 destroyed by fire 2/83
BJH 104F	7T456403	DN C52F	(182/74)	5/68	Davis, London SW16 (N)	New Enterprise, Tonbridge (K) 3/78, destroyed by fire 1/80
BJH 105F	7T453940	Pn C45F	(688627)	"	Redbridge, Clayhall 8 (N)	Sherwoods Parsons, Barking (XN) 1/77
BJH 998F	7T451282	DN C52F	(182/64)	"	Parkinson, Welwyn Garden City (N)	Frankish, Brandesburton (B) wdn 6/80
BKX 179F	7861383	"	(179/87)	6/68	Dreelan, Langley (N)	Sykes, Appleton Roebuck (ZB) 1/82
BKX 777F	7T451613	Pn C52F	(688590)	5/68	Jeffways, High Wycombe (N)	Buggy, Castlecomer (I) as 251 CIP, 7/79
BMA 903F	7T451469	Pn C49F	(688583)	"	Bullock, Cheadle (C)	Private owner (caravan), London SE15 (XN) by 10/81
BMB 461F	7T453875	Pn C51F	(688607)	3/68	Niddrie, Middlewich (C)	Tam O'Shanters Jazz Band, Cannock (XD) c7/80
BMB 560F	7860245	Pn C52F	(688541)	4/68	Bostock, Congleton 19 (C)	Cass, Hull (B) 8/78, wdn 8/79
BMB 561F	7T450890	"	(688571)	2/68	" 18 (C)	Fosdike, Bramfield (F) 5/72, disused on premises since 1/75
BUR 469F	7855637	"	(688529)	"	Knightswood, Watford (N)	Field, Paulton (H) 1/71, wdn 10/79
CAR 546F	7T450698	DN C52F	(182/14)	3/68	Kirby, Bushey (N)	Gibson, Moffat (M) by 1/74, sold 5/76
CAR 547F	7T450200	"	(182/15)	"	"	Harding, Bagborough (H) 12/75, sold 1/80
CAR 548F	7T451910	"	(182/16)	"	"	Kirby, Busheyheath (N) sold 7/74
CAR 549F	7863629	"	(182/10)	"	"	Claireaux, Hadleigh (ZF) 4/80, partially dismantled by 8/83
CRO 161F	7864153	"	(182/49)	4/68	Premier, Watford (N)	Car transporter (X?) by 9/80
CRO 162F	7T450778	"	(182/50)	"	"	Kinsman, Bodmin (H) c6/81 (7/82)
DHB 863F	7817698	Pn C52F	(672567)	12/67	Morlais, Merthyr 22 (G)	Balgownie, Bridge of Don (L) 10/78
DJH 731F	7T457715	"	(688638)	6/68	Fox, Hayes (N)	Lewis, Rhydlewis (G) 11/72 (9/81)
DJH 732F	7T457279	"	(688639)	"	"	Littlemead School, Chichester (XK) 7/77, wdn by 3/79
DJH 734F	7T456135	"	(688606)	8/68	Morris, Harlow (N)	Oliver, Waltham Cross (N) 5/73, wdn 5/74
DJH 735F	7T457703	"	(688640)	6/68	Fox, Hayes (N)	Crown Tours, Frome (H) 4/82
DLG 652F	7T450931	DN C52F	(182/46)	4/68	Pride of Sale, Sale (C)	Campbell, E Kilbride (M) 6/76, sold, burnt out 8/78 and scr
EMB 233F	7T456573	Pn C52F	(688600)	6/68	Naylor, Stockton Heath (C)	Drabble, Sheffield (B) by 7/79, wdn 12/80
FEC 900F	7856181	DN C52F	(182/41)	4/68	Brown, Ambleside (A)	Bush, Lenham (K) 6/72, to seat store 10/79, sold 4/80
GCK 453F	7T450085	Pn C49F	(688597)	3/68	Ferguson, Preston (C)	Reality Furniture (mobile showroom), St Helens (XC) c6/80
GCU 964F	7862893	DN C52F	(182/5)	/68	Mallam, South Shields (A)	Weeks, Sutton Valence (K) 5/78, to Warburton and sold by 12/81
GEF 595F	7T450253	"	(182/13)	3/68	Beeline, Hartlepool (A)	Jopling, Birtley (A) by 7/81
GEF 596F	7T455534	Pn C52F	(688641)	6/68	"	Williams, Ewyas Harold (ZD) 12/79, sold to breaker 1/81
GEF 597F	7T456205	"	(688642)	"	"	Gill & Munden, Wadebridge (H) 1/82
GEF 598F	7T456228	"	(688643)	"	"	Turnbull, Murton (A) 12/75 (7/79)
GEF 599F	7T456484	"	(688644)	"	"	Jones, Peterlee (A) 7/77
GSY 22F	7855923	DN C52F	(182/34)	4/68	Hunter, Loanhead (M)	Stock car transporter, seen in Colchester (XF?) 7/83
GSY 141F	7T450894	Pn C52F	(688569)	/68	Allan, Gorebridge (M)	'Reflex Racing with Cannon' (transporter) (X?) by 6/82
HMJ 469F	7T453723	"	(688572)	5/68	Taylor, Meppershall 69 (F)	Cole, Bexleyheath (ZN) 12/79 exported –/80
HPR 306F	7860000	DN C52F	(182/54)	/68	Rendell, Parkstone (K)	Beeline, Southborough (K) 2/72 sold 1/81
HPR 307F	7829608	"	(182/55)	/68	"	Furlong, Wantage (K) 2/74, sold 12/78
HTF 448F	7834879	"	(179/65)	4/68	Robinson, Great Harwood 148 (C)	Cleverly, Pontypool (G) 9/76, sold 7/78
HTF 449F	7834609	"	(179/67)	"	" 149 (C)	Martin, Cross Ash (ZG) by 10/81
HTH 279F	7858628	Pn C52F	(688536)	11/67	Jones, Login (G)	Jones, Login (G) burnt out 2/74
HTJ 741F	7856233	"	(688534)	2/68	Jackson, Chorley (C)	Grievson, Horsford (F) 4/79 (4/80)
HTJ 742F	7860836	Pn C49F	(688537)	4/68	"	Flint, Nettleton (H) 3/79 (2/82)

Reg	Chassis	Body	Batch	Date	Owner	Later
HXG 305F	7T452351	Du C52F		3/68	Begg, Thornaby (A)	Octavia Home, Wisbech (XF) by 3/78
JBM 937F	7T453916	DN C52F	(182/79)	6/68	Buckmaster, Leighton Buzzard (E)	Wall, Manchester (C) 5/74 sold for scr by 3/82
JCT 874F	7861670	"	(179/85)	12/67	Searson, Barkston (E)	Autotransit, Grimsby (XE) by 8/80
JCW 135F	7T455562	Pn C52F	(688589)	6/68	Bracewell, Padiham (C)	Kavanagh, Tipperary (I) by 7/75
JDR 285F	7T456352	"	(688631)	"	Embankment, Plymouth (H)	Lavery, Dublin (I) 1/80 ex Tours, Douglas (IOM) as 111 KMN
JDR 418F	7T458480	"	(688632)	"	"	Lavery, Dublin (I) 1/80 ex Tours, Douglas (IOM) as 111 HMN
JER 584F	7T451074	"	(688582)	3/68	Young, Rampton (F)	Miller, Foxton (F) 5/71 (4/80)
JGV 167F*	6803689	Pn C49F	(669317)	8/67	Morley, West Row (F)	Morley, West Row (F) from new, still there 4/80
JJE 55F	7T452955	DN C52F	(182/45)	4/68	Kenzie, Shepreth (F)	Sanders, Holt (F) 9/79, wdn 11/82, sold by 5/83
JND 207F	7T452407	Pn C52F	(688616)	"	Manchester City Transport 207 (C)	Shaw, Maxey (F) 6/72, wdn 6/83
JND 208F	7T452464	"	(688618)	"	" 208 (C)	" "
JND 209F	7T453283	"	(688617)	"	" 209 (C)	" "
JND 210F	7T453289	"	(688619)	"	" 210 (C)	" "
JND 211F	7T453598	"	(688621)	"	" 211 (C)	Mobile caravan, Wickwar (XH) by 11/82
JND 212F	7T453635	"	(688620)	"	" 212 (C)	Shaw, Maxey (F) 6/72 to seat store on premises by 8/81
JNE 11F	7T450543	"	(688568)	3/68	Fingland, Rusholme (C)	Cannon, New Malden (N) 6/82
JNM 888F	7T458789	DN C52F	(182/88)	7/68	Baxter, Moggerhanger (F)	Underwood, North Walsham (F) 3/77
JTB 400F	7T450439	Pn C52F	(688595)	2/68	Tatlock, Whitefield (C)	Squires, Stainforth (B) 5/79, wdn 6/80
JTC 501F	7859821	DN C52F	(182/1)	3/68	Battersby-Silver Grey, Morecambe (C)	Whaites, Settle (B) 2/75
JTC 502F	7T451574	"	(182/19)	"	"	Nuttall, Modbury (H) 6/79 (7/82)
JTC 890F	7T451521	Pn C52F	(688610)	"	Davies & Mawson, Little Hulton (C)	Turner, Bury (C) 4/77
JTJ 700F	7T450721	"	(688592)	"	Tatlock, Whitefield (C)	Tatlock, Whitefield (C) wdn 8/70
JVR 250F	7859260	"	(688538)	1/68	Mayfair, Wythenshawe (C)	J J Kavanagh, Urlingford (I) 12/78
KCE 377F	7T451134	"	(688603)	5/68	Fox, Manea (F)	Mobile shop, Todmanton (XE) by 4/81
KDK 547F	7T450751	Pn C49F	(688573)	/68	Yelloway, Rochdale (C)	Wilby, Hibaldstow (ZE) by 11/80
KDK 548F	7T450853	"	(688574)	/68	Creams, Rochdale (C)	Non-PSV owner, Beetley (ZF) 8/80, later burnt out
KFA 776F	7T453501	"	(688599)	5/68	Viking, Burton (D)	Newman, Ravenshead (E) 9/69 burnt out -/78
KFA 777F	7T454646	"	(688580)	"	11 (D)	Ironside, Sevenoaks (N) 6/76, wdn 8/80
KRF 706F*	7833482	DN C52F	(179/69)	1/68	Turner, Brown Edge (D)	Swanbrook, Staverton (ZH) by 7/79, sold 9/79
KTB 100F	7T450302	Pn C52F	(688591)	3/68	Tatlock, Whitefield (C)	Grogan, Rainhill (C) 2/72, wdn 2/76
KTC 361F	7861867	DN C52F	(179/88)	4/68	Hadwin, Ulverston (A)	Revill, Langtoft (B) 5/77 (10/80)
KTC 362F	7860703	"	(179/86)	"	"	Marsh, Wincanton (H) 6/78 (3/83)
KTC 549F	7T452239	"	(182/22)	5/68	Bold, Melling (C)	Bishop, Oxhey (N) 4/79 wdn by 5/81
KTC 550F	7T453559	"	(182/48)	4/68	"	Clarkson, Dinnington (B) 5/76, wdn 6/77
KWV 506F	7859862	"	(179/80)	"	Browning, Box (H)	Taylor, Sutton Scotney (ZK) 5/78, sold 5/78
LAW 105F	7860514	"	(182/37)	1/68	Whittle, Highley (D)	Semmence, Wymondham (F) 12/82
LAW 106F	7862325	"	(182/38)	"	"	Tranther (mobile caravan), Halstead, Kent (XK) 9/80
LAW 107F	7862080	"	(182/39)	"	"	Parco, Gosport (K) 6/73, burnt out 11/74
LAW 120F	7862369	"	(182/40)	"	"	Page, Penryn (H) 11/78, wdn 11/79
LAW 897F	7854063	"	(182/6)	3/68	Jones, Market Drayton (D)	Pavilion Social Club, Abergavenny (XG) 9/81
LCF 999F	7863144	"	(182/7)	5/68	Mulley, Ixworth (F)	JDW, Ipswich (F) 6/75, wdn 12/81
LCG 101F	7861912	Pn C44F	(688528)	9/67	Coliseum, Southampton (K)	Thorne, Pewsey (H) 2/79 (12/82)
LCG 585F	7855893	DN C52F	(182/33)	10/67	Martin, West End (K)	Bone, Hook (K) 11/75 (9/79)
LFV 450F	7857178	"	(179/73)	4/68	Newton, Blackpool (C)	Heaps & Brewer, Cheshunt (N) 4/80 (1/81)
LHA 588F	7843963	Pn C52F	(672571)	8/67	Ashmore, Smethwick 29 (D)	Ashmore, Smethwick (D) from new, still there c-/83
LMR 731F	7T454109	DN C49F	(182/65)	4/68	Wilts & Dorset 920 (H)	Hills, Manchester (C) 11/79
LMR 732F	7T454070	"	(182/66)	"	" 921 (H)	Warrington Driver Training Group (XC) 11/76, wdn -/80
LMR 733F	7T454093	"	(182/67)	"	" 922 (H)	Jeffery, Fordham (ZF) for spares 4/81
LMR 734F	7T454046	"	(182/68)	"	" 923 (H)	Hamlett, Middlewich (C) 11/79
LOR 633F	7860333	DN C52F	(182/57)	1/68	Margo, London SW16 90 (N)	Hammond, Farenden & Newton, Waltham Cross (N) 5/78, wdn 3/80
LOR 637F	7864313	Pn C52F	(688563)	/68	Barfoot, Southampton (K)	Marchwood, Totton (K) sold 11/79
LOR 640F	7T450878	"	(688585)	2/68	Summerbee, Southampton (K)	Day, Hoddesdon (N) 10/74, wdn 11/75
LTC 534F	7T456526	DN C52F	(182/78)	6/68	Walls, Wigan (C)	Barnett, Kettering (E) 10/78, wdn 4/79

Reg	Chassis	Body	Batch	Date	Operator	Later history
LUX 999F	7T450326	DN C52F	(182/21)	3/68	Price, Wrockwardine Wood (D)	Watkins, Meliden (C) 9/71 (8/77)
MAA 252F	7T451416	"	(182/62)	"	Watson, Southampton (K)	New Enterprise, Tonbridge (K) 2/80 sold 5/82
MAA 256F	7T453850	Pn C52F	(688609)	"	Banstead Coaches, Banstead (N)	Davies, Puriton (H) 1/79 sold for scr by 3/82
MAA 260F	7T451297	"	(688601)	4/68	Soul, London SW19 (N)	Brooks, Failsworth (C) 11/78
MCG 35F	7856416	"	(688532)	1/68	Buckmaster, Leighton Buzzard (E)	Clarke, Great Ashfield (F) 2/76 (4/80)
MCJ 800F	7T453899	"	(688624)	5/68	Yeomans, Canon Pyon 17 (D)	Lavery, Dublin (I) as 216 CZA 11/80
MDF 210F	7863680	DN C52F	(182/12)	4/68	Princess Mary Coaches, Bristol (H)	R R Wiltshire (ex S G Wiltshire), Staple Hill (H) 4/79 (12/82)
MEL 987F	7T450802	"	(182/52)	"	Shamrock & Rambler, Bournemouth (K)	Jefferiss, Southall (N) 4/81, believed withdrawn 7/82
MEL 988F	7T451017	"	(182/53)	3/68	Charlie's Cars, Bournemouth 88 (K)	Egerton Hospital Equipment, Bromley (XN) by 4/78
MEL 989F	7T451007	"	(182/56)	"	" 89 (K)	Tanner & Allpress, Sibford Gower (E) 11/75
MFU 196F	7T451063	"	(182/17)	1/68	Daisy, Broughton (E)	Stifford Sea Scouts, Grays (XN) 8/82
MHU 926F	7861143	"	(182/51)	"	Wessex, Bristol (H)	Primrose Valley, Filey (B) 5/77, broken up 4/80
MNW 700F*	7816727	Pn C52F	(672548)	/68	Wallace Arnold, Leeds (B)	Hodgson, Millom (A) 11/71 wdn by 8/82
MNW 701F	7T451686	"	(688576)	"	"	Barry Kestrels Jazz Band (XG) by -/82
MNW 702F	7T454262	"	(688577)	"	"	M & M, Braintree (F) 2/79, operations ceased 2/83
MNW 703F	7T454918	"	(688578)	"	"	Barlow, Lichfield (D) 7/77 wdn 9/79 to farm at Huddlesford by 7/82
MSF 223F	7T455138	DN C52F	(182/83)	6/68	Edinburgh Corporation 223 (M)	Exported to Eire by 6/75
MSF 224F	7T455623	"	(182/84)	"	" 224 (M)	Kinsman, Bodmin (H) 5/81 (7/82)
MSF 225F	7T454029	"	(182/91)	7/68	" 225 (M)	Gray, Clackmannan (M) 3/75 (3/81)
MUJ 473F	7T455485	Pn C52F	(688625)	6/68	Foxall, Bridgnorth (D)	Matthews, Blaenavon (G) by 6/82
NAA 304F	7857384	DN C52F	(179/72)	/68	Hodge, Sandhurst (K)	Meredith Greens Jazz Band, Kidderminster (XD) by 7/81
NAA 305F	"	"		/68	"	Abingdon Coaches, Abingdon (K) 2/80 sold 4/80
NBO 754F*	7817717	Pn C52F	(672573)	6/68	Malcolm Margo, Croydon (N)	Oliver, Welwyn Garden City (N) 2/78, wdn by 7/81
NCY 222F	7T450061	"	(688593)	2/68	Davies, Morriston (G)	Wilding, Clayton-le-Moors (C) 3/78
NDD 522F	7859089	"	(688535)	3/68	Wiltshire, Bristol (H)	Henderson, Penygraig (G) 9/80 (9/81)
NDF 630F	7853586	DN C52F	(182/2)	"	Western Roadways, Patchway (H)	L Keogh, Thurles (I) 11/78
NJN 68F	7T451334	"	(182/23)	5/68	Victoria, Southend (F)	Priory, Christchurch (K) 7/75
NJU 848F	7T451718	Pn C52F	(688586)	3/68	Howlett, Quorn 32 (E)	Underwood, North Walsham (F) 11/77 sold 2/81
NNV 999F	7857156	DN C52F	(179/81)	11/67	Jeffs, Helmdon (E)	Burton, Haverhill (F) 7/73 sold 4/81
NOR 635F	7T455361	Pn C52F	(688611)	6/68	Richmond, Epsom (N)	Russell, Chichester (K) 11/74, wdn 11/76
NVA 561F*	7837032	DN C52F		3/68	Galloway, Harthill (M)	Pollard, St Ives (H) 9/74, wdn 5/75
NVD 648F	7860792	Pn C52F	(688539)	3/68	Park, Hamilton (M)	Greenshaw High School, Sutton (XN) 8/80
NWN 601F	7856394	DN C52F	(179/77)	4/68	Morris Bros, St Thomas (G)	Kinsman, Bodmin (H) c6/81 (7/82)
NWN 786F	7T451692	Pn C52F	(688596)	5/68	Demery, Morriston (G)	Morris, St Thomas (G) 5/69, burnt out 7/77
NXD 660F	7855014	"	(688527)	8/67	Seamarks, Westoning (F)	Ford, Gunnislake (H) 5/80, wdn 8/80
OAD 173F	7T450500	DN C52F	(182/77)	6/68	Western Roadways, Patchway (H)	Morgan, Great Bedwyn (H) 7/77, wdn 9/78
OAY 405F	7T455249	"	(182/29)	7/68	Bishop, Watford (N)	Spratt, Wreningham (F) 10/74, wdn 2/80
OCR 499F	7T456620	"	(182/87)	/68	Jacobs, Bitterne Park (K)	Collins, Hemingborough (B) 4/81, sold by 2/82
ODF 143F	7T456297	Pn C52F	(688542)	7/68	Lock, Eastington (H)	Church, Gloucester (XH) c-/80
OJU 366F	7T452526	"	(688579)	6/68	Bishop, Watford (N)	Cook, Leigh-on-Sea (ZF), storeshed at Canvey depot by 8/83
ONR 350F	7T457335	DN C52F	(182/85)	7/68	Baxter, Moggerhanger (F)	Kendrick (mobile catering unit), Crowle (XD) by 8/81
ONV 320F	7T452588	"	(182/25)	3/68	Johnson, Rushden (E)	Campbell Consultants, Watford (ZN) 5/77
ORM 100F	7T453318	Pn C52F	(688584)	"	Messenger, Aspatria (A)	Barsby, Derby (E) 10/75 wdn by 5/79; seen in Oxford 6/80
ORM 365F	7T454694	DN C52F	(182/26)	4/68	Titterington, Blencow (A)	Lindley Racing (transporter), East Ardsley (XB) 3/82
ORM 988F	7T454807	"	(182/18)	5/68	Rae, Whitehaven (A)	Gingerbread Group, Liverpool (XC) 7/80
ORX 94F	7T453666	Pn C52F	(688602)	"	Windsorian, Windsor (K)	Godding, Cwm (G) by -/80, wdn by 9/80
OUD 553F	7T453376	Pn C49F	(688612)	4/68	Grayline, Bicester (E)	Gregory, Timsbury (H) 6/75 (2/82)
OUS 685F	7T453437	DN C52F	(182/27)	3/68	Haldane, Glasgow (M)	Jardine 'Aquamasters Ski Sports Team', Leicester (XE) by 10/82
OUU 399F	7863921	Pn C52F	(688557)	11/67	Garrard and Hollis, Hillingdon (N)	Tally Ho!, Kingsbridge (H) 11/81 (12/82)
OXD 126F	7854537	DN C52F	(182/32)	/67	Vauxhall Motors, Luton (N)	Easey, March (F) 5/76, scr on premises 1/81
OYD 139F	7T450350	Pn C44F	(688562)	1/68	R & S, London SW7 (N)	Spall (transporter), Dallinghoo (X?) 11/79
OYD 140F	7T450277	"	(688570)	/68	"	Godding, Cwm (G) by 4/75, burnt out 12/75
OYF 262F*	7807704	M1 B40D	(B3978)	9/67	BEA, Ruislip 6561 (XN)	Williamson (mobile caravan), New Malden (XN) 5/82

Reg	Chassis	Body		Batch	Date	Owner	Later history
OYF 263F*	7806125	Ml B40D	(B3977)	8/67	BEA, Ruislip 6562 (XN)	Whyte, Colnbrook 69 (XN) 9/80 (10/81)
OYF 264F*	7806271	"	(B3984)	10/67	" 6564 (XN)	" 70 (XN) "
OYF 265F*	6871772	"	(B3980)	9/67	" 6565 (XN)	Air Anglia, Norwich (XF) 12/78
OYF 266F*	6869540	"	(B3982)	10/67	" 6566 (XN)	Whyte, Colnbrook 71 (XN) 9/80 (10/81)
OYF 267F*	6872377	"	(B3983)	"	" 6567 (XN)	" 72 (XN) "
OYF 268F*	7802601	"	(B3981)	"	" 6568 (XN)	Air UK, Norwich (XF) 12/78 sold 2/82
OYF 269F*	6871458	"	(B3979)	9/67	" 6569 (XN)	Whyte, Colnbrook 73 (XN) 9/80 wdn by 11/82
PTG 658F*	7837409	DN C52F	(179/70)	/68	Creamline, Tonmawr (G)	B Kavanagh, Urlingford (I) as 3123 IP by 8/76
PTX 295F	7T450032	Pn C52F	(688594)	1/68	Thomas, Gorseinon (G)	Telford Lavender Belles Jazz Band (XD) 9/79
PUE 952F	7T456169	DN C52F	(182/76)	5/68	Priory, Leamington (D)	Prentice, West Calder (M) 4/79 wdn 2/81 and being used for spares
PUW 30F	7854305	"	(182/36)	1/68	Bexleyheath Tpt, Bexleyheath (N)	Neville, Sutton Coldfield (D) 9/73 wdn 10/80
PUW 31F	7855455	"	(182/35)	3/68	" 39 (N)	New Enterprise, Tonbridge (K) 3/76, wdn by 4/78
PXE 478F	7856743	"	(179/74)	"	Hillside, Luton (N)	Sheredes School, Hoddesdon (XN) 3/80
RDJ 828F	7T454751	"	(182/47)	4/68	St Helens Co-op, Wigan (C)	Unknown owner (horsebox), Burrelton (XL) 11/81
RRR 637F	7T450458	Pn C52F	(688635)	5/68	Moxon, Oldcotes (E)	Barlow, Lichfield (D) 1/76, wdn 12/78
RYB 668F	7T454973	DN C52F	(182/82)	6/68	Crown Tours, Frome (H)	Field, Paulton (H) 7/82
RYD 624F	7T455028	Pn C52F	(688629)	"	Berry, Taunton (H)	Hicks & Newman, Heathfield (K) 3/78 (9/79)
SBJ 813F	7863100	DN C52F	(179/89)	3/68	Braybrooke, Mendlesham (F)	Gilley Law Cavaliers Jazz Band (XA) by 6/83
SFD 618F	7T459124	"	(182/93)	7/68	Kendrick, Dudley (D)	Kendrick, Dudley (D) wdn 9/81 sold for scr 2/83
SFD 619F	7T459011	"	(182/92)	"	"	Kendrick, Dudley (D) sold 2/83
SGO 344F	7T450479	Pn C52F	(688554)	11/67	Ellis, Barking (N)	Sheppard & Plaister (ex Sheppard), Broad Town (H) 1/82 (12/82)
SJJ 587F	7T451767	Pn C49F	(688558)	6/68	Timpson, London SE6 (N)	Wilby, Hibaldstow (E) 8/75, wdn by 12/79
SJJ 588F	7T451816	"	(688559)	"	"	GeeTee Signs, Bucknall (XE) by 10/82
SJJ 589F	7T451881	"	(688560)	"	"	Wing, Sleaford (E) 3/76 sold 3/80
SJJ 590F	7T451863	"	(688561)	"	"	Timpson damaged by fire -/70, scr 7/71, parts to Australia by 2/77
SNN 219F	7T455304	DN C52F	(182/81)	"	Sherwood, Worksop (E)	Loughborough Multiple Sclerosis (XE) -/75
SNY 818F	7T456213	"	(182/28)	5/68	Brewer, Caerau (G)	Jones, Login (ZG) for spares c3/82
SPK 750F	7858586	"	(179/90)	1/68	Safeguard, Guildford (N)	Smith, Adderbury (E) by 7/81, out of use later in 7/81
SWP 729F	7T450969	"	(182/69)	5/68	Regent, Redditch (D)	Peace, Kirkwall (L) by 10/82, derelict by 10/82
SWP 730F	7T453697	"	(182/70)	"	"	Langston & Tasker, Steeple Claydon (E) 9/69
SWP 734F	7T452295	Pn C52F	(688622)	4/68	"	Piper, Sheerness (K) 4/82
SWP 735F	7T454392	"	(688623)	5/68	"	New Enterprise, Tonbridge (K) 9/82
SWU 654F*	7863431	Wk B56F	(CF1590)	11/67	Wigmore, Dinnington (B)	Leon, Finningley (B) 5/71 wdn 11/79
SYA 900F	7T459135	Pn C52F	(688645)	7/68	Somervale, Midsomer Norton (H)	Chivers, Midsomer Norton (H) 12/74 (2/82)
SYG 754F	7T453642	"	(688581)	4/68	Anderton, Keighley (B)	Thwaites, High Laver (N) 9/80 wdn by 5/81
SYX 576F*	7806449	Pn C51F	(672514)	1/68	George Ewer, London N16 (N)	Cathedral, Gloucester (H) 5/75 (2/82)
SYX 577F*	7810348	DN C49F	(179/62)	12/67	"	Mobile caravan, Witham (XF) 10/80
TDH 411F	7T451374	DN C52F	(182/24)	2/68	Mason, Darlaston (D)	Dinner, Launceston (H) 3/80 (2/82)
TGH 3F	7857406	Pn C52F	(688543)	3/68	Wilmot, Southall (N)	Jackson, London SE20 (N) 8/79 (1/81)
TGJ 364F	7864230	DN C52F	(182/8)	"	Essex Coachways, London E15 (N)	Regent, Whitstable (K) 7/74, wdn 5/78, sold 1/80
TGJ 365F	7862848	Pn C52F	(688551)	6/68	"	Morgan, Bognor Regis (K) 9/70 wdn for scr 6/81
TGJ 367F	7863379	"	(688545)	"	County, Brentwood (N)	Jeffery, Fordham (F) 4/78, wdn after accident 7/83, seat store 8/83
TGX 841F	7861427	DN C52F	(179/82)	3/68	Margo, London SE20 52 (N)	Netherfield Coaches, Netherfield (E) 5/77, wdn by 7/78
TGX 861F	7861188	"	(179/84)	"	Berger, London N7 (N)	Green, Aston Ingham by 9/81, wdn 1/82
TGX 877F	7856446	"	(179/56)	6/68	Super, Upminster (N)	Lavery, Dublin (I) as 144 UZJ 10/80
TGX 878F	7857858	"	(179/75)	4/68	"	Draper, Bromley (N) 8/78 (8/80)
THX 751F	7T451423	"	(182/63)	2/68	Foley, Cranford (N)	Bluebird, Hessle (E) 1/74 (2/81)
TMY 364F	7856972	Pn C52F	(688531)	6/68	Blackford, Isleworth (N)	Linnelly, Ardee (I) 12/77
TPA 968F	7861625	"	(688540)	3/68	Thomas, Ewell (N)	Carter & Floris, Luton (N) 3/76, wdn 2/77
TPE 189F	7T450143	DN C52F	(182/58)	2/68	Warner, Milford (K)	Pied Pipers & Ladybirds Dance Troupe, Partington (XC) 11/79
TPK 333F	7855818	"	(182/4)	"	Beach, Staines (N)	Holvey, Bristol (H) 3/77, wdn 12/81 broken up on premises 3/82
TWR 696F*	7809839	Pn C52F	(688530)	12/67	Stockdale, Selby (B)	Moore, Thorp Arch (XB) by 2/80
TYG 863F	7855657	DN C52F	(182/3)	3/68	Whiteley, Maltby (B)	French, Hellaby (B) 1/78, wdn 4/80

UPF 43F	7863870	DN C52F	(182/9)	4/68	White, Camberley 16 (K)	Harris, Hillingdon (N) 10/79, broken up for spares 4/80
UPJ 997F	7T456465	"	(182/75)	6/68	Stanley, Hersham (N)	Nuttall, Modbury (H) 2/79 (7/82)
URO 922F*	7807035	Pn C52F	(672513)	7/67	Penmaenmawr Mtr Co, Penmaenmawr (C)	Spennymoor Rangers Juvenile Jazz Band (XA) by 8/80
URO 926F*	6872628	"	(672492)	8/67	Penmaenmawr Mtr Co, Penmaenmawr (C)	Pritchard, Bethesda (C) 12/68 (8/77)
URO 927F*	7853824	"	(688526)	10/67	Clarke, London SE20 (N)	Sonner, Chatham (K) 1/70 wdn by 10/72
URO 928F	7862123	"	(688544)	5/68	Brewer, Cobham (N)	Dorset Racing (transporter) (XH) by 4/82
URO 929F	7837558	DN C52F	(179/71)	6/68	Alexandra, Enfield (N)	Myall, Bassingbourn (F) 9/75 (4/80)
UWT 675F*	7823150	Du C52F	(179/54)	3/68	Wood, Pollington (B)	Exported to Eire by 10/74
UWX 276F	7857603	DN C52F	(182/44)	5/68	Murgatroyd, Thuscross (B)	Shaw, Maxey (F) 10/73 (9/80)
UWX 980F	7T454156	Pn C52F	(688613)	"	Mosley, Barugh Green (B)	Willis, Bodmin (ZH) by 10/80 (12/82)
UWX 981F	7T454133	"	(688614)	"	"	Evans, Rhyl (C) 6/71 (8/77)
UYG 657F	7T454863	"	(688636)	"	Beecroft, Fewston (B)	Beecroft, Fewston (B) from new, still there 2/81
VWT 145F	7T455514	"	(688587)	"	Billies, Mexborough (B)	Hemlington Zodiacs Juvenile Jazz Band (XA) 6/81
VWT 146F	7T455466	"	(688588)	6/68	"	Johnson, Shaw (C) by 6/81
VWW 477F	7T458664	"	(688615)	"	Pepper, Thurnscoe (B)	Caravan, noted Pembroke Dock (XG) by 8/81
VWW 732F	7T458499	DN C52F	(182/89)	"	Store, Stainforth (B)	Thorne, Newhaven (XK) by 3/82
VWW 982F	7T455647	Wk B56F	(CF1627)	"	Wigmore, Dinnington (B)	Hulley, Baslow (B) 3/76, sold to breaker 1/79
WNU 243F	7T455587	Pn C52F	(688608)	"	Briggs, Chesterfield (B)	Digby, Sevenoaks (N) 2/78, sold for scr 4/80
WRA 91F	7856950	DN C52F	(182/42)	4/68	Bull, Tideswell (E)	D Coaches, Morriston (G) 12/78 to seat store by 11/82
WRA 316F	7T458417	Pn C52F	(688634)	6/68	Branson, Chesterfield (B)	Shephardson, Barton-on-Humber (E) 11/77 wdn by 4/81
XUP 91F	7854782	DN C52F		4/68	Fulton, Sacriston (A)	Fulton, Sacriston (A) wdn 5/69
XUP 457F	7855237	Pn C52F	(688552)	5/68	Martindale, Ferryhill (A)	Falcons Jazz Band (XG) by 8/80
XUP 458F	7855689	"	(688553)	"	"	Barnes, Aldbourne (H) 4/75, wdn 8/77
YNK 631F	7864280	"	(688556)	6/68	Parnaby, Tolworth (N)	Jones, Rochford (F) 11/80
YNK 634F	7T451086	DN C52F	(182/61)	3/68	T H Bruton, London SW11 (N)	Margo, Thornton Heath (N) wdn 12/76
YNK 636F	7829014	"	(182/31)	"	Biss, Bishops Stortford (N)	Hardie, Aberchirder (L) 4/73 (11/81)
YNK 637F	7834579	"	(182/30)	"	"	Prentice, West Calder (M) by 3/78, wdn by 11/78, scr -/78
YNK 647F	7T450522	Pn C52F	(688555)	"	Thompson, London N18 (N)	Eady, Washington (A) 7/78
YNK 648F	7T450373	"	(688598)	6/68	Grasshopper, Ilford (N)	Horton (stock car transporter), Wybunbury (X?) by 6/80
AHM 40G	9T465587	Pn C53F	(692478)	2/69	Bexleyheath Tpt, Bexleyheath (N)	Thornaby Royals Jazz Band (XA) by 4/82
AWT 998G	9T468685	DN C53F	(200/30)	6/69	Pyne, Starbeck (B)	Caravan, Bradford (XB) 2/82
BRB 674G	7T459067	Wk DP56F	(CF1820)	3/69	Tailby and George, Willington (E)	Caravan, noted Parkstone (XK) by 5/80
CPO 184G	9T466577	DN C53F	(200/108)	7/69	Gale, Haslemere (K)	Static cafe on A43 at Silverstone (XE) by 6/83
DJH 742G	9T462100	Pn C53F	(692430)	2/69	Thompson, London N18 (N)	White Heather, Southsea (K) 5/74 wdn 5/81 being scr 8/82
DJH 744G	9T464153	DN C53F	(200/66)	"	Hunt, Hayes (N)	Guscott, Halwill (H) 4/78
DJH 745G	9T464449	"	(200/16)	3/69	Barber, Mitcham (N)	Sleep, Bere Alston (H) 1/72 (12/82)
DJH 747G	7T461645	Pn C52F	(692471)	4/69	Essex Coachways, London E15 (N)	Ward Freeman School, Buntingford (XN) 7/81
DJH 749G	7T460193	Pn C53F	(692405)	"	"	Watson, Annfield Plain (A) 2/72 (7/79)
DPT 746G	7T459201	"	(692410)	2/69	Voy, Newton Aycliffe (A)	New Enterprise, Tonbridge (K) 9/79 scr by 3/83
DUP 390G	9T464050	"	(692436)	3/69	Jewitt, Spennymoor (A)	Semmence, Wymondham (F) 12/77 (9/80)
ERO 499G	7T458733	DN C52F	(182/86)	9/68	Gilbert, Bovingdon (N)	Bush, Lenham (K) 4/77 scr 9/81
FHD 856G	9T463642	Co C53F		3/69	Gath, Dewsbury (B)	Whitstable Majorettes (K) by 4/82
FPT 625G	9T468808	DN C53F	(200/28)	6/69	O'Hara, Spennymoor (A)	Knutsford Morris Dancers, Knutsford (XC) 9/80
GJC 993G	9T468396	"	(200/95)	7/69	Penmaenmawr Mtr Co, Penmaenmawr (C)	Talks, Enfield (N) 4/79 wdn 12/81
GNK 238G	7T460161	Pn C52F	(692411)	12/68	Sworder, Walkern (N)	Sworder, Walkern (N) written off 3/78, scr on premises 11/80
HMB 989G	9T463494	Pn C53F	(692446)	1/69	Bullock, Cheadle (C)	James, Sherston (H) 3/75 (7/82)
HNK 149G	7T459398	"	(692406)	3/69	Sonners, Chatham (K)	Newland, Crow (K) 5/74 damaged by fire 1/82
HTU 88G	9T462816	"	(692415)	"	Pleasureways, Altrincham 88 (C)	?Priory, Christchurch (K)? 2/76
HTU 89G	9T462931	"	(692416)	"	" 89 (C)	Vaughan, Copthorne (N) 12/81
HTU 90G	9T462871	"	(692417)	"	" 90 (C)	Kim, Sandown (K) 10/80
HTU 91G	9T462394	"	(692418)	"	" 91 (C)	Williams, Chirk (C) 1/80
HTU 92G	9T462390	"	(692419)	"	Jackson, Altrincham 92 (C)	P Kavanagh, Urlingford (I) 11/78
HTU 96G	9T462140	"	(692413)	"	" 96 (C)	Valeside, London NW10 (N) 11/78 wdn 3/81

Reg	Chassis	Body	Body No	Date	First Owner	Later History
HTU 97G	9T462254	Pn C53F	(692414)	3/69	Jackson, Altrincham 97 (C)	Jackson, Altrincham (C) wdn 7/70
HTU 98G	9T462361	"	(692420)	"	Shearing, Altrincham 98 (C)	Hammond, Farenden & Newton, Waltham Cross (N) 9/79, wdn 3/80
HTU 99G	9T462319	"	(692421)	"	" 99 (C)	Shearing, Altrincham (C) wdn 8/71
HTU 762G	9T465091	Pn C52F	(692450)	1/69	Bostock, Congleton 6 (C)	White, Keady (NI) -/80
HTU 763G	9T465131	"	(692451)	"	" 14 (C)	Light, Shaftesbury (H) 10/79, wdn 4/82
HTU 764G	9T465100	"	(692452)	"	" 17 (C)	Cotton, Bilton (D) 3/73 for sale 2/81
HTU 765G	9T465118	"	(692449)	"	" 20 (C)	Caines (transporter) (X?) by 2/83
JAR 618G	7T460219	DN C53F	(200/3)	4/69	Thorpe, London E17 (N)	Norris, Hawkhurst 68 (K) 11/78 (12/80)
JAR 619G	8T461526	"	(200/21)	6/69	West, Woodford (N)	Gill & Munden, Wadebridge (H) 9/80 (2/82)
JAR 620G	9T465895	Pn C53F	(692480)	5/69	Davis, London SW16 (N)	Decimals Morris Troupe, Skelmersdale (XC) 2/82
JCK 280G	9T462886	DN C53F	(200/13)	3/69	Fergusson (Overland), Preston (C)	Hunt, Chislehurst (N) c7/78, wdn 4/79
JMB 399G	9T465240	"	(200/11)	"	Pride of Sale, Sale (C)	Jones, Login (G) 9/75 (9/81)
JUR 510G	9T468373	Pn C53F	(692493)	6/69	Brunt, Hatfield (N)	Gateway, Tingewick (E) 9/80 (11/81)
JUR 581G	9T466589	DN C53F	(200/34)	"	Pagan, Sutton (N)	Worthing Coaches, Worthing (K) 8/76 wdn 6/81
JUR 582G	9T467755	"	(200/35)	"	"	Jones, Ynysybwl (G) 10/79 (9/81)
JUR 583G	9T468378	"	(200/37)	"	"	Mid Wales, Newtown (C) 11/75 (8/77)
JUR 584G	9T468625	"		"	"	Fleetwood Sea Cadets (XC) 7/81
JUR 587G	9T469275	DN C52F	(200/51)	"	Fox, Hayes (N)	Norris, Hawkhurst 70 (K) 4/79 (12/80)
JUR 588G	9T469288	DN C53F	(200/53)	"	"	Kendrick (mobile catering unit), Crowle (XD) by 8/81
JUR 589G	9T469372	"	(200/54)	"	"	Willis, Bodmin (H) 11/80 (12/82)
KCP 251G	7T459457	Pn C53F	(692407)	1/69	Sheard, Halifax (B)	Clayton, Mabe (H) 9/80 (2/82)
KNK 362G	9T466524	DN C50F	(213/30)	6/69	All Seasons, London W2 (N)	South Stanley Starlights Jazz Band (XA) 11/82
KNK 363G	9T466697	"	(200/39)	"	"	Gray, Clackmannan (M) 5/78 (3/81)
KPR 352G	9T466149	Pn C53F	(692481)	5/69	Rendell, Parkstone (K)	Wort & Hillier (preservationists), Verwood (PK) 3/83
KPR 353G	9T466765	"	(692482)	"	"	Tally Ho!, Kingsbridge (H) 9/79 (3/83)
KPR 354G	9T463721	DN C53F	(200/82)	3/69	"	O'Mara, Limerick (I) 10/77
KPR 355G	9T463777	"	(200/83)	"	"	Bristol Unicorns Marching Band (XH) by 10/81
LBM 828G	9T465534	"	(200/72)	"	Sproat, Bedford (F)	Morley, Whittlesey (F) 10/75, wdn on premises 6/83
LGS 418G	9T467774	Pn C53F	(692442)	4/69	King, Dunblane (L)	Transporter (X?) 4/80
LLG 699G	9T466606	DN C53F	(200/31)	6/69	Naylor, Stockton Heath (C)	Griffin, Lydbrook (H) 8/76 (2/82)
LVE 617G	9T465606	Pn C53F	(692476)	4/69	Kenzie, Shepreth (F)	Cook, Leigh-on-Sea (F) 3/76, wdn 6/82, scr 7/82
LVR 9G	9T463565	"	(692437)	1/69	Fingland, Rusholme (C)	Howells, Ynysddu (G) 2/77, wdn by 8/80
LVU 885G	9T465356	"	(692467)	3/69	Mayfair, Wythenshawe (C)	Shephardson, Barton-on-Humber (E) 4/79 (5/80)
LXJ 574G	9T465294	Pn C52F	(692477)	"	Holt, Rusholme (C)	Isaac, Morriston (G) 12/77, sold 12/78
MBR 702G	9T466336	Pn C53F	(692465)	5/69	Carney, Roker (A)	C J & B J Clarke, Elmswell (F) 4/75 (4/80)
MEB 148G	9T463998	"	(692448)	6/69	Internat'l Progressive, Cambridge(F)	Transporter, North Crawley (XE) by 3/82
MEB 149G	9T465167	"	(692463)	"	"	Russell, Sutton Coldfield (D) 2/78, wdn 12/80
MEB 150G	9T465224	"	(692464)	"	"	Gastonia, Cranleigh (K) 4/74, scr 4/76
MND 213G	9T466175	Pn C52F	(692490)	5/69	Manchester City Transport 213 (C)	Hughes, Rhyl (C) 9/78
MND 214G	9T466196	"	(692491)	"	" 214 (C)	Sidat & Afzal, Blackburn (C) 5/78, wdn 5/78
MVM 824G	9T466413	"	(692492)	6/69	Connolly, Gorton (C)	Evans, Shifnal (D) 9/82
MXG 108G	7T459599	DN C53F	(200/4)	4/69	Begg, Thornaby (A)	Pyne, Harrogate (B) 5/70
NCF 794G	7T460109	Pn C53F	(692404)	1/69	Morley, West Row (F)	Morley, West Row (F) from new, still there 7/83
NDL 313G	9T466524	"	(692461)	3/69	Seaview Motor Services, Seaview (K)	Seaview Motor Services, Seaview (K) from new, still there 12/80
NDL 360G	9T466876	DN C53F	(200/27)	4/69	Moss, Sandown (K)	Moss, Sandown (K) from new, still there 12/80
NDL 361G	9T465551	"	(200/26)	"	"	Moss, Sandown (K) from new, still there 12/80
NDL 556G	8T461121	Pn C53F	(692428)	"	Shotter, Brighstone (K)	Moss, Sandown (K) 3/74 (12/80)
NDL 557G	8T461285	"	(692429)	5/69	"	Moss, Sandown (K) 3/74 (12/80)
NDL 699G	9T466370	DN C53F	(200/100)	/69	Coaches (IOW), Thorness Bay (K)	P Kavanagh, Urlingford (I) 9/78
NDL 700G	9T466206	"	(200/101)	/69	"	Tapping (stock car transporter), Aylestone (XE) 7/82
NED 537G	7T459578	Pn C53F	(692403)	11/68	Cooper, Warrington (C)	Mobiles (dining vehicle), Wembley (XN) -/81
NGV 916G	9T465368	DN C53F	(200/25)	7/69	Burton, Haverhill (F)	Jeffery, Fordham (F) 5/80 (8/83)
NUX 105G	9T462565	"	(200/47)	2/69	Whittle, Highley (D)	Penniston, Melton Mowbray (ZE) 9/81

Reg	Chassis	Body	(No.)	Date	Operator	History
NUX 106G	9T464079	DN C53F	(200/48)	2/69	Whittle, Highley (D)	Porter, Dummer (K) 2/77, wdn 7/80
NUX 107G	9T464132	"	(200/49)	"	"	Griffin, Lydbrook (H) by 4/82
NUX 120G	9T462432	"	(200/50)	"	"	Wood, Kirby-le-Soken (F) 11/78, wdn 3/80, became shed on premises
OFR 457G	7T459521	"	(200/7)	4/69	Slack, Blackpool (C)	Mobile caravan (X?) by 4/82
OFR 553G	9T465145	"	(200/15)	"	Murray, Blackpool (C)	Churchill, Shepperton (N) 10/77 (8/80)
OHR 672G	9T468063	Pn C52F	(692487)	5/69	Rimes, Swindon (H)	Hadaway, Yiewsley (N) 2/80 (1/81)
OMW 438G	9T465341	DN C53F	(200/92)	6/69	Browning, Box (H)	Bassett & Sluggett, Holsworthy (H) 6/80 (2/82)
OOR 320G	7T450828	Pn C52F	(688604)	11/68	Gale, Haslemere (K)	West Wight, Totland Bay (K) 5/71 (12/80)
OOU 856G	7T459544	DN C53F	(200/2)	9/68	Skinner, Harvey & Boyes, Oxted (N)	Skinner & Harvey, Oxted (N) from new, still there 10/81
OOU 858G	8T461501	"	(200/20)	10/68	G A Weston, Wickford (N)	Coastal Continental, Barry (G) 6/77, wdn by 5/79, burnt out 8/79
OOX 956G	9T464611	"	(200/81)	1/69	Meddings, Birmingham (D)	Sayer, Ipswich (F) 12/76, wdn 10/79
ORU 579G	9T464220	DN C49F	(200/44)	"	Hants and Dorset 921 (K)	H A & E W Jones, Menai Bridge (C) 8/80
ORU 580G	9T464267	"	(200/45)	"	" 922 (K)	Tanner & Allpress, Sibford Gower (E) 6/76, wdn by 7/78
ORU 581G	9T464243	"	(200/46)	"	" 923 (K)	Chilcott, Neacroft (K) 3/78, sold 4/79
OTD 861G	8T463592	Pn C53F	(692444)	"	Walls, Wigan (C)	Barnett, Kettering (E) 10/78
OTT 252G	9T465801	DN C53F	(200/70)	3/69	Trathen, Yelverton (H)	Emerald Ambassadors Marching Band, Plymouth (XH) by 6/82
OUX 383G	7T460125	"	(200/5)	5/69	Foxall, Bridgnorth (D)	Holvey, Bristol (H) 4/81 sold 6/82
PBE 873G	9T464638	"	(200/14)	2/69	Williams, Scunthorpe (E)	Sanders, Holt (F) 5/80, broken up 8/81
PEL 903G	9T465747	DN C49F	(200/41)	4/69	Wilts and Dorset 924 (H)	St Matthews Morris Troupe, Stretford (XC) 4/80
PEL 904G	9T466318	"	(200/40)	"	" 925 (H)	Phelan, Graiguenamanagh (I) as 3370 IP, 4/76
PEL 905G	9T466284	DN C53F	(200/42)	5/69	" 926 (H)	Wrexham Rugby Football Club (XC) 1/80
PEL 906G	9T466307	"	(200/43)	"	" 927 (H)	Royals Jazz Band, Stoke-on-Trent (XD) by 5/81
PEL 994G	9T465513	DN C49F	(200/77)	"	Shamrock & Rambler, Bournemouth (K)	Caravan, unknown owner (X?) c6/82
PEL 995G	9T465497	"	(200/78)	"	"	Tanner & Allpress, Sibford Gower (E) 6/76
PEL 996G	9T465460	"	(200/75)	"	"	Tanner & Allpress, Sibford Gower (E) 5/76
PEL 997G	9T465481	"	(200/76)	"	"	Workshop, Southall (XN) 11/82
PFU 163G	9T465372	Pn C50F	(692434)	3/69	Appleby, Conisholme (E)	Appleby, Conisholme (E) from new, wdn 8/81
POC 827G	9T462760	Pn C53F	(692431)	"	Bowen, Birmingham (D)	Queen & Harris, Faversham (K) 12/73
POM 808G	8T461456	"	(692422)	2/69	Brown, Birmingham (D)	Kemp, Clacton (F) 1/78, burnt out 10/79
POT 502G	9T465006	DN C53F	(200/73)	4/69	Hodge, Sandhurst (K)	Lewis, Llanerchymedd (C) 9/79
POT 503G	9T466469	"	(200/74)	/69	"	Wyness, Poole (K) 1/77 wdn c3/81
POT 505G	8T463471	"	(200/71)	1/69	Watson, Southampton (K)	Langdon, Shanklin (K) 2/82
POU 39G	9T466113	Pn C52F	(692443)	3/69	Milton Keynes, Leighton Buzzard (E)	James, Sherston (H) 9/77 wdn for scrap by 4/82
PPY 551G	9T464860	Co C53F		5/69	Eddie Brown, Helperby (B)	Squibb (transporter), Eastleigh (XK) by 12/82
PSC 228G	9T466390	DN C53F	(200/60)	7/69	Edinburgh Corporation 228 (M)	Hircock, Upwell (F) 9/79 (4/80)
PSC 229G	9T468853	"	(200/64)	"	" 229 (M)	Salmon, Blackpool (C) 10/79
PSC 230G	9T466264	"	(200/109)	"	" 230 (M)	Appleby, Conisholme (E) 1/76 (5/80)
PTB 869G	7T460139	"	(200/8)	2/69	Wrigley, Irlam (C)	Roberts, Aylesham (K) 11/79, wdn 10/80, scr -/82
PTC 597G	7T461020	"	(200/10)	3/69	Hadwin, Ulverston (A)	Wren, London NW9 (N) 10/82
PTC 598G	7T459482	"	(200/9)	"	"	Alston, Halton (C) 4/79
PTE 370G	9T463670	Pn C53F	(692445)	"	Holmes, Garstang (C)	Easton, Brandiston 10/77 wdn on premises 11/82
PTJ 442G	9T465569	DN C53F	(200/12)	4/69	C & H, Fleetwood (C)	Worthington, Collingham (E) 11/78, exported to Eire 11/79
PTO 667G	7T454005	"	(200/1)	11/68	French, Nottingham (E)	Hoggarth, Bolton (C) 6/76, wdn 5/78
RAA 177G	9T466631	Pn C53F	(692479)	4/69	Margo, London SW16 102 (N)	Wrigglesworth, Carlton (E) 6/77 sold 9/81
RAA 178G	9T466046	"	(692453)	"	" 101 (N)	Tally Ho!, Kingsbridge (H) 10/78 (3/83)
RAA 179G	9T466786	Pn C52F	(692472)	3/69	Farnborough Cs, Farnborough (K)	Thorn (Ultra), Gosport (XK) 6/78
RAF 102G	7T459258	DN C53F	(200/6)	"	Jennings, Bude (H)	Barrett, Deal (K) 7/81 wdn by 5/83
RBC 345G	7T455192	DN C52F	(182/80)	4/69	Cook, Dunstable (N)	Abbey, Selby (B) 12/76 (2/81)
RDF 870G	8T460859	DN C53F	(200/33)	5/69	Warner, Tewkesbury (H)	Warner, Tewkesbury (H) from new, still there 12/82
RDF 878G	9T465311	Co C53F		"	Western Roadways, Patchway (H)	Howard, Whitby (B) 8/74 wdn 12/80
RDF 879G	9T465276	"		"	"	McLaughlin, Hillhead (NI) 6/81
RDF 880G	9T465257	"		"	"	Wills, Bow (H) 4/76, wdn 4/77
RDF 881G	9T464953	"		"	"	Dave Fuell Racing (transporter), Redditch (XD) as HAB 154X 4/81

Reg	Chassis	Body	Batch	Date	Operator	History
RNR 935G	9T464106	DN C53F	(200/67)	4/69	Hart, Donisthorpe (E)	Hyke, Lincoln (E) 12/79 wdn by 4/81
ROT 352G	9T466552	"	(200/29)	5/69	Hutchinson, London SE25 (N)	Douglas, Ramsgate (K) c9/81
ROT 353G	9T464417	"	(200/22)	4/69	Martin, West End (K)	West Wight, Totland Bay (K) 6/72 (12/80)
ROT 356G	9T466660	Pn C52F	(692489)	"	Banstead Coaches, Banstead (N)	Hinckley Venture Scouts (XE) (rebuilt to C29FT) 11/80
RRH 475G	9T465444	Pn C53F	(692468)	"	Danby, Hull (B)	Watt, Glasgow (M) 2/81
RTB 553G	9T463829	"	(692433)	3/69	Battersby-Silver Grey, Morecambe (C)	Short, Wingland (XF) 7/82
RTB 554G	9T462648	"	(692432)	"	Atkinson, Morecambe (C)	Bammant, Fakenham (F) 6/74 (4/80)
RTC 409G	9T463692	Co C53F		4/69	Bold, Melling (C)	Crabbe, Stockton (A) ?/??
RTD 759G	7T466719	DN C53F	(200/96)	5/69	Timewell, Maghull (C)	Galloway, Mendlesham (F) 10/79 (4/80)
RUA 713G	7T459144	Pn C49F	(692401)	/69	Wallace Arnold, Leeds (B)	Clayton, Leicester (E) 4/72, destroyed by fire 7/76
SCR 29G	9T465957	DN C53F	(200/98)	6/69	Jacobs, Bitterne Park (K)	Farm Restaurant, Boggle Hole nr Whitby (XB) 9/82
SHP 761G	9T466537	"	(200/102)	"	Shaw, Coventry (D)	Evans, Swansea (G) 4/80 wdn by 7/80
SHP 762G	9T466643	"	(200/103)	"	"	Bates, Rothwell (E) 3/79, sold 4/81
SHP 763G	9T468064	"	(200/104)	"	"	Godding, Cwm (G) 9/78 wdn -/82
SHP 764G	9T466081	"	(200/105)	"	"	Sing, Cardiff (G) sold 1/83
SHP 765G	9T468322	"	(200/106)	"	"	Sing, Cardiff (G) 1/82
SNV 310G	9T467740	Pn C53F	(692485)	4/69	Coales, Wollaston (E)	McAleer, Luton (N) 4/79 wdn 9/80
SNV 777G	8T462289	DN C53F	(200/68)	3/69	A G H Head, Lutton (E)	Holt, Newport (B) 4/80 (5/81)
SOR 341G	9T465837	"	(200/80)	6/69	Marchwood Motorways, Totton (K)	Marchwood, Totton (K) from new, still there 12/80
SOR 877G	9T468647	"	(200/52)	"	"	Marchwood, Totton (K) from new, still there 12/80
SRP 310G	9T467694	Pn C53F	(692484)	4/69	Coales, Wollaston (E)	Pathfinders Alsatian Club, Northampton (XE) 5/82
STB 450G	9T465727	Co C53F		6/69	Nor West Hovercraft, Fleetwood (C)	Jones, Oakley (K) 11/76 sold 7/81
SUB 666G	9T464579	Pn C53F	(692455)	4/69	Wallace Arnold (Woburn), Leeds (B)	Hallam, Newthorpe (E) 12/77 wdn 6/81
SUB 667G	9T464510	"	(692456)	"	"	W & M Jackson, Blackpool (C) 11/79
SUB 668G	9T465036	"	(692462)	"	"	Robinson, Kimbolton (F) 9/73 (7/83)
SUD 594G	9T462232	DN C53F	(200/85)	2/69	Carterton Coaches, Carterton (E)	Hehir, Kilkenny (I) 11/78
SUD 595G	9T462704	"	(200/84)	"	"	Wood & Elsmere, Bognor Regis (K) 3/78, wdn 2/80
SVD 20G	9T466740	Pn C53F	(692440)	4/69	Park, Hamilton (M)	Griffiths, Port Dinorwic (C) 5/78
SVD 21G	9T468018	"	(692441)	"	"	Greenhalgh, Ottershaw 4 (N) 7/78 (1/81)
SXE 848G	7T459653	DN C52F	(182/90)	10/68	Vauxhall Motors, Luton (N)	Shaw, Silverdale (C) 5/73, wdn 9/78
TAC 344G	9T464906	Pn C53F	(692457)	2/69	Shirley, Meriden (D)	Kinsman, Bodmin (H) 10/80 (7/82)
TAC 345G	9T465065	"	(692458)	"	"	Dickson, Stoke Mandeville (E) 2/80 (11/81)
TAC 346G	9T465186	"	(692459)	"	"	Shirley, Meriden (D) from new, wdn 2/72
TBD 310G	9T468445	"	(692486)	5/69	Coales, Wollaston (E)	Chivers, Stratton-on-the-Fosse (H) 6/80 (2/82)
TBW 718G	9T463619	Co C53F		4/69	Grayline, Bicester (E)	Bailey, Biddisham (H) 9/78, wdn 9/79
THA 209G	9T465428	DN C53F	(200/93)	5/69	Mann, Smethwick (D)	Coleman, Yeovil (H) 7/77 (2/82)
THA 210G	9T465407	"	(200/94)	"	"	Hallam & Smith, Ilkeston (E) 8/80
TJB 78G	9T463113	Co C53F		/69	Bryan, Didcot (K)	Burnt out, remains to Willetts, Yorkley (ZH) 10/72
UAL 628G	8T461435	DN C53F	(200/69)	12/68	Lindrick, Langold (E)	Bluebird, Hessle (B) 4/75 (2/81)
UBL 95G	9T466895	Pn C53F	(692475)	5/69	Windsorian, Windsor (K)	MacKnight, South Mimms (N) 11/79 (1/81)
UFD 436G	8T461573	DN C53F	(200/19)	3/69	Mills, Gornal Wood (D)	Striplin, Tavistock (H) 1/79
UNX 481G	9T466230	"	(200/49)	5/69	Marvin, Rugby (D)	Marvin, Rugby (D) from new, still there 8/80
UUE 664G	9T470790	"	(200/17)	7/69	Priory, Leamington (D)	Williams, Bethesda (C) 6/80
UYC 799G	7T458531	Co C52F		3/69	R & S, London W8 (N)	Thistle, Doncaster (B) 3/79
VDJ 748G	7T458842	DN C53F	(200/23)	4/69	St Helens Co-Op, Goose Green (C)	Mobile caravan, noted Leeds (XB) by 4/82
VMV 612G	7T456149	Pn C53F	(692408)	10/68	Margo, London SE20 (N)	Newman, Ravenshead (E) 7/70 burnt out -/78
VNY 987G	9T465203	"	(692469)	5/69	Jenkins, Skewen (G)	Hyke, Lincoln (E) 1/79 (5/80)
VTX 195G	9T465781	DN C53F	(200/79)	6/69	"	Finlay, -?- (I) by 9/74
VYH 58G	9T462181	Pn C53F	(692423)	2/69	Jones, Deal (K)	Harling, London SE1 (N) 3/70, wdn 6/76
VYH 59G	9T463881	"	(692447)	/69	"	Harling, London SE1 (N) 3/70, wdn 6/76
VYT 430G	9T466258	"	(692483)	4/69	Margo, London SE19 (N)	Smith, Murton (A) -/75, derelict at depot c-/80
VYT 485G	7T459422	"	(692402)	"	"	Adams, Handley (H) 3/71 written off in accident 12/72
VYT 493G	9T462268	DN C53F	(200/87)	5/69	Richmond, Epsom (N)	Leach, Harold Wood (N) 10/73 (1/81)

Reg	Chassis	Body	(No.)	Date	Operator	History
VYT 494G	9T465919	DN C53F	(200/88)	5/69	Richmond, Epsom (N)	Filer, Stanton Wick (H) 9/79 (2/82)
VYT 495G	9T464329	"	(200/86)	"	"	Sutton Eagles Jazz Band (XE) by 6/81
WPF 872G	7T460231	Pn C52F	(692412)	12/68	Safeguard, Guildford (N)	Light, Shaftesbury (H) 12/80 (7/82)
WUY 478G	9T465982	DN C53F	(200/89)	5/69	Marsh, Harvington (D)	Tanner & Allpress, Sibford Gower (E) 11/80
WUY 479G	9T466810	"	(200/91)	"	"	Turnbull, Murton (A) 11/78 wdn by 11/81
WWU 787G	7T460209	Wk B56F	(CF1816)	10/68	Wigmore, Dinnington (B)	Dorset County Council Education Department (XH) ?/??
WWY 114G	9T464178	Pn C53F	(692425)	12/68	Abbey, Selby (B)	Cobholm, Great Yarmouth (ZF) for spares 8/82
WWY 115G	9T464196	"	(692426)	1/69	"	Croda, Snaith, staff bus (XB) 8/73
XEH 348G	9T466018	DN C53F	(200/24)	5/69	Procter, Hanley (D)	Phillips, Dormston (D) 1/81
XNP 545G	9T465112	Pn C53F	(692470)	4/69	Harding and Dyson, Redditch (D)	V M D Maddren, Billingham (A) by 7/81, sold for scr 11/81
XPB 350G	8T461233	DN C53F	(200/18)	3/69	Beach, Staines (N)	Bone, Hook (K) 11/77 (9/79)
XPK 77G	9T466857	Pn C53F	(692488)	5/69	Bicknell, Godalming (K)	Roberts, Douglas (IOM) as MAN 958F, 10/75 (1/80)
XYN 536G	9T466359	"	(692435)	6/69	Safeway, Hornchurch (N)	Craker, Shepway (K) 4/82
YRB 203G	7T460118	Wk DP56F	(CF1821)	10/68	Tailby and George, Willington (E)	Gilbert, Bingham (E) 5/75, wdn 1/81, dumped at depot by 9/82
YWJ 665G	8T461401	Pn C53F	(692427)	4/69	Shalesmoor, Sheffield (B)	Millward, Sheffield (B) 12/78, exported to Pakistan 9/79
YWU 292G	9T464546	"	(692438)	3/69	Baddeley, Holmfirth 96 (B)	Allan, Thrapston (E) 12/81 (1/83)
YWU 293G	9T464478	"	(692439)	"	" 97 (B)	G Jones, Blaenau Ffestiniog (C) 8/80 wdn 6/81
YWY 615G	9T468767	"	(692474)	5/69	Mosley, Barugh Green (B)	Juniper, Chatteris (F) 6/80
YWY 949G	9T465390	Wk B56F	(CF1889)	4/69	Wigmore, Dinnington (B)	Dorset County Council (school bus) (XH) -/73
AAL 110H	9T469786	Pn C53F	(708364)	3/70	Brumpton, Dunham (E)	Howard, Whitby (B) 4/77 (5/81)
AJW 547H	9T472408	DN C53F	(213/18)	2/70	Hazeldine, Bilston (D)	McBrearty, Londonderry (NI) as IH 117 11/82
AUK 447H	9T472637	"	(213/17)	3/70	"	Pollard, Hayle (H) by 4/82 (7/82)
AYH 958H	0T473380	"	(211/23)	5/70	Essex Coachways, London E15 (N)	Brown & Bennett, Gloucester (H) 10/79 (2/82)
BDJ 279H	0T473196	"	(213/19)	3/70	St Helens Co-Op, Goose Green (C)	Unknown owner (hot-rod transporter) (X?) by 7/81
BNP 869H	9T471049	"	(213/8)	2/70	Marsh, Harvington (D)	Bell, Silksworth (A) 4/79
BWU 314H	9T468635	Wk B56F		8/69	Wigmore, Dinnington (B)	Dorset County Council Education Dept (XH) ?/??
CBJ 859H	0T474056	DN C53F	(213/37)	5/70	Shreeve, Lowestoft (F)	Shreeve, Lowestoft (F) from new, still there 9/80
CGK 563H	9T466444	"	(200/59)	8/69	Godfrey, Croydon (N)	Goodsir, Holyhead (C) 5/79
CWU 391H	9T472671	Pn C53F	(708376)	1/70	Anderton, Keighley (B)	Williams, Southampton (K) 9/79 sold 8/81, to snack bar 2/83
CYG 980H	9T471765	DN C53F	(213/12)	3/70	N & R, Elsecar (B)	Sanders, Holt (F) 9/81 (7/83)
DWE 328H	0T473988	Pn C51F	(708391)	"	Andrew, Sheffield (B)	Hall & Lord, Blackpool (C) 6/73 (7/78)
DWR 116H	0T476646	Pn C53F	(708404)	"	Abbey, Selby (A)	Leighfield (preservationist), Grittenham (P?) 8/82
DWR 461H	9T470934	"	(708366)	"	Baddeley, Holmfirth 106 (B)	Baker, Hopton (F) 5/78 (7/83)
DWT 776H	0T476978	"	(708406)	6/70	Shaw, Dobcross (B)	Lunn, Rothwell (B) 8/74
DWT 890H	0T477039	Pn C51F	(708396)	4/70	Kirkby, Harthill (B)	Richards, Moylgrove (G) 1/78 (11/81)
DWW 431H	9T471505	Pn C53F	(708378)	5/70	Bingley, Kinsley (B)	Fowler, Holbeach (F) 6/80 (7/83)
HJM 772H	9T472616	"	(708375)	12/69	Brown, Ambleside (A)	Rowland & Goodwin, St Leonards (K) 3/77 (8/83)
HNO 31H	0T473001	"	(708384)	4/70	Boon, Boreham (F)	Don, Dunmow (F) 2/79, burnt out at Felstead 6/79
HXC 957H	9T468675	"	(692494)	9/69	Ardenvale, Knowle (D)	Caravan, Levenshulme (XC) 5/82
JUP 351H	0T476035	DN C53F	(213/27)	6/70	General, Chester-le-Street (A)	Robinson, Wigan (C) 9/79
KNK 379H	9T471508	Pn C53F	(708357)	4/70	Thompson, London N18 (N)	Cathedral, Gloucester (H) 7/77 (2/82)
LEW 232H	9T469763	DN C53F	(200/58)	9/69	Duncan, Huntingdon (F)	Clarke, Elmswell (F) 4/80, disused on premises 9/82
LEX 991H	9T466481	"	(200/32)	3/70	Caroline, Great Yarmouth (F)	Palace Bingo, Gorleston (XF) 5/82
LXC 583H	9T472508	Co C53F		"	Ardenvale, Knowle (D)	Worthing Boys' Home (XK) 5/81
MEN 327H	0T475020	Pn C52F	(708398)	"	Fairclough, Radcliffe (C)	Edwards, Soham (F) 11/79 (4/80)
MEN 329H	0T475561	Pn C53F	(708392)	4/70	"	Guscott, Halwill (H) 6/79 (3/83)
MJT 225H	9T470930	"	(708393)	2/70	Adams, Handley (H)	Adams, Handley (H) from new, still there 2/82
MPR 531H	9T471884	"	(708365)	6/70	Rendell, Parkstone (K)	Gay, Northlew (H) 10/78 (2/82)
MPR 532H	9T471932	"	(708367)	"	"	Knight, Hazelbury Bryan (H) 10/72 (7/82)
MPR 533H	0T473318	"	(708380)	"	"	Hogg, Benington (E) 2/77 wdn 5/80
MPR 534H	0T473288	"	(708381)	"	"	Fussey, Lockington (B) 4/77 (2/81)
MPR 535H	0T473220	"	(708382)	"	"	Bruce, Airdrie (M) by 9/82
MPR 536H	0T471449	"	(708383)	"	"	Brown & Bennett, Gloucester (H) 1/82

Reg	Chassis	Body	Batch	Date	Operator	Notes
MUR 191H	9T471740	DN C53F	(213/10)	2/70	Hunt, Hayes End (N)	Caravan, seen in Chesterfield (XB) 7/82
MUR 198H	9T471455	Pn C53F	(708355)	"	Alexandra, Enfield (N)	Hewitt, Birmingham (D) 9/80, burnt out 10/80
MUR 210H	9T471470	DN C53F	(213/9)	4/70	Thorpe, London E17 (N)	Norris, Hawkhurst 69 (K) 11/78 (12/80)
NER 823H	9T471434	Pn C53F	(708359)	2/70	Young, Rampton (F)	Steve Stockdale, Selby (B) 2/77 (10/80)
NNK 754H	9T472008	"	(708372)	1/70	Margo and Plaskow, Edgware (N)	Prentice, West Calder (M) 1/73 (4/81)
NUR 471H	0T477388	"	(708408)	3/70	Limebourne, London SW1 1 (N)	Adams, Handley (H) 1/73 (2/82)
NUR 472H	0T477249	"	(708409)	"	" 2 (N)	Jones, Login (G) 3/74 (9/81)
NUR 473H	0T477427	"	(708411)	"	" 3 (N)	Unknown Jazz Band (XA) by 6/83
NUR 474H	0T477468	"	(708412)	"	" 4 (N)	Religious Travel, London E12 (XN) 11/79
NUR 477H	9T472928	"	(708385)	4/70	Hall, London SW19 (N)	Piper, New Malden (N) 2/78 (1/81)
NUR 478H	0T474156	"	(708388)	3/70	Davies, London SW16 (N)	Explorer, Croydon (N) 4/78 wdn 3/81
OAR 67H	0T475741	DN C53F	(213/44)	5/70	Premier-Albanian, Watford (N)	Skew, New Milton (K) 1/79 (12/80)
OAR 68H	0T477164	"	(213/45)	"	"	Clue, Menheniot (H) 3/81 (2/82)
OAR 69H	0T478812	"	(213/46)	7/70	"	Whiteford, Lanark (M) 10/78
OCT 990H	9T469696	"	(200/56)	9/69	Wing, Sleaford (E)	Excelsior, Dinnington (B) 9/80 (2/81)
OKX 234H	9T464958	Co C53F		3/70	Bletchley Self Drive, Bletchley (E)	Galloway, Oxford (E) 6/82
ORO 797H	9T471584	Pn C53F	(708370)	/70	Plaskow and Margo, Edgware (N)	Higgs, Clevedon (H) 11/76 (7/82)
OTM 649H	0T477443	DN C53F	(213/43)	7/70	Stringer, Ampthill (F)	Banstead Coaches, Banstead (N) 1/72 wdn 11/81
OVU 858H	0T472724	Co C53F		"	Stubbs, Manchester (C)	Glynne, Glasgow (M) 9/73
PAR 821H	9T471965	Pn C53F	(708369)	4/70	Supreme, Hadleigh (F)	Trinity Georgians Jazz Band, Fazeley (XD) 8/81
PAR 824H	0T473342	DN C53F	(213/36)	5/70	Sightseeing, London W13 (N)	Shreeve, Lowestoft (F) 3/75 (6/83)
PAR 825H	9T471364	"	(213/15)	"	"	" (F) 9/73 (6/83)
PAR 826H	9T470745	Pn C53F	(708371)	"	"	Transporter/caravan, Worksop (XB) 7/82
PDL 351H	0T473758	DN C52F	(213/35)	2/70	Southern Vectis 410 (K)	Southern Vectis 410 (later 120) (K) from new, wdn 10/82
PDL 816H	0T473336	DN C53F	(213/31)	4/70	Moss, Sandown (K)	Moss, Sandown (K) from new, still there 12/80
PDL 823H	9T471438	"	(213/5)	5/70	Seaview Motor Services, Seaview (K)	Kim, Sandown (K) 10/80
PJH 451H	9T471464	Pn C53F	(708354)	4/70	Wilmot, Southall (N)	Mitchell, Exeter (H) 6/78, wdn 9/80
PJH 454H	0T476212	DN C52F	(213/29)	5/70	WHM (Brentwood), Hutton (N)	Lavender & Horton, Cheslyn Hay (D) 6/78, wdn 2/81
PJH 459H	0T475492	Pn C53F	(708395)	"	Dolling, Uxbridge (N)	Stoodley & Whatford, Coldwaltham (K) 6/80, exported to Eire 3/82
PJH 470H	0T476138	DN C53F	(213/28)	"	Ward, London N11 (N)	Cleverly, Cwmbran (G) 4/81 (8/81)
PLG 762H	9T469724	Pn C53F	(708362)	3/70	Bostock, Congleton 12 (C)	S S & B E Smith, Pylle (H) 12/76 (12/82)
PLG 763H	9T470856	Pn C52F	(708363)	"	" 16 (C)	Sparkes, Bath (H) 5/81 (12/82)
PLG 764H	9T471106	"	(708361)	"	" 22 (C)	Smith, Adderbury (E) 4/80
PNK 317H	0T474889	DN C53F	(213/42)	11/70	Parker, London NW9 (N)	Shillingford, Elstree (N) 7/81 (10/81)
PWH 834H	9T464648	Pn C53F	(692454)	6/70	Hargreaves, Bolton (C)	Hircock, Upwell (F) 8/78 (6/83)
RAR 671H	9T471449	"	(708356)	7/70	Sonner, Chatham (K)	Fuell (transporter), Redditch (XD) -/82
RAR 674H	9T471052	DN C53F	(213/2)	6/70	Stanley, Hersham (N)	Eschman & Walsh, Lancing (XK) 11/78
RAR 675H	9T471370	"	(200/110)	"	Pagan (Cavalier), Sutton (N)	Ellis & Lewis, Cliftonville (K) 4/74, burnt out -/79
RAR 676H	9T470939	"	(200/65)	"	"	Rowland & Goodwin, St Leonards (ZK) for spares 7/83; being stripped
RMB 699H	0T475036	"	(213/41)	7/70	Naylor, Stockton Heath (C)	Chilcott, New Milton (K) 11/80
SDV 263H	9T471675	"	(213/7)	5/70	Trathen, Yelverton (H)	Sheppard & Plaister (ex Sheppard), Broad Town (H) 1/82 (12/82)
SED 562H	9T471050	Pn C52F	(708358)	4/70	Cooper, Warrington (C)	Stowell, Warrington (C) 5/80, written off -/81
SKG 709H	7T460201	Pn C53F	(692409)	"	Pagan, Sutton (N)	Wilby, Hibaldstow (E) 9/79 (5/80)
SLJ 756H	0T473878	DN C49F	(213/32)	"	Wilts and Dorset 928 (H)	Stillmeadow Equestrian Centre (XB) by 8/82
SLJ 757H	0T475910	"	(213/33)	5/70	" 929 (H)	Hughes, Penmaenmawr (C) 11/79
SLJ 758H	0T477179	"	(213/34)	6/70	" 930 (H)	Sergent, Wrinehill (D) 5/81
SNT 925H	0T477080	Pn C53F	(708407)	"	Foxall, Bridgnorth (D)	Contractus, Stevenage (N) 8/82
SRU 252H	0T476745	DN C49F	(213/25)	3/70	Shamrock & Rambler, Bournemouth (K)	Abbey, Selby (B) 1/77 (2/82)
SRU 253H	0T475872	"	(213/26)	"	"	Abbey, Selby (B) 1/77 (2/82)
SSF 235H	0T473271	DN C53F	(213/22)	6/70	Edinburgh Corporation 235 (M)	Rule, Boxford (F) 3/80, wdn 5/82
SSF 236H	0T474867	"	(213/38)	"	" 236 (M)	New Enterprise, Tonbridge (K) 11/81
SSF 237H	0T474940	"	(213/39)	"	" 237 (M)	Brown, Builth Wells (G) 10/78 (8/81)
SUO 155H	9T469630	"	(200/62)	"	Snell, Newton Abbot (H)	Damaged by flood; to Brown, Builth Wells (ZG) for spares 8/80

TJU 283H	9T468667	DN C53F	(200/57)	10/69	Drewery, Woodford Bridge (N)	Robertson, Romford (N) 8/72 (10/81)
TUT 888H	9T473933	Pn C53F	(708390)	2/70	Weston, Leicester (E)	Weston, Leicester (E) from new, still there 12/79
UAA 755H	9T472572	"	(708374)	11/69	Marchwood Motorways, Totton (K)	Marchwood, Totton (K) from new, still there 12/80
UAO 755H	9T467990	Wk B53F	(CF1941)	/70	British Gypsum (XA)	Robinson, Appleby (A) 7/75, broken up 10/76
UFL 498H	9T470870	Pn C53F	(708360)	1/70	Whippet, Hilton (F)	Leech, Newcastle (XA) 10/79
UJU 149H	9T471430	DN C53F	(213/13)	3/70	Alpha, Brighton (K)	Burton, Haverhill (F) 10/75 sold 10/81
UJU 931H	0T476586	Pn C53F	(708402)	5/70	Howlett, Quorn 37 (E)	Smith & Ball, Waterhouses (D) 1/79, wdn 9/79
UOL 400H	0T478844	"	(708413)	"	Smith, Birmingham (D)	Gill & Munden, Wadebridge (H) 1/82
UOR 21H	9T470630	DN C53F	(200/63)	1/70	Fleet Coaches, Fleet B29 (K)	JAB Refiners, Sheffield (XB) by 8/81 (at Milford Haven) wdn by 4/82
UOR 604H	0T477227	Pn C52F	(708410)	4/70	Banstead Coaches, Banstead (N)	Explorer, Croydon (N) 4/79 (8/80)
UOR 606H	0T473143	DN C53F	(213/21)	3/70	Watson, Southampton (K)	Coastal & Country, Whitby (B) 3/76 sold 1/83
UOU 997H	0T472401	"	(213/16)	11/69	Coliseum, Southampton (K)	Sanders, Holt (F) 5/80, sold for scrap 7/83
URL 450H	0T473084	Pn C53F	(708377)	5/70	Stevens, St Ives (H)	Hopley, Mount Hawke (H) 1/76 (7/82)
UTB 921H	9T469483	DN C50F	(200/61)	10/69	Holmeswood, Rufford (C)	Parker, Hindolveston (F) 8/79, wdn 11/82
UUT 500H	0T475660	Pn C53F	(708401)	5/70	Wood, Wigston (E)	Phillips, Ruskington (E) 5/79 (5/80)
VAA 107H	9T472366	Co C53F	(290)	3/70	Cowdrey, Gosport (K)	Daisy, Broughton (E) 3/72, burnt out 7/78
VBD 310H	0T476066	Pn C48F	(708400)	4/70	Coales, Wollaston 50 (E)	Leicester & District Multiple Sclerosis Society (XE) 5/76
VEG 244H	9T471173	Pn C53F	(708368)	2/70	Whippet, Hilton (F)	Watt, Clydebank (M) 2/81, used for spares and as seat store 9/82
VFL 548H	0T474281	"	(708387)	4/70	"	Pangbourne Coaches, Pangbourne (K) 11/78 (12/80)
VHT 911H	9T470995	DN C53F	(213/1)	3/70	Wessex, Bristol (H)	Abbey, Selby (B) 2/77 (2/82)
VHU 666H	9T468768	Co C53F		11/69	G P Smith, Bristol (H)	Vinall, East Grinstead (N) 7/77, wdn 7/78
VOT 508H	9T471374	DN C53F	(213/4)	5/70	Warren, Alton (K)	Warren, Alton (K) from new, written off after accident 12/81
VTC 445H	9T471384	DN C49F	(213/3)	4/70	Walls, Wigan (C)	Barlow-Myers, Maidenhead (XK) by 5/77
VTC 446H	9T477482	"	(213/11)	"	"	Lansdown, Tockington (H) 6/74 (7/82)
VTJ 611H	0T473124	DN C53F	(213/20)	"	Hadwin, Ulverston (A)	Hadwin, Ulverston (A) from new, wdn by 7/81
VTJ 612H	0T474921	"	(213/40)	6/70	"	McEntee, Haverfordwest (XG) 3/80
VVA 259H	9T470794	"	(213/6)	1/70	Galloway, Harthill (M)	Clark & Herrington, Flushing (H) 8/78, sold 7/80
VVD 200H	0T473365	Pn C53F	(708405)	3/70	MacPhail, Newarthill (M)	Brown & Bennett, Gloucester (H) 3/80 (2/82)
WAO 122H	9T471409	DN C53F	(213/14)	4/70	Kirkpatrick, Brigham (A)	Kirkpatrick, Brigham (A) from new, still there -/79
WHA 216H	0T477306	"	(213/49)	7/70	Morris, Bearwood (D)	Air Training Corps squadron, Devon area (XH) by 3/83
WHA 440H	9T470977	"	(200/107)	5/70	Mann, Smethwick (D)	Enterprise, Chatteris (F) 5/77 (4/80)
WRM 91H	0T476002	Pn C53F	(708397)	4/70	Hamilton, Workington (A)	Brockbank, Chesterfield (B) 4/76
WRM 92H	0T475600	"	(708399)	"	"	Smith, Didsbury (C) 5/78, wdn 6/80
XRX 3H	0T475804	"	(708394)	5/70	Pangbourne Coaches, Pangbourne (K)	Pangbourne Coaches, Pangbourne (K) from new, still there 12/80
XTB 626H	0T474414	DN C53F	(213/24)	4/70	Bold, Melling (C)	Pratt, Frampton-on-Severn (H) 3/79 (7/82)
XTC 530H	0T476509	Pn C53F	(708403)	"	Shaw, Silverdale (C)	Caravan (X?) 9/82
XTG 922H	9T464298	"	(692466)	"	Porthcawl Omnibus Co, Porthcawl (G)	Porthcawl Omnibus Co, Porthcawl (G) from new, still there 11/81
XUB 559H	0T475233	"	(708389)	7/70	Shilton, Leeds (B)	Carolinas Jazz Band, Kirkby (XC) 6/81 scr after accident 3/82
XYD 926H	9T470990	"	(708353)	3/70	Pow, Paulton (H)	Berkeley, Paulton (H) 12/72 (2/82)
YLT 333H	9T470742	DN C53F	(200/55)	4/70	Rowson (Blueline), Hayes (N)	Adamson, Edinburgh (M) 3/79
YTG 528H	0T474378	Pn C53F	(708386)	"	Jenkins, Skewen (G)	Axon, Chertsey (N) 7/78 (8/80)
YYB 239H	9T472384	Co C53F		3/70	Clevedon Motorways, Clevedon (H)	Gould, Pilton (H) 5/79 (2/82)
YYX 997H	9T470867	Pn C53F	(708352)	5/70	Margo, London SW16 108 (N) (Note 5)	Ardcavan, New Ross (I) re-registered KZR 677 3/77
YYX 998H	9T470688	"	(708351)	"	" 109 (N) (Note 5)	Margo, Thornton Heath (N) wdn 5/76
AAA 707J	1T483469	DN C52F		3/71	Watson, Southampton (K)	Gay, Northlew (H) 6/80 (2/82)
ABW 185J	1T484913	Pn C53F	(712408)	"	Carterton Coaches, Carterton (E)	Chivers, Wallington (N) 6/73 (8/80)
ABW 186J	1T485368	"	(712409)	"	"	Howard, Whitby (B) 12/77 (5/81)
ABW 187J	1T485923	"	(712410)	"	"	Deeble, Upton Cross (H) 11/80 (2/82)
ABW 188J	1T485432	"	(712411)	"	"	Sheppard & Plaister, Broad Town (H) 2/82 (12/82)
ACG 784J	0T480436	"	(718379)	4/71	Holman, London N8 (N)	Holman, London N22 (N) from new, sold 9/82
AEG 371J	1T483620	"	(712378)	"	Whippet, Hilton (F)	Bluebird, Hull (B) 11/81
AEG 564J	1T483212	"	(712380)	"	"	Smurthwaite, Copthorne (N) 2/79 (10/81)
AEG 565J	1T483794	"	(712379)	"	"	Freeman, Uffington (K) 9/76 (9/79)

Reg	Chassis	Body		Batch	Date	Operator	Later history
AFL 384J	1T485474	Pn	C53F	(712394)	5/71	Whippet, Hilton (F)	Underwood, North Walsham (F) 1/77 (9/80)
AFL 385J	1T484162	"		(712395)	"	"	Machin, Ashby-de-la-Zouch (E) 12/77 (12/79)
AFL 386J	1T484200	"		(712396)	6/71	"	Tattersall, Threshfield (B) 3/79 exported to Eire 8/81
AHA 667J	1T483824	DN	C53F	(229/44)	4/71	Mann, Smethwick (D)	Selden Fisheries, Kendal (XA) by 7/82
AHA 668J	1T483526	"		(229/31)	"	"	Arma, Aberdeen (L) 5/83, wdn 5/83
AKB 700J	1T483333	"		(229/26)	8/71	James, Liverpool (C) (note 6)	Jones, Login (G) 3/77 (9/81)
AVA 238J	1T484052	"		(229/18)	4/71	Park, Hamilton (M)	Abbey, Selby (B) 1/77 (2/81)
BAA 885J	1T485454	Pn	C53F	(712400)	6/71	Hutchinson, London SE25 (N)	Stevens, Bristol (H) 2/81 (12/82)
BBW 939J	1T483104	Co	C53F	(71/50)	5/71	Hambridge, Kidlington (E)	Kearney, Cork (I) -/81
BHO 670J	1T489281	DN	C53F	(229/16)	8/71	Castle, Waterlooville (K)	Down, Mary Tavy (H) 5/80 (2/82)
BVF 678J	1T483557	Pn	C53F	(712406)	7/71	Spratt, Wreningham 23 (F)	Woodcock, Buxton (F) 1/79 (9/80)
CFD 300J	1T483351	Co	C53F	(71/37)	5/71	Mills, Gornal Wood (D)	Easton, Brandiston (F) 3/77, wdn 3/81
CTF 901J	1T485600	DN	C53F		3/71	Battersby-Silver Grey, Morecambe (C)	Prentice, West Calder (M) 7/75 wdn 2/82, being used for spares
CTF 902J	1T483551	"		(229/27)	4/71	"	Prentice, West Calder (M) 9/75 wdn 2/81, being used for spares
CTF 903J	1T485571	"		(229/28)	"	"	Bishop, Oxhey (N) 10/80
CWD 574J	1T489156	"		(229/13)	6/71	Cotton, Bilton (D)	Harris, Fleur-de-Lys (G) by 6/75, sold 11/77
DTJ 632J	1T483188	"			4/71	Hadwin, Ulverston (A)	?Unknown non-PSV owner, Milford Haven (XG) 12/80?
DTJ 633J	1T483172	"			"	"	Hadwin, Ulverston (A) from new, wdn 11/80
DTX 504J	1T487569	Pn	C53F	(712412)	5/71	Jenkins, Skewen 4 (G)	House, Hilton (H) 4/79 (7/82)
DTX 942J	1T487339	DN	C53F	(229/4)	"	" 5 (G)	Long, Skibbereen (I) 2/81
DYD 249J	1T484408	DN	C53F	(229/38)	3/71	Osmond, Curry Rivel (H)	Freeman, Uffington (K) 11/80
ETB 223J	1T483059	DN	C53F	(229/34)	4/71	Coupland, Fleetwood (C)	Fearon (Indoor Gardening), Carlisle (XA) 12/82
ETC 554J	1T484362	DN	C53F	(229/30)	"	Walls, Wigan (C)	Eady, Washington (A) 10/80, sold by 2/82
ETF 717J	1T488193	"		(227/17)	5/71	Coupland, Fleetwood (C)	Oldham Aces Morris Troupe (XC) 6/80
FAL 183J	1T483416	DN	C53F		3/71	Clarke, Newthorpe (E)	Williams, Bethesda (C) 12/79
FDJ 966J	1T483982	DN	C53F	(229/37)	"	St Helens Co-op, Goose Green (C)	Pemberton, Willenhall (D) 10/77, sold for scr 12/81
FWU 843J	0T478875	DN	C53F	(213/47)	8/70	Shaw, Dobcross (B)	Sportsman, Whiston (C) 4/76
FYG 663J	0T480197	Wk	B56F	(CF2364)	10/70	Wigmore, Dinnington (B)	Abbey, Selby (B) 12/72 (2/81)
FYT 987J(1)	1T484662	DN	C53F	(229/8)	2/71	Atlas, Edgware (N) (note 7)	
FYT 987J(2)	1T483019	DN	C53F	(229/39)	8/71	West Kent, Biggin Hill (N) (note 7)	Collingwood, Wheatley Hill (A) 6/80, disused 4/83
FYW 800J	1T485514	Pn	C53F	(718415)	4/71	Bexleyheath Tpt, Bexleyheath 63 (N)	Tally Ho!, Kingsbridge (H) 9/79 (3/83)
FYW 801J	1T485542	"		(718416)	"	" 64 (N)	Seward, Dalwood (H) 2/80 (12/82)
GUY 321J	1T483032	"		(712399)	5/71	Beoley Garage, Beoley (D)	P & R, Hartlepool (ZA) acquired for spares by 1/83
GWP 956J	1T487645	DN	C53F	(229/55)	6/71	Watts, Stourbridge (D)	Morley, Whittlesey (F) 3/75 (7/83)
GWX 159J	0T480178	Wk	B56F		11/70	Wigmore, Dinnington (B)	Turnbull, Lockerbie (M) 4/74, wdn by 1/75, exported to Eire 5/76
HBJ 174J	1T487199	DN	C53F	(229/10)	6/71	Classic, Lowestoft (F)	Shreeve, Lowestoft (F) 6/77 (6/83)
HWU 519J	1T485039	Wk	B56F	(CF2366)	2/71	Wigmore, Dinnington (B)	Gilbert, Bingham (E) 1/77, wdn 6/80, out of use at depot by 9/82
JHC 900J	1T484466	Pn	C53F	(712421)	5/71	Harmer, Bexhill (K)	Harmer, Bexhill (K) from new, wdn by 2/83, disused at depot by 8/83
JHF 649J	1T482975	Du	C53F		4/71	Douras, Wallasey (C)	Biggs, St Albans (N) 3/81 wdn by 12/82
JWT 725J	1T485874	Pn	C53F	(712382)	"	Baddeley, Holmfirth 109 (B)	Catchpole, Tydd St Giles (F) 5/79 (4/80)
KWE 130J	1T489074	DN	C53F	(213/52)	7/71	Musselwhite, Sheffield (B)	Beeston, Hadleigh (ZF) 1/82
KWE 169J	1T487525	Pn	C53F	(712417)	"	"	Abingdon & Caldicott, Abingdon (K) 10/76 (9/79)
LEC 151J	1T483588	"		(712404)	3/71	Brown, Ambleside (A)	Brooks, Failsworth (C) 1/79, wdn by 10/81
LEK 68J	1T485895	"		(712397)	5/71	Liptrot, Bamfurlong (C)	Hurst, Wigan (C) 5/77 wdn 6/80, burnt out and scr ?/??
NJY 992J	1T485791	DN	C53F	(229/35)	"	Embankment, Plymouth (H)	Turner & Butcher, Kenninghall (F) 5/79 (9/80)
OJT 411J	1T484433	Pn	C53F	(712414)	6/71	Rendell, Parkstone (K)	Hogg, Benington (E) 2/78 wdn by 7/82 after accident
OJT 412J	1T487146	"		(712415)	"	"	Unknown Jazz Band, Stockton (XA) 4/82
OJT 413J	1T487413	"		(712416)	"	"	Withers, Leicester (E) 6/79 (12/79)
OJT 416J	1T483693	"		(712376)	"	"	Primrose Valley, Filey (B) 10/75 (5/81)
PJE 470J	0T481391	"		(712405)	2/71	Miller, Foxton (F)	Miller, Foxton (F) from new, still there 4/83
PVE 592J	1T483386	"		(712377)	4/71	Young, Rampton (F)	Hogan (Shamrock), Thurles (I) as 2566 FI, -/79
RAR 679J	0T478780	"		(708414)	9/70	McIntyre, Harlow (N)	Havering Corps of Drums (XN) 9/79, for sale 8/82
RAR 688J	1T483273	DN	C53F	(229/25)	3/71	"	Jones, London N15 (N) 3/82

Reg	Chassis	Body	Body No	Date	Owner	History
RAR 690J	?T461819	VH C51F	(4465)	1/71	All Seasons, London W2 (N)	Boulton, Cardington (D) 11/76 (7/81)
RGR 620J	1T485680	DN C53F	(229/43)	5/71	Carney, Roker (A)	Sanders, Holt (F) 10/78, wdn on premises 7/83
SDL 743J	1T487476	Pn C53F	(712383)	6/71	Southern Vectis 410 (K)	Southern Vectis 110 (K) from new, wdn 10/82
SDL 744J	1T487913	"	(712384)	"	" 411 (K)	Southern Vectis 111 (K) from new, wdn 10/82
SDL 838J	1T483303	"	(712422)	3/71	Seaview Services, Seaview (K)	Seaview Services, Seaview (K) from new, still there 12/80
TAR 183J	1T483434	"	(712385)	/71	Guards, London WC1 (N)	Sherman, Warwick (D) 4/78
TAR 184J	1T483446	"	(712386)	2/71	"	Grayline, Bicester (E) 8/78
TAR 185J	1T483245	"	(712387)	"	"	Lavery, Dublin (I) as 134 TZO by 5/82
TAR 186J	1T484333	"	(712388)	"	"	Havering Corps of Drums, Hornchurch (XN) 3/78, for sale 8/82
TAR 187J	1T484855	"	(712389)	3/71	"	Morris Green, Bolton (C) 2/76 (7/78)
TAR 188J	1T484952	"	(712390)	"	"	Kim, Sandown (K) 6/81
TAR 189J	1T483010	"	(712391)	"	"	Perry, Blackwood (G) 4/79 (11/81)
TFV 475J	1T487259	DN C53F	(229/32)	5/71	Murray, Blackpool (C)	Jackson, Blackpool (C) 7/73 (7/78)
UMR 554J	1T483634	Pn C53F	(712393)	4/71	Barnes, Aldbourne (H)	Hawthorn Travel, Barry (G) 3/79 (9/81)
URO 845J	1T484347	"	(718418)	"	Alexandra, Enfield (N)	Light, Shaftesbury (H) 4/82 wdn 4/82
URO 852J	1T485399	"	(712413)	"	Stanley, Hersham (N)	Stanley, Hersham (N) from new, still there 10/81
UVJ 800J	1T485487	DN C53F	(229/41)	5/71	Wye Valley, Hereford (D)	Shaw, Warwick (D) 11/77 wdn 2/81
VBO 660J	1T485761	"	(229/45)	4/71	T.J., Cardiff (G)	Miller, Whitchurch (H) 8/71 (7/82)
VED 598J	1T483335	Pn C53F	(712419)	7/71	Cooper, Stockton Heath (C)	Littlemead School, Chichester (K) by 3/79
VKR 538J	0T477128	DN C53F	(213/50)	9/70	Browne, Willesborough (K)	Cook, Leigh-on-Sea (F) 3/72 (8/83)
VLJ 231J	1T483072	DN C49F	(229/1)	6/71	Shamrock & Rambler, Bournemouth (K)	Shamrock & Rambler, Bournemouth (K) wdn 12/77
VLJ 232J	1T488561	"	(229/4)	"	"	Kime, Folkingham (E) 9/81
VLJ 233J	1T489338	"	(229/5)	7/71	"	Lewis, Carriglefn (C) 7/78
VNK 911J	1T484662	DN C53F	(229/8)	5/71	Plaskow & Margo, Edgware (N)(note 7)	Richardson (caravan), Louth (XE) 10/82
VUO 298J	1T483333	"	(229/26)	7/71	Hibberd, Morchard Bishop (H)(note 6)	Hibberd wdn 8/71; re-registered AKB 700J (q.v.)
WAF 734J	0T474821	Co C53F		8/70	Brown and Davies, Truro (H)	VMW Motors (racing car transporter), Kingswood (XH) as VMW 10, 3/78
WAR 673J	1T487669	DN C53F	(229/46)	7/71	Feltham Haulage, Feltham (N)	Bithell, Llandudno Junction (C) 7/77
WEL 802J	1T488478	DN C49F	(229/19)	6/71	Wilts and Dorset 62 (H)	Elkin, Macclesfield (C) 1/81
WEL 803J	1T488404	"	(229/20)	7/71	" 63 (H)	Hants & Dorset (K) wdn by 2/82
WEL 804J	1T488511	"	(229/2)	"	Hants and Dorset 1095 (K)	Alpha Dentonian, Denton (C) 2/80
WEL 805J	1T488762	"	(229/3)	"	" 1096 (K)	Lightfoot, Winsford (C) 6/78
WJH 129J	1T483751	DN C53F	(229/15)	6/71	Gilbert, Bovingdon (N)	Transporter (X?) by 8/82
WNK 471J	1T488019	"	(229/40)	8/71	Cavalier, Sutton (N)	Smith, Emneth (F) 6/76, damaged by fire, wdn 6/81
WNK 472J	1T488310	"	(229/42)	"	"	Tidworth Coaches, Tidworth (H) 4/75 (12/82)
WNK 473J	1T487833	"	(229/49)	"	"	Fairway, Biggleswade (F) 12/77, wdn 8/82
WNK 474J	1T488634	"	(229/51)	"	"	Harrod, Wormegay (F) 2/80
WNK 475J	1T487348	"	(229/52)	"	"	Collingwood, Wheatley Hill (A) 3/80, exported to Eire 6/81
WNK 476J	1T486532	"	(229/48)	"	"	Smith, Emneth (F) 2/77, derelict at Wisbech St Mary 7/82
WOU 989J	0T474223	Pn C53F	(708373)	8/70	White, Camberley 4 (K)	Prout, Port Isaac (H) 9/76 (7/82)
WTU 690J	1T483661	Pn C52F	(708370)	3/71	Bostock, Congleton 24 (C)	Nuttall, Modbury (H) 7/77 (7/82)
WUR 870J	1T488944	DN C53F	(229/14)	10/71	Lee-Lozone, Cheshunt (N)	Kirkhill Lodge Hotel (horsebox/executive suite), Dyce (XL) by 11/81
XKO 295J	1T485661	Pn C53F	(712381)	4/71	Browne, Willesborough (K)	Browne, Brabourne (K) wdn 12/81
XMB 989J	1T484641	DN C53F	(229/33)	8/71	Naylor, Stockton Heath (C)	Edwards, Bwlchgwyn (C) 12/76
XNK 513J	1T487606	"	(229/6)	7/71	Camping, Brighton (K)	Tanner & Allpress, Sibford Gower (E) 11/80
XOR 466J	0T478783	"	(213/51)	9/70	Budden, West Tytherley (K)	Foster, Glastonbury (H) 5/79 (2/82)
XRH 826J	1T483154	Pn C53F	(718420)	5/71	Danby, Hull (B)	Anchorians Junior Jazz Band, Newcastle (XA) -/82
YAF 303J	1T483505	"	(718419)	4/71	Stoneman, Nanpean (H)	Berkeley, Paulton (H) 3/75 (2/82)
YAY 769J	1T487167	DN C53F	(229/12)	6/71	Castle, Horndean (K)	Guildford Sea Cadet Corps Band (XN) by 3/82
YCV 940J	1T488200	"	(229/5)	"	Brown and Davies, Truro (H)	Williams, St Agnes (H) 9/75 (12/82)
YHP 3J	1T484110	"	(229/50)	5/71	Shaw, Coventry (D)	Collingwood, Wheatley Hill (A) 5/80, believed sold for scr 6/83
YHP 6J	1T485967	"	(229/40)	1/72	"	Pyne, Harrogate (B) 3/73
AXC 516K	2T471346	"	(241/23)	3/72	Ardenvale, Knowle (D)	James, Cardiff (G) 5/78 (9/81)
BJU 578K	1T492155	"	(241/1)	4/72	Lee-Lozone, Cheshunt (N)	Rampling, Ramsgate 1/78 sold for scr 12/81

Reg	Chassis	Body	Body No	Date	Operator	History
CAR 359K	2T471883	Pn C53F	(728393)	2/72	McIntyre, Roydon (N)	Perry, Blackwood (G) 4/78 (11/81)
CAR 360K	2T472906	"	(728410)	6/72	"	Thomas, Calne (H) 5/76 (12/82)
CAR 433K	2T472544	"	(728392)	3/72	Coats, London N22 (N)	Coats, London N22 (N) wdn 3/75
CAT 952K	2T470856	DN C53F	(241/21)	4/72	Danby, Hull (B)	Nuttall, Modbury (H) 4/77 (7/82)
CDD 235K	2T472907	Pn C53F	(728384)	5/72	Grindle, Cinderford (H)	Chivers, Midsomer Norton (H) 10/77 (2/82)
CRO 690K	2T471076	DN C53F	(241/6)	4/72	Alexandra, Enfield (N)	Abbey, Selby (B) 6/77 (2/81)
DAA 967K	2T470302	"	(241/18)	1/72	Hutchinson, London SE25 (N)	Craven, Preston (C) 7/77
DAO 706K	2T470272	"	(241/11)	11/71	Kirkpatrick, Brigham (A)	Kirkpatrick, Brigham (A) from new, still there 3/79
DMB 860K	2T470496	Pn C52F	(728390)	1/72	Bostock, Congleton 18 (C)	Prentice, West Calder (M) 8/75 wdn 2/82, being used for spares
DMB 861K	2T470229	"	(728391)	"	" 14 (C)	Bostock, Congleton (C) from new, wdn 4/75
DOE 111K	2T471384	Pn C53F	(728388)	4/72	Smith, Birmingham (D)	Smith, Birmingham (D) from new, wdn 2/82
DRM 561K	1T491027	DN C53F	(229/53)	1/72	Stephenson, Maryport (A)	Flint, Nettleton (H) 1/80 (2/82)
DUR 122K	2T471844	"	(241/26)	7/72	Gilbert, Bovingdon (N)	Edkins, Rubery (D) 8/80, wdn 5/81
DUR 961K	2T472686	Pn C53F	(728408)	5/72	Plaza, London W2 (N)	Tanner & Allpress, Sibford Gower (E) 11/80
DUR 962K	2T472839	"	(728409)	"	"	Tanner & Allpress, Sibford Gower (E) 11/80
DUR 975K	2T471089	"	(728385)	7/72	Paul, Dane End (N)	Tally Ho!, Kingsbridge (H) 1/79 (3/83)
DUR 980K	2T472644	"	(728397)	6/72	Stanley, Hersham (N)	Cannon, New Malden (N) 10/82
DWN 253K	2T471639	DN C53F	(241/24)	4/72	Lewis, Morriston (G)	Royal Red, Llandudno (C) 5/75
EHA 600K	2T471371	"	(241/19)	"	Mann, Smethwick (D)	Barrett, Deal (K) 6/80
EHO 626K	2T472142	"	(241/25)	5/72	Banstead Coaches, Banstead (N)	Owen, Yateley (K) 2/78 (12/80)
EHO 808K	1T492669	Pn C53F	(728382)	2/72	Watson, Southampton (K)	Chisholm, Swanley (N) 4/80 (8/80)
FAR 724K	2T473072	DN C53F	(241/29)	10/72	Langley Coach Co, Slough (N)	Thomas, Calne (H) 11/76 (12/82)
FAR 733K	2T473479	"	(241/31)	8/72	Quondam, Cheshunt (N)	Heseltine, Featherstone (B) 10/77 sold 7/81
FCG 839K	2T471612	"	(241/22)	3/72	Castle, Waterlooville (K)	Brown, Builth Wells (G) 6/79 (8/81)
FLG 360K	2T471048	Pn C52F	(728394)	"	Bostock, Congleton 19 (C)	Sheppard & Plaister (ex Sheppard), Broad Town (H) 1/82 (12/82)
FOU 220K	2T473098	DN C53F	(241/36)	6/72	Budden, West Tytherley (K)	Norris, Hawkhurst 73 (K) 8/80 (12/80)
HLG 812K	2T470731	Pn C53F	(728398)	"	Naylor, Stockton Heath (C)	Lakelin, Felindre (G) 10/77 (9/81)
JHX 4K	1T491000	DN C53F	(213/48)	8/71	Soviet Trade Deleg'n, London N6 (XN) (note 8)	Motorcycle transporter, Halstead (XF) 4/83
KLK 468K	2T471862	"	(241/7)	4/72	Drewery, Woodford Bridge (N)	King, New Malden (N) 6/80 (1/81)
KLU 756K	1T492415	"	(241/4)	12/71	West Kent, Biggin Hill (N)	West Kent, Biggin Hill (N) from new, still there 10/81
KMM 308K	2T470594	"	(241/17)	3/72	Bexleyheath Tpt, Bexleyheath (N)	Piper, Sheerness (K) 4/82
KTC 121K	2T470209	"	(241/12)	12/71	Battersby-Silver Grey, Morecambe (C)	Hudson, Rowlands Castle (K) 9/79
KTC 122K	2T470107	"	(241/14)	"	"	McBrearty, Bridge End (I) as 1H 118 c8/81
KTC 123K	2T471028	"	(241/15)	"	"	Watt, Horsham (N) 12/81
KTE 305K	1T492246	"	(241/5)	1/72	Walls, Wigan (C)	Tanner & Allpress, Sibford Gower (E) 11/80
LDJ 892K	2T470800	"	(241/16)	3/72	St Helens Co-op, Goose Green (C)	Cotgrave Joypegs Jazz Band (XE) -/83
LPF 338K	2T471602	"	(241/3)	6/72	Harding, Betchworth (N)	Hallfield, Redhill (N) 8/76 (1/81)
MAL 629K	1T492561	Pn C53F	(728377)	4/72	Moxon, Oldcotes (E)	Grimshaw, Burnley (C) 6/79
MEK 651K	2T471908	"	(728381)	2/72	Liptrot, Bamfurlong (C)	Wolstenholme, Carlton (C) 9/76
NEC 237K	2T472881	"	(728386)	4/72	Brown, Ambleside (K)	Thomsett, Deal (K) 1/82
OPT 806K	1T489038	DN C53F	(213/38)	8/71	Fir Tree, Crook (A)	Tanner & Allpress, Sibford Gower (E) 11/80
OWT 297K	2T472031	Pn C53F	(728395)	4/72	Bingley, Kinsley (B)	Fowler, Holbeach Drove (F) 6/79 (7/83)
PEW 946K	1T489249	"	(712398)	12/71	Whippet, Hilton (F)	Fosdike, Bramfield (F) 10/77 (4/80)
PWU 443K	2T471932	"	(728396)	5/72	Bingley, Kinsley (B)	Griffiths, Port Dinorwic (C) 4/79
REW 222K	2T470244	"	(728389)	3/72	Dew, Somersham (F)	Newbury & Cooper, Maiden Bradley (H) 8/76 (7/82)
RPR 738K	1T488607	"	(712418)	4/72	Rendell, Parkstone (K)	Eke, Attleborough (F) 5/77 (4/80)
RPR 739K	2T470261	"	(728399)	"	Rendell, Corfe Mullen (K)	Hillier, Foxham (H) 4/77 (7/82)
RPR 741K	1T492199	"	(728376)	6/72	Rendell, Parkstone (K)	Cadwallader, Bridgend (G) 5/82 sold 2/83
RPR 748K	1T487547	"	(728380)	"	"	Field, Paulton (H) 12/74, wdn by 7/82, removed from depot 9/82
TVG 69K	2T470195	Pn C52F	(728387)	3/72	Mascot, Norwich (F)	Probets, Portishead (H) 7/80, sold by 10/81
UTL 283K	1T488736	Pn C53F	(712392)	1/72	Delaine, Bourne 70 (E)	Turnbull, Marton (A) 10/80
VDX 115K	2T473089	DN C53F	(241/33)	5/72	Classic, Lowestoft (F)	Shreeve, Lowestoft (F) 4/78 (4/83)

WDK 476K	1T491836	DN C53F		4/72	Bywater, Rochdale (C)	Tanner & Allpress, Sibford Gower (E) c11/82
XAW 505K	1T492381	"	(241/8)	2/72	Whittle, Highley (D)	Hallfield, Redhill (N) 12/80
XAW 506K	1T492308	"	(241/9)	"	"	Evans, Llanrhaeadr (C) 8/73 (8/77)
XAW 514K	2T472170	"	(241/10)	4/72	"	Evans, Shifnal (D) 11/81 wdn 2/83
XAW 550K	2T471956	"	(241/13)	3/72	Corvedale, Ludlow (D)	Pollard, Hayle (H) 5/81 (7/82)
XFR 289K	2T473175	"	(241/27)	7/72	J Jackson, Blackpool (C)	Clarke, Great Ashfield (F) 9/82
XHR 79K	2T471690	"	(241/20)	3/72	Barnes, Aldbourne (H)	Barnes, Aldbourne (H) from new, still there 2/82
XUR 290K	2T471136	Pn C53F	(728379)	1/72	Morgan, Bognor Regis (K)	Kim, Sandown (K) 6/81
YED 779K	2T471971	"	(728378)	3/72	Cooper, Stockton Heath (C)	Charlesworth, Melksham (H) 7/81 (2/82)
YHL 927K	1T491712	DN C53F	(229/9)	8/71	Birdsall, Ossett (B)	Dorset County Council Education Dept (XH) ?/??
YVC 18K	2T470042	Pn C53F	(728383)	6/72	Shaw, Coventry (D)	Primrose Valley, Filey (B) 9/75 (5/81)
ANO 395L	2T473270	"	(732405)	7/73	McIntyre, Roydon (N)	Baker, St Albans (N) 5/82
FAR 739L	2T474230	DN C53F	(241/37)	10/72	Quondam, Cheshunt (N)	Mitchell, Broxburn (M) 12/82
FFL 248L	2T474198	"	(241/38)	5/73	Kiddle, St Ives (F)	Kiddle, St Ives (F) from new, still there 4/83
GAF 107L	2T473039	"	(241/32)	10/72	Brown and Davies, Truro (H)	Easton, Cromer (F) 12/78 (6/83)
GAT 502L	2T474319	Pn C53F	(732404)	4/73	Danby, Hull (B)	Perry, Blackwood (G) 4/83
GUR 483L	2T473016	DN C53F	(241/35)	10/72	Ward, Ickenham (N)	Ward, Ickenham (N) from new, still there 10/81
HWD 531L	1T492931	"	(241/28)	8/72	Webb, Armscote (D)	Wahl, Armscote (D) 6/82
JRO 380L	2T472929	"	(241/30)	12/72	Doyle, London Colney (N)	Parkinson, Welwyn Garden City (N) 9/74 (1/81)
LOU 776L	2T473189	Pn C53F	(732403)	3/73	Castle, Horndean (K)	Gibson, Ramsdell (K) 3/78 (9/79)
LUR 510L	2T473363	"	(732402)	5/73	Brunt, Potters Bar (N)	Evans, Rhyl (C) 5/79
LUR 600L	2T473391	"	(732084)	2/73	McIntyre, Roydon (N)	P Kavanagh, Urlingford (I) 5/79
MJH 289L	2T473346	DN C53F	(241/34)	3/73	Keburn, Worsley (C)	
MRO 200L	2T473280	Pn C53F	(732885)	7/73	McIntyre, Roydon (N)	Greenhalgh, Ottershaw (N) 8/81
RBY 42L	2T473322	"	(732396)	4/73	Exclusive, Hounslow (N)	White Heather, Southsea (K) 1/75 (12/80)
RBY 43L	2T473197	"	(732397)	"	"	Murphy, Rowlands Gill (A) 9/79 (8/83)
RBY 44L	2T474303	"	(732398)	"	"	Sunstar, London NW10 (N) 6/81, wdn by 3/83
RPB 222L	2T473290	"	(732085)	5/73	Chivers, Elstead (K)	Rowland & Goodwin, St Leonards (K) 3/83 (8/83)
SAN 913L	2T473235	"	(732401)	2/73	Drewery, Woodford Bridge (N)	Drewery, Woodford Bridge (N) from new, still there 8/80
TTK 708L	2T473401	"	(732400)	1/73	Adams, Handley (H)	Sheppard & Plaister (ex Sheppard), Broad Town (H) 1/82 (12/82)
UFX 360L	2T473507	"	(732399)	2/73	Ward and Tarr, Parkstone (K)	West Wight, Totland Bay (K) -/80
YVC 19L	2T471365	"	(728406)	8/72	Shaw, Coventry (D)	Clarke, Pailton (D) 3/76, wdn 3/80
YVC 20L	1T492952	"	(728407)	"	"	Perry, Blackwood (G) 2/75 (11/81)

NOTE 1 - 7 KX was new to Todd, Whitchurch (E), and retained its registration until sold to St Austell Garages, St Austell (H) in 6/75. When later it passed to Clue, Menheniot (H) it had been re-registered 814 XAF.

NOTE 2 - AWT 351B was delivered with the registration 144 GWX, but was re-registered before entry into service.

NOTE 3 - EDL 783D was new to Vauxhall Motors, Luton (XN) as a demonstrator, and in this form was exhibited by Vauxhall at the New York World's Fair as described in the text. It was first registered by Moss of Sandown in 1966.

NOTE 4 - LWY 820D was offered for sale unused by Phillipson, and was purchased by Whittle, Highley (D) who re-registered it JNT 252E (q.v.).

NOTE 5 - YYX 997/998H carried each other's registrations from new until early 1977, when they were corrected.

NOTE 6 - VUO 298J of Hibberd, Morchard Bishop (H), was acquired secondhand by James, Liverpool (C) in 8/71, and was re-registered AKB 700J by them.

NOTE 7 - There were two vehicles which successively bore the registration FYT 987J. FYT 987J(1) was new in 2/71 to Atlas, Edgware (N) and consisted of chassis 1T484662 and Duple Northern C53F body 229/8. In the following month FYT 987J(2) was delivered to Baker's (dealers) of Bordon, with chassis 1T483019 and Duple Northern C53F body 229/39; this vehicle continued to carry FYT 987J throughout its life. FYT 987J(1) was re-registered VNK 911J, and in this form it was delivered to Plaskow & Margo, Edgware (N); subsequent reference to this vehicle is as VNK 911J.

NOTE 8 - In addition to JHX 4K, the USSR Trade Delegation, London N6 (XN) had an earlier Bedford VAL70 coach, 9T468696, with Duple Northern body no. 200/90, delivered in 1969. It is not known whether this vehicle was used in London, or indeed in Britain, and if so what registration number it carried.

Appendix 2 — Irish and Isle of Man re—registrations

Several VALs carried two or more registrations during their careers; those that were re-registered while remaining within mainland Britain are detailed in Appendix 1 and in the notes at the end of that Appendix. The purpose of this section is to list those that were re-registered on passing to operators in the Isle of Man, Northern Ireland and Eire.

Re-registration has been compulsory for vehicles imported into the Isle of Man throughout the period of this book, and for vehicles imported into Eire since about 1976. Re-registration is not compulsory for vehicles imported into Northern Ireland, but a few examples are known.

This Appendix is organised in four sections; mainland Britain to Isle of Man; mainland Britain to Northern Ireland; mainland Britain to Eire; and Isle of Man to Eire. (In the last-named case the original mainland registrations of the vehicles concerned are shown in brackets, before the Isle of Man registrations).

Mainland Britain to Isle of Man

KCU 701 to MAN 615; 52 XNN to BMN 111; GNP 140C to MAN 72D; FWH 354D to MMN 111(1); JAX 384D to OMN 111; JAX 898D to NMN 111; JBF 671D to MAN 618; JWO 794D to JMN 111(2); MFD 218E to HMN 111; ULG 23E to MN 8964; JDR 285F to 111 KMN; JDR 418F to 111 HMN; MCJ 800F to PMN 111; TGX 877F to EMN 111(2); XPK 77G to MAN 958F; AJW 547H to MAN 111E; KTC 122K to JMN 111(3). Bracketed numbers after a registration indicate that the vehicle was the second, third etc PSV to bear this registration in the Isle of Man.

Mainland Britain to Northern Ireland

LVX 320C to KIA 1777 (later to Eire); FDL 585D to FJI 1262; FBM 706E to GIA 9946.

Mainland Britain to Eire

1462 TF to VZL 179; 111 DAY to NIR 53; 649 DCE to CZO 890; 132 FUA to VZL 192; AES 339B to SIY 920; ATV 49B to 3124 IP; CTD 576B to VZL 191; DMA 280B to 101 AIU; ANM 575C to VMI 950; BVD 829C to YIY 684; CAL 227C to 1129 ZB; CUJ 313C to UMI 890; CUK 506C to 933 ID; CEK 57D to MLI 220; EUG 915D to 3276 IP; GND 111E to 3277 IP; KHM 23D to 419 MZD; MFD 218E to SZP 117; BKX 777F to 251 CIP; PTG 658F to 3123 IP; PEL 904G to 3370 IP; YYX 997H to KZR 677; PVE 592J to 2566 FI; TAR 185J to 134 TZO.

Isle of Man to Eire

(FWH 354D) MMN 111(1) to 284 HZC; (JWO 794D) JMN 111(2) to 858 AZE; (MCJ 800F) PMN 111 to 216 CZA; (TGX 877F) EMN 111(2) to 144 UZJ; (AJW 547H) MAN 111E to IH 117; (KTC 122K) JMN 111(3) to IH 118.

As noted previously, the above reports of re-registrations in Eire account for only a proportion of those Bedford VALs which are known to have been exported there. Some of the others may not have been used in Eire since re-registration became compulsory.

Appendix 3
Australian VALs

BEDFORD   VAL COACHES KNOWN TO HAVE BEEN DELIVERED NEW TO OPERATORS IN AUSTRALIA

(Known details of VALs which were exported to other countries outside the British Isles are set out in Chapter 10).

MO.219	VAL70		PMC RB53F	(1518)	7/72	Evans, Nimmatabel, NSW, Australia
MO.3434	"	?T493202	CCMC RC49F	(72.132)	3/73	Duffy's Bus Lines, NSW, Australia
MO.5129	"		Coachmaster B49F	(1010)	/68	Offner's Bus Service, Wellington, NSW
mo.064	VAL70	?T488993	CCMC RB51D	(71.457)	12/71	Gosper, Windsor, NSW, Australia
mo.581	VAL70		"	(72.82)	9/72	"
mo.4820	VAL14	1477S	Coachmaster B50D	(583)	/64	Kogarah Bus Service, NSW, Australia
mo.5393	VAL70	?T458896	CCMC C48F	(69.94)	7/69	Katen and Heath, NSW, Australia
mo.5653	VAL70	?T471247	CCMC B50D	(70.86)	5/70	Chester Hill-Bankstown, NSW, Australia
mo.5703	VAL70	?T473579	CCMC C48F	(71.11)	8/71	"
mo.5821	VAL70	?T491399	CCMC DP50D	(71.674)	5/72	"
mo.5827	VAL70	707243	CCMC B50D	(72.161)	7/72	"
mo.5849	VAL70	720923	CCMC RC48F	(73.550)	8/73	Hubbard, Milton, NSW, Australia
mo.5973	"	715280	CCMC RC48F	(73.470)	/74	Katen and Heath, NSW, Australia
TV.501	VAL14	1721S	Coachmaster C44F	(727)	/66	Kogarah Bus Service, NSW, Australia
TV.619	VAL70	0T477195	Van Hool C49F	(4833)	/71	Pykes Motor Tours, Sydney, Australia
TV.620	"	0T476731	"	(4832)	/71	"